D0212791

COLLEGE
ATHLETES FOR HIRE

COLLEGE ATHLETES FOR HIRE

THE EVOLUTION AND LEGACY OF THE NCAA's AMATEUR MYTH

ALLEN L. SACK AND
ELLEN J. STAUROWSKY

FOREWORD BY KENT WALDREP,

President, National Paralysis Foundation

Westport, Connecticut
London

HICKSVILLE PUBLIC LIBRARY
HICKSVILLE, N.Y.

Library of Congress Cataloging-in-Publication Data

Sack, Allen L.
     College athletes for hire : the evolution and legacy of the NCAA's
amateur myth / Allen L. Sack and Ellen J. Staurowsky ; foreword by
Kent Waldrep.
        p. cm.
     Includes bibliographical references and index.
     ISBN 0–275–96191–5 (alk. paper)
     1. College sports—Corrupt practices—United States. 2. College
sports—Moral and ethical aspects—United States. 3. National
Collegiate Athletic Association. I. Staurowsky, Ellen J., 1955– .
II. Title.
GV351.S23 1998
796.04′3′0973—dc21   97–43956

British Library Cataloguing in Publication Data is available.

Copyright © 1998 by Allen L. Sack and Ellen J. Staurowsky

All rights reserved. No portion of this book may be
reproduced, by any process or technique, without the
express written consent of the publisher.

Library of Congress Catalog Card Number: 97–43956
ISBN: 0–275–96191–5

First published in 1998

Praeger Publishers, 88 Post Road West, Westport CT 06881
An imprint of Greenwood Publishing Group, Inc.

Printed in the United States of America

∞™

The paper used in this book complies with the
Permanent Paper Standard issued by the National
Information Standards Organization (Z39.48–1984).

10 9 8 7 6 5 4 3 2 1

796.043
S

To Gina, Aaron, and Ethan
—*Allen*

For Carl and the Scout
—*Ellen*

Contents

Foreword

On October 26, 1974, at Legion Field in Birmingham, Alabama, I ran my last play as a Texas Christian University (TCU) football player. On fourth and long, I took a pitchout from our quarterback and tried to turn Alabama's left end. I plunged into a wall of red jerseys, hurtled through the air, and landed on my head as I had many times before.

This time, however, I broke my neck and I was left a quadriplegic. Only eleven months after my injury, I was informed by TCU that it had no insurance and was not liable for my present or future medical bills. The fact is that until the early 1990s, no scholarship athlete was, or had ever been, covered by catastrophic injury insurance despite assurances often given by many recruiters to the contrary.

Wherever American jurisdiction prevails, federal law mandates that each state must provide for some type of workers' compensation scheme. Liability is imposed on an employer because protection of workers is considered good for society. If the TCU athletic director had tripped on his way to the press box on the day of my injury and had suffered a fate similar to mine, he would have been covered by workers' compensation, as would the groundskeepers, the coaches, and the many others who run the multimillion-dollar college sport industry.

Why, then, does the National Collegiate Athletic Association (NCAA) continue to this day to put its revenue-producing athletes at risk by denying them coverage under any state workers' compensation system? My answer is that the NCAA and its member institutions have consciously fabricated a myth that scholarship athletes are merely amateurs and have much more in common with intramural frisbee players than with the professional athletes they have in fact become.

Championing this myth is a cast of characters ranging from athletic directors (the industry's fund raisers) to big-time coaches (the field representatives for Nike, Adidas, and other apparel manufacturers). The bottom line is profit. By insisting that scholarship athletes are amateurs, universities have been able to keep labor costs to a minimum. Although this may not be slavery, so to speak, the fact is that the coach has indeed become the boss and the player has become the employee. The key to this employer-employee relationship is the coaches' ability to use scholarship money to control the day-to-day activities of their athletes and to set a cap on how much athletes can earn.

Walter Byers, the former executive director of the NCAA, has recently published a book entitled *Unsportsmanlike Conduct: Exploiting College Athletes*, in which he acknowledges the pervasive influence of money in college sports. He further contends that athletic scholarships are little more than a "national money-laundering scheme," which funnels money to so-called amateur athletes. Byers's book, which has not received the attention it deserves, was a step in the right direction.

Professors Allen L. Sack and Ellen J. Staurowsky have picked up the flag where Byers left off and have produced a rigorous scholarly analysis of how the amateur myth emerged and how it hurts student athletes. Books such as these will raise the consciousness of the American public. The power to demand change lies in the hands of the moms and dads who entrust the well-being of their talented children to the NCAA. My sons will never be subjected to what I have endured, and your child should not either.

On March 23, 1993, the Texas Workers' Compensation Board ruled in my favor that "Kent Waldrep was an employee of TCU" when he was injured. This case is still in the appeals process. Whatever the outcome of my case, the amateur myth is under considerable attack from many directions and will ultimately fall. Perhaps Sack and Staurowsky's book will help to hasten its demise.

Kent Waldrep
President, National Paralysis Foundation
Dallas, Texas

Preface

My involvement in college sport spans thirty-five years, and my experiences as an athlete, an advocate for athletic reform, a college professor, and an NCAA faculty athletics representative have focused my attention on the issue of sport in higher education. In the mid-1960s I attended the University of Notre Dame on a football scholarship. As a member of Ara Parseghian's 1966 national championship football team, I had opportunities that most young athletes can only dream about.[1]

My last football game was against the University of Southern California before a sellout crowd of over 100,000 spectators in the Los Angeles Coliseum. We won 51 to 0. The night before the game, the team was invited to a private screening of a film that was about to be released by Universal Studios. Robert Mitchum, one of the stars of the movie, joined us in the screening room and talked with the players as if we were old friends. I leaned back in the soft leather seats, watched the movie, and marveled at how well football players are sometimes treated.

During my four years at Notre Dame, I traveled first class and stayed in luxury hotels. I remember meals on the road where the choice was steak or lobster. Wherever we stayed we were treated as celebrities. During one trip the pilot even altered our flight plan just so that we would get a better aerial view of the Grand Canyon. I can well understand why other college students, especially female college athletes, who often carpooled to games at their own expense, resented what they perceived to be the privileged lives of big-time college athletes.

Of course, there was another side to playing such big-time college football. Many nights I limped to the library after practice and fell asleep with my face on a desktop. I remember grueling late summer scrimmages when to quench our thirst we sucked water out of the same wet towels that we used for wiping blood off cuts and scrapes. In late autumn, chilling rains would form icicles on my face mask and leave me with a perpetual sore throat. Pain and physical exhaustion are an integral part of college football. I would be lying if I said that I had enough energy left after practice to give serious attention to Kierkegaard and Nietzsche.

Big-time college sport in the 1960s had its share of abuses, but the NCAA was still hanging onto some semblance of what I would call an educational model of sport. When I played football, there was no freshman eligibility and Notre Dame refused to play in bowl games. Both of these policies reflected my university's commitment to the academic needs of its athletes. The fact that I received a four-year scholarship further underscores the concern for athletes' welfare that existed in the 1960s. Several players that I knew while at Notre Dame were badly injured and had to give up football. NCAA rules at the time prohibited taking away their scholarships.

The 1970s saw a total abandonment of amateurism in the world of big-time college sport. As the revenue and exposure from television increased, the NCAA passed rules that placed the corporate needs of commercial sport over the academic needs of athletes.[2] In 1972 freshman eligibility was introduced, thus allowing a seventeen-year-old to play football on national television in the fall before he had even attended his first college class. In 1973 the four-year scholarship went the way of the flying wedge. This change allowed coaches to withdraw scholarships from injured athletes and from those not skilled enough to play at the so-called big-time level. College athletes could now be "fired."

During my senior year at Notre Dame, I was drafted by the Los Angeles Rams, but I could not picture my 205-pound body playing defensive end in the National Football League (NFL). I decided (wisely, I think) to pursue a doctorate in sociology at Penn State and to become a college professor. While my teammates went off to professional football or to a variety of other careers, I remained in higher education and saw on a day-to-day basis the ways that college sport often subverts educational values and exploits young athletes. What I found especially reprehensible was the NCAA's claim that big-time college athletes are merely amateurs engaged in playful recreation.

In 1981 I took a leave of absence from the University of New Haven to accept a job in the South Bronx as director of the Center for Athletes' Rights and Education (CARE). As director of CARE, an organization funded by a $250,000 grant from the U.S. Department of Education and cosponsored by the National Football League Players Association, I took the position that athletic scholarships constitute employment contracts and that as employees college athletes deserve the same benefits as other workers, including workers' compensation when injured, the right to form labor unions, and the right to bargain over salaries, benefits, and conditions of employment.

CARE survived for only two short years but managed to touch a nerve that sent NCAA attorneys scampering for legal opinions from Mission, Kansas, to Washington, D.C. Walter Byers, executive director of the NCAA from 1952 to 1987, has admitted in a recent book that CARE's efforts to organize college athletes led the NCAA to issue a "red alert."[3] What I learned from the NCAA's response to CARE's reform efforts is that media exposés, and the blue-ribbon commissions that often follow in their wake, have minimal impact on NCAA policy. Court action, government intervention, and any efforts to organize college athletes, on the other hand, are tactics that the NCAA takes very seriously and moves quickly to counter.

CARE was an aggressive advocate for Title IX, a federal law passed in 1972 that requires that women have equal access to sports in educational institutions. But our vigorous advocacy of employment rights for big-time college athletes created tension between CARE and certain feminists in the sports community. As these women saw it, CARE's proposals had the potential to divert money away from nonrevenue-producing sports, including many women's programs, into what they felt were the already bloated budgets of men's football and basketball. Some women asked how it made sense to increase benefits for football players when women's programs were starved for resources.

CARE, during its short history, never did adequately address that question. And it took me another ten years to realize that Title IX and the struggle for gender equity have a greater potential for restoring the educational integrity of college sport than any single reform passed by the NCAA over the past 100 years. This book, coauthored by a feminist scholar, will attempt to reconcile the views of those who want to end the exploitation of big-time college athletes with those for whom gender equity is the major priority. To accomplish this, we are convinced that the myth of amateurism upon which the current system is based must be replaced by a model of amateurism that will meet the educational needs of universities in the twenty-first century.

Allen L. Sack

When Allen Sack asked me to be coauthor of this book, I accepted without hesitation. As a former athletics director turned academic, I welcomed the opportunity to undertake a rigorous examination of the dilemmas posed by intercollegiate sport. I also hoped that through our mutual investigation, we might suggest valid changes that could assist institutional decision makers in handling college sport more effectively within the confines of modern higher educational settings. As is the case with Allen, I have traveled my own path in intercollegiate athletics and those experiences have advised my approach and commitment to this undertaking.

I am the daughter of a woman who played for the legendary college coach Eleanor Snell. For those unfamiliar with Snell's legacy and record of achievement, suffice it to say that decades before Title IX of the Education Amendments Act of 1972 was passed, she was a progressive educator who entertained the belief that competitive athletics for women was appropriate and important.

Miss Snell was hired in 1931 by Ursinus College, where she had a distinguished career teaching physical education and coaching field hockey, basketball, softball, and tennis. Her lifetime career coaching record of 674 wins, 194 losses, and 42 ties easily places Snell in the company of other great college coaches including the likes of Bear Bryant and John Wooden. The fact that she compiled such a record of success at a time when many perceived female athleticism to be taboo is a testament to her vision and to the women who played for her.

Because my mother had been one of "Snell's Belles," a term adopted with affection and pride by the Ursinus women who played for Snell, my introduction to college sport came early in life, at age 4, to be precise. I have warm and vivid memories of accompanying my mother, along with my two older brothers and sister, to her field hockey officiating assignments at colleges located in the Philadelphia area. The year was 1959.

While my mother patrolled the sidelines, intent on the game in progress, I found myself each time surrounded and embraced by a community of female college athletes. They became my baby-sitters, my instructors, my entertainers, and ultimately my symbols of possibility. Those afternoons watching my mother officiate served as formative and definitive moments that shaped my conceptions of education, sport, and life.

Based on my four-year-old worldview from the bench, I actually got the impression, albeit short-lived, that competitive intercollegiate athletics was the domain of women. I was aware that boys could be athletes as well, due in part to the fact that my brothers and neighborhood boys were my backyard teammates. But it was these women who I saw racing downfield, exalting in victory, and finishing in fatigue who left no doubt in my mind that women competed seriously as athletes. And, yes, it was also these female athletes who fed me milk and cookies while they socialized after each contest.

Those early experiences firmly established in my mind a belief that sport and education, without regard to gender, were seamlessly blended, naturally compatible, and complementary. I had grasped within the first five years of my life the essence of the student-athlete ideal. My conclusion—people, women and men, were meant to be athletes as surely as they were meant to be scholars. And quite clearly, they were meant to be both.

In the intervening thirty-six years since those officiating trips with my mother, many things have happened. Our family grew from four to eight children. Despite the challenges created by such a brood, my mother continued to officiate and became the first woman to umpire men's fast pitch softball in the Philadelphia area in the 1970s. In various turns of fate, I became a multisport student athlete at Ursinus College, went on to become a college coach, later became an athletics director, and somewhere in the midst of all of that earned my doctorate. Having been exposed at age four to a version of athletics that provided equitable access for females as a matter of course, I was ill prepared to discover how greatly a person's gender influences decision making in college sport.

In college in the mid-1970s, I became aware of the deferential treatment received by male athletes. As a point of comparison, while my coauthor and his Notre Dame teammates experienced the thrill of traveling first class, my college team discovered the fine art of caravaning, an accepted mode of transportation for women's teams at the time, wherein coaches and players would frequently travel to games in their own vehicles. By our caravaning, the accumulated risks and costs of an athletic team's travel were borne by the participants and the coaches, not by the institution. Although speeding along behind a leaden-footed coach whose preoccupation with the upcoming game made her oblivious to warning lights and stop signs may have helped a young woman like myself build character, the ride itself often made entering a game in a relaxed and focused state of mind rather remote. Equally remote and even inconceivable was the idea that our athleticism would gain us easy access to posh restaurants or luxury hotels.

Having only partially recovered from my initial surprise over the inconsistency of a system that excessively privileges some while providing minimally for others, I have come to understand that the issue of gender in intercollegiate athletics often evokes a level of debate and controversy that is unmatched by any other topic. The intensity of this debate is in part due to the perception that gender equity can be attained only at the expense of male athletes. But the fact that such discussions of gender equity inevitably expose the myth of amateurism and its inherent inconsistencies also fuels this controversy. For instance, if college sport is an integral component of an amateur student athlete's education, why have academic institutions so readily chosen to provide fewer of these educational opportunities to females? Similarly, if college sport is educational and is not a form of professional entertainment, why is a sport's revenue-generating capacity given such weight in determining the allocation of resources between men's and women's athletic programs?

Discussions about gender in college sport have the capacity to lay bare the forces that not only seek to limit female athletic involvement but serve to exploit male athletes as well. In effect, an objective examination of gender equity reveals not only the limiting and exclusionary practices that influence female athletic development; it exposes also the parallel exploitative practices that at their worst subvert the interests and abilities of male athletes and transform these men into expendable commodities. Both sets of practices corrupt the integrity of higher education by separating college sport from the educational enterprise it was theoretically intended to be.

Our joint purpose in writing this book has been to revisit the educational premise that has historically defined the fundamental amateur ideal, to refashion a model of athletics that proceeds first from the standpoint of a student athlete's welfare, and to relocate college sport again on a firm educational foundation. Through this process, which involves a close look at how the term "amateurism" has been used and abused, we believe that American colleges and universities will be more fully equipped to meet the challenges of the twenty-first century.

Ellen J. Staurowsky

Acknowledgments

This book is not intended to be a history of collegiate sport. We believe, however, that any attempt to formulate social policy has to be set in a historical context. Our treatment of the early years of male and female collegiate sport owes a great deal to others whose histories of both collegiate sport and women's physical education served as our starting point, including Pearl Berlin, Susan Cahn, Jack Falla, Jan Felshin, Ellen Gerber, Joan Hult, Mabel Lee, Carole Oglesby, Benjamen Rader, Ron Smith, Adryn Sponberg, John Thelin, Waneen Wyrick, and Patricia Vertinsky.

We owe a very special note of gratitude to sport historian Ron Smith for graciously allowing us to use notes and documents that he has been painstakingly collecting from university archives for over the past twenty years. Of particular relevance to our work was material that Professor Smith shared with us from presidential papers in the university libraries at Brown, Harvard, the University of North Carolina at Chapel Hill, Georgia Tech, Stanford, and the University of Virginia.

This project could not have been undertaken and completed without the support of our respective institutions. We would like to thank the University of New Haven for the support it provided through its sabbatical leave and summer research programs, as well as the Ithaca College Instructional Development Program. We would like to acknowledge the generous assistance of archivists and reference librarians from the Association for Intercollegiate Athletics for Women Archives at the University of Maryland, the Constance Applebee papers at Bryn Mawr College, the Cornell University Archives, the

Hobart and William Smith Library, the National Collegiate Athletic Association in Kansas, the Ursinusiana Collection at Ursinus College, the Archives at Yale University, and the Yale Department of Athletics.

We would like to thank David Westby and Cynthia Wells for reading significant portions of this manuscript in its earlier stages. Their comments and criticisms were greatly appreciated. Others who have patiently listened to us or argued with us or whose work has had a significant influence on this book include Patricia and Peter Adler, Ruth Bruner, Bonnie Calmer, Walter Byers, Harry Edwards, Cary Goodman, Robert Hoffnung, Michael Morris, Mark Naison, Roy Perry, Nelson Sack, Jack Scott, Fred Shults, Eleanor Snell, Murray Sperber and Rick Telander. Gina Sack and Betty Keyser Staurowsky deserve special mention in this regard. Many others could be added to this list.

We would, finally, like to acknowledge the significant contributions of our students (both athletes and nonathletes), who have educated us about the importance of dispelling the amateur mythology that so affects their lives. As the next generation of social policy shapers and decision makers, they have inspired us with the promise they possess to create a more humane and just future in the arena of collegiate sport.

COLLEGE
ATHLETES FOR HIRE

Introduction: The Different Faces of Collegiate Sport

THE BIG TEN AND THE LITTLE THREE

A visit to a Wesleyan University football game on one autumn weekend, followed by a trip to a University of Michigan game the next, would yield for sports observers some striking contrasts. It is only a slight overstatement to say that the only factor that these two contests share in common is the shape of the football. A typical game, for example, between any two teams of the "little three"—Wesleyan, Amherst, and Williams—might attract a few thousand spectators, a relatively small percentage of whom would actually pay to see the game. Revenues generated would be minuscule. Concessions and other merchandising would likely be handled by team members selling popcorn, hot dogs, and T-shirts to raise money for their yearly trips.

The atmosphere at the "little three" game, as one manifestation of the disparity among divisions in college athletics, stands in sharp contrast to the atmosphere that one might expect to find at a Big Ten game (that is, among Division IA, commonly referred to as "big-time"). A Michigan–Penn State game could on average attract over 100,000 spectators and generate gate receipts of over $2 million.[1] Television revenues, corporate sponsorships, concessions, licensed merchandise, parking, and other promotions add millions more.[2] Wolverine Stadium holds almost as many people as live in the city of New Haven, Connecticut. When these fans stream into Ann Arbor, its hotels, restaurants, and related businesses prosper, and crowded streets take on the ambiance of a major resort.

Few would argue that a Wesleyan football game can compete with a Michigan game as a form of mass commercial entertainment. The average size and speed of Big Ten players, the intensity of the crowds, the media coverage that transforms players and coaches into national celebrities—these simply cannot be duplicated in games among the little three. Nor can these contests be compared in terms of what it costs to stage them.[3] Big-time college football generates millions in revenue, but even the average Division IA athletic program barely breaks even after costs are taken into account.[4] (Various NCAA division levels are discussed more comprehensively later in this Introduction.) The football program at Michigan requires a level of funding that is unimaginable at such colleges as Wesleyan and Amherst.

These differences in the level of commercialism, that is, the amount of revenue generated in big-time as compared to smaller colleges' football programs, are fairly obvious to the general public. What is less apparent but of profound importance is the degree to which athletes at the big-time level have been transformed into paid entertainers. The very linchpin of big-time college sport, and the employer–employee relationship that serves as its foundation, is the athletic scholarship. The athletes entertaining the crowds at a Michigan game are paid for their services in the form of room, board, tuition, and fees. This financial package can be taken away immediately if an athlete decides for one reason or another to give up sports.

In contrast, athletes at schools such as Wesleyan enjoy the freedom that one usually associates with amateurism. If Wesleyan football or field hockey players find that their dream of graduating magna cum laude is threatened by the time demands of sports, they can give up varsity sport with absolutely no financial loss. National Collegiate Athletic Association rules prevent such Division III colleges as Wesleyan from awarding athletically related financial aid to any student. Division III sport is an avocation that is free from financial constraints. Athletic scholarships, on the other hand, give coaches considerable control over athletes' behavior both on and off of the field and create conditions that make big-time college sport virtually indistinguishable from any other employment.

The profound differences between big-time and small-time collegiate athletic programs seem beyond dispute. What is remarkable is that despite these differences, the NCAA has been able to convince the public, including judges and members of Congress, that it is perfectly logical and ethical to apply the term "amateur" to athletic programs as disparate as those found at Wesleyan and at the University of Michigan. This misuse of the word "amateurism" has implications that go well beyond academic debates about the meanings of words.

By being allowed to take shelter under the same amateur umbrella as the Wesleyans of the world, the business of professional college sport enjoys special privileges not available to other industries. For instance, a recent complaint brought by the Federal Trade Commission (FTC) against the College Football Association for antitrust violations was dismissed in part on the grounds that the "amateur" nature of college sport placed it outside the jurisdiction of the FTC.[5] Universities have also used the amateur label to shield themselves from workers' compensation claims by seriously injured college athletes,[6] to avoid federal taxation of sport sponsorship revenues,[7] and to delegitimize efforts by athletes to unionize or to demand a greater share of college sports revenue.[8]

Given the obvious economic interests of big-time college sport, there is no mystery why sport-governing bodies such as the NCAA and the major collegiate conferences cling to the amateur myth and send lobbyists to Congress to ensure that the myth is perpetuated. Another reason that the myth of amateurism has escaped sustained criticism and scrutiny is honest confusion over the distinction between sport as a leisure activity and sport as a form of employment. This confusion is not peculiar to college sport. Throughout the history of labor negotiations in professional sports leagues, there has been a powerful undercurrent of public opinion that sport is not a form of work in the same sense that working in a factory or in an office is. Sport, in the minds of many people, is associated more closely with play than with employment.

UNTANGLING CONCEPTS

A clearer understanding of current issues confronting college sport must begin by exploring the relationship between sport as a leisure activity and sport as a form of employment. Most scholars agree that leisure activities are free from the practical or pragmatic concerns of making a living.[9] Some writers define leisure as "free time." Others prefer to view leisure as "an activity pursued during free or unobligated time." Regardless, there is considerable agreement that during leisure, feelings of compulsion are minimal. In leisure, there is considerable room for discretion.[10]

But as the sociologist Bennett Berger correctly points out, the notion that leisure is free or unobligated activity is in need of qualification. No activity, according to Berger, is ever totally free of normative constraint. Even leisure activities are shaped by the norms, values, and group relations of society and culture. What distinguishes work (including working for some individual or corporate body, i.e., employment) from leisure is not the presence or absence of constraints but the kinds of constraints that characterize these activities.[11]

The constraints placed on leisure activity tend to be normative in nature. When a coach exhorts his team to "win one for the Gipper" or elicits conformity by suggesting that a player is somehow "letting down the team," he or she is using normative constraint. Normative constraint can also refer to standards and belief systems that have become deeply internalized. Athletes who push themselves to the extremes of human endurance because of an inner sense of pride or determination are also responding to normative constraints. Leisure, according to Berger, refers precisely to those activities that we feel "ethically (as opposed to expediently) constrained to do."[12]

Professional employment may or may not be normatively constrained, depending on such factors as the degree to which a worker identifies with and gets intrinsic satisfaction from the job. What distinguishes leisure from employment, however, is that the latter is always subject to what can be called instrumental constraint.[13] Instrumental constraint is based on the control of material rewards and resources. Professional athletes may love their jobs, but their day-to-day activities are controlled by employers who can impose fines, determine salaries, and ultimately terminate employment. It is not whether an activity is perceived to be enjoyable that distinguishes employment from leisure. Rather, it is the presence or absence of instrumental constraint.

According to this formulation, sport under some conditions is a form of leisure activity; under others, it is professional employment. Amateur sport, as the term has been defined historically and as it is currently defined in the *NCAA Manual*, is an "avocation," meaning that it is a form of leisure activity.[14] This does not mean that amateur sport is taken less seriously than professional sport. Amateur rock climbers have risked their lives on shear cliffs and have endured frostbite to reach a summit. Amateur rugby players risk serious injury and thrive on intense competition. What separates the amateur from the professional is the absence of remunerative, or instrumental, constraint, not the absence of desire.

Although amateur athletes can become obsessed with their sports, they generally can walk away from athletic involvement without fear of financial loss. For this reason, amateur sport is the model that is most consistent with the stated mission of universities. Students who do not depend on sport for their daily living expenses have greater latitude to make education their top priority. It can be argued that the amateur model *is* the educational model of college sport. Schools that offer athletic scholarships have embraced a form of professionalism, and have made a conscious decision to use paid performers to attract revenue and/or publicity to their schools.

One final term that needs clarification is "commercialism." To say that college sport has become commercialized simply means that some universities have been fairly successful in attracting sports revenue and spectators to their campuses. The quality of the sport entertainment product is generally enhanced by offering athletes financial inducements such as scholarships, but commercial college sport is possible without them. For instance, Ivy League football at such a school as Yale University can generate considerable revenue from gate receipts, sponsorships, and occasional television and radio broadcasts. The Ivy League's commitment to education, however, does not allow professionalism in the form of athletic scholarships.

Conversely, there are athletic programs that offer athletic scholarships (are professionalized) but make very little money. Nonrevenue sports at Division I schools, including most women's programs, are examples. The approach to collegiate sport that is shared by the 373 members of the NCAA's Division III makes little or no money and offers no athletic scholarships. The Division III athletic philosophy, as stated in the *NCAA Manual*, is to emphasize the impact of athletics on participants rather than on spectators.[15] Some of the most prestigious academic institutions in the country belong to Division III, including the "little three" institutions that were discussed earlier.

The primary defining characteristic of what will be referred to as "corporate college sport" throughout this book is that it is both commercialized and professionalized. Division IA football and basketball are examples. Division IA football programs are required by the NCAA to have stadiums with permanent seating capacities of at least 30,000 and to have averaged 17,000 paid attendance per home game during the immediate past four-year period.[16] Television is a major source of revenue in these programs. The NCAA's $1.75 billion deal with CBS which began in 1996 to broadcast the men's basketball tournament gives a good idea of the revenue-producing potential from televising such games.

In addition, these corporate college sport programs award athletic scholarships to "blue chip" athletes, who as a group often have a markedly different demographic profile than that of the rest of the student body. Teams tend to have a higher proportion of blacks than can be found on their campuses as a whole. Also, the overall gap between athletes and nonathletes in academic preparedness tends to be rather large.[17] Athletes in the corporate model are recruited differently, are subsidized differently, and are admitted to college for very different reasons than for other students. They are, essentially, paid professionals.

FOCUSING ON THE PROBLEM

Many books have been written on the "evils" of commercialism in collegiate sport. Many of the scholars and historians who have contributed to this extensive literature have also focused on the hypocrisy of under-the-table payments from alumni, boosters, agents, and a variety of other sources outside the university.[18] But almost no attention has been given to the process by which the NCAA itself has incorporated professionalism into its constitution and bylaws. In other words, there remains a considerable gap in the historical record when it comes to the evolution of "NCAA-sponsored" professionalism in the form of athletically related financial aid.

Because the role of athletic scholarships in professionalizing college sport has not received the attention it deserves, the NCAA is often perceived as an embattled defender of amateurism, holding its ground against "greedy athletes, unscrupulous agents, and overzealous alumni." NCAA-sanctioned payments are obscured by amateur rhetoric. There is no better evidence that the myth of amateurism is still alive and well than the fact that seriously injured collegiate athletes continue to be denied workers' compensation benefits on the grounds that they are amateurs, not employees. This myth exerts a powerful influence over public policy in collegiate sport and is accepted uncritically by millions of Americans both in and outside of academe.

The major purpose of this book is to examine the evolution of college athletes into university employees and to put to rest once and for all the NCAA-fabricated mythology that scholarship athletes are amateurs. This book also analyzes how the amateur myth has exploited athletes financially, has undermined educational integrity, and has transformed some of America's most prestigious universities into centers of fraud and hypocrisy. A subtheme is that certain women, such as those who created the Association for Intercollegiate Athletics for Women (AIAW), have been a major source of resistance to the corporate model. A close examination of the history and current realities of women's collegiate sport helps to place the contradictions in the corporate model in sharper relief and provides guidance as to where college sport should go in the future.

The first section of this book examines the historical roots of myths and ideologies that have exploited men and excluded women in the area of collegiate sport. Chapter 1 examines the decline of the "amateur spirit" in Great Britain and the United States as well as the causes of the rampant professionalism that characterized college sport in America in the late nineteenth century. Chapter 2 traces the history of athletic subsidization from 1906, the year of the first NCAA Convention, to 1956, when the NCAA substituted a counterfeit version of amateurism for the real thing. This chapter looks at the economic and political forces that led to the watershed decision to allow financial inducements for college athletes in the form of room, board, tuition, and fees.

While men were hard at work fashioning an amateur mythology to defend the economic interests of the emerging college sport cartel, women were fashioning a model of collegiate sport that while intertwined with sexist practices and assumptions of that era, nonetheless placed the educational needs of athletes first. Chapter 3 looks at the origins of women's collegiate sport in light of the Victorian and other patriarchal values that dominated higher education in the late 1800s. Chapter 4 looks at the distinctive "sport-for-women philosophy," which evolved as a creative response to female exclusion. Considerable attention is given to the 1923 Platform of the Women's Division of the National Amateur Athletic Federation and its emphasis on the educational needs of athletics rather than on the entertainment needs of spectators.

In the second part of the book, the focus is on the dramatic changes in college sport in the decades following the introduction of athletic scholarships. The NCAA legislated professionalism into college sport in 1956. But it was not until 1967 that college athletes were transformed into employees in the strict sense that the term "employee" is used in a court of law. Chapter 5 looks at the legislative changes made by the NCAA to establish control over the college athlete workforce as well as the legal and ethical consequences of those changes. Several key workers' compensation cases involving injured college athletes are discussed to illustrate how the NCAA and its attorneys have misrepresented the nature of corporate college sport in order to deny athletes their rights.

The educational fallout of the NCAA's veiled professionalism is the topic of Chapter 6. Whereas athletic scholarships undeniably created opportunities, they also set talented athletes apart from other students in ways that were academically problematic. Admitted by different and often lower academic standards and subjected to athletic demands that interfere with academic performance, scholarship athletes have been pushed into the academic periphery. Chapter 6 documents the conflicts inherent in the student-athlete role, discusses the NCAA's efforts to create minimum standards for freshman eligibility, and argues that universities have been far more concerned with exploiting the athletic talent of the black community than with nurturing its academic potential.

Chapter 7 addresses one of the most complex issues facing college sport today, that is, the issue of gender equity. Starting with the late 1960s, this chapter traces the rise and fall of the American Association for Intercollegiate Athletics for Women, the impact of Title IX, and the growing professionalism in women's sport. This chapter also documents women's often unsuccessful struggle to gain gender equity without abandoning their long-standing commitment to academic principles. Although court decisions have increased athletic opportunities for women at all levels, these laws have also at times thwarted women's efforts to avoid the hypocrisy of the corporate model, with its athletic scholarships, lowered academic standards, and tendency to create obstacles to intellectual and personal growth. This chapter argues that the NCAA takeover of the AIAW put an end to this women's experimental model of collegiate sport that placed the human and educational needs of students above the commercial needs of the college sport industry.

The final chapter, Chapter 8, combines insights derived from the history of college sport with an analysis of current trends to suggest models of college sport that can best meet the educational needs of college women and men in the twenty-first century. The central argument of this final chapter is that the concept of amateurism, when misapplied to athletic systems whose main goal is the production of high-performance athletes, spawns hypocrisy and exploitation. Thus, the amateur concept has no place in such venues as the Olympic Games and is totally inappropriate in big-time college sport. No meaningful reform is possible without first addressing this issue.

Once the amateur myth has been put to rest, universities can explore a number of alternative strategies. One would be to actually "turn amateur" in the truest sense. What this would mean is abandoning athletic scholarships for some form of need-based aid. Chapter 8 will argue that reinventing amateurism would offer college presidents at most schools a cost-effective alternative to the current athletic "arms race" and would help to manage escalating athletic department costs, including those associated with attaining gender equity. Chapter 8 argues, in short, that amateurism deserves serious consideration.

Another alternative to the current system is for the relative handful of schools that actually make money from college sport to abandon the pretense of amateurism and allow athletes to engage in the same kinds of entrepreneurial ventures pursued by coaches and the many others who make their livings from collegiate sport. Chapter 8 will offer suggestions for how this can be done without increasing costs, threatening the survival of male and female nonrevenue-producing sports, or denying college athletes an opportunity to receive the same quality of education as other students. The main premise of this chapter is that college sport does not have to be corrupt in order to perform its many valuable functions for higher education.

Part I

Rules of the Game for Men and Women

1

The Decline of the Amateur Spirit

In the late nineteenth century, the United States experienced rapid industrialization, and the competitive and acquisitive values of the marketplace began to pervade all of America's social institutions, including its colleges and universities. In this competitive environment, the traditional concept of amateurism, which had been so vital to liberal education, including sports, in British public schools and universities, came increasingly under attack in American schools. Die-hard advocates of amateurism (including elitist anglophiles as well as some faculty and college presidents) fought against athletic recruiting, athletic scholarships, under-the-table payments, lowered admission standards, and the other trappings of professionalism. Their efforts were futile. By 1905, the year in which the NCAA was created, rampant professionalism had spun out of control.

AMATEURISM AND THE GENTLEMAN-ARISTOCRAT

According to Barrington Moore, Jr., the amateur ideal, while most clearly associated with the British aristocracy, was probably embraced by the leisure classes in most preindustrial civilizations.[1] At the very center of this ideal was the notion that aristocratic status indicates a "qualitatively superior form of being, whose qualities were hereditary rather than the fruit of individually acquired merits. . . ."[2] Thus, the gentleman-aristocrat was not expected to put forth too great an effort in any single direction. He could strive for excellence, but not just in one activity and as a consequence of prolonged training. The aristocrat took great pains to distance himself from the highly trained professional, the latter being viewed as a mere "segment of a man—overdeveloped in one direction, atrophied in all others."[3] Investing too much time and effort in one specialized activity would be plebeian.

Also central to the amateur ethos was the belief that leisure activities are qualitatively superior to those associated with making a living or whose motive is material gain. The gentleman-amateur was free to explore a wide range of human possibilities, and leisure was felt to be a prerequisite for living a worthy life. As Thorstein Veblen observed in his classic, *The Theory of the Leisure Class*, abstention from productive labor had become a sign of superior status among landed aristocrats from the time of the ancient Greeks.[4] The aristocrat, unlike the tradesman and the mechanic, had time to appreciate art for art's sake and to study the aesthetic dimensions of life merely for the love of it. To be an aristocrat was to be an amateur.

There is probably no country in the world where the traditional concept of the amateur has had a more lasting effect than Great Britain.[5] In the nineteenth century, Britain was ruled by a leisure class composed of titled nobility and landed gentry. As the owners of large country estates, the British ruling class had a great deal of time for leisure pursuits. Country gentlemen found time for literature, science, and agricultural experiments and for laying out gardens.[6] They also engaged in outdoor sports and recreations. Consistent with amateur predilections, the British aristocrat tried to do everything well but generally avoided professional drill and methodical instruction.

During the nineteenth century, the amateur ideal was often credited with reinforcing character traits that produced success in spheres ranging from science to warfare. The Duke of Wellington's seemingly banal comment linking victory at Waterloo to the playing fields of Eton, one of England's most prestigious schools for young aristocrats, reflects this positive assessment of the virtue of the amateur ideal. As historian John Keegan has suggested, Wellington's comment speaks more to the role of aristocratic character than to the complex military strategies in the British victory. What made the difference at Waterloo was "coolness, endurance, and the pursuit of excellence for its own sake," and these were the traits that English gentlemen acquired in game-playing.[7]

Of course, amateurism had its detractors, and their numbers were to increase as the British aristocracy began to show signs of decline in the late nineteenth century. Following humiliating military setbacks in the Boer War in 1889, the Honorable George C. Brodrick, Warden of Merton College, wrote a scathing indictment of what he labeled "a nation of amateurs." "The young English gentleman," said Brodrick, "is no dandy and no coward, but he is an amateur born and bred, with an amateur's lack of training, an amateur's contempt for method. . . ."[8] In Brodrick's view, the amateur spirit had not only crippled the army's officer corps but had infected the whole of professional and public life in Britain. The disasters in South Africa were only symptomatic of a general weakness in British culture resulting from the carelessness inherent in the amateur ideal.[9]

Brodrick's attack on the amateur spirit came at a time when the British leisure class was beginning to falter. International competition was bringing agricultural prices down, thereby increasing economic pressures on the owners of landed estates. A new middle class was also challenging aristocratic dominance in professions ranging from the civil service to the military.[10] In a world increasingly dominated by giant corporations and complex bureaucracies, the highly skilled specialist, recruited on the basis of merit and working to make a living, began to replace the cultured dilettante. In this new industrial age, the gentleman-amateur was simply no match for the paid professional.

AMATEUR SPORT IN BRITISH COLLEGES AND UNIVERSITIES

There is a long and rich tradition of sport in British society, and the traditions of amateur sport are the product of Britain's leading universities and public schools. Students at Oxford and Cambridge engaged in versions of such sports as boating, cricket, horse racing, football, and tennis as early as the sixteenth, seventeenth, and eighteenth centuries. Students at two of the "Great Public Schools," the elite preparatory schools of Eton and Westminster, had competed in cricket as early as 1788.[11] The Oxford–Cambridge cricket match at Lord's Ground in London in 1827 was probably the first intercollegiate athletic contest ever. Two years later, Oxford and Cambridge met again at the Henley Regatta, along the Thames River, for the first intercollegiate rowing race.[12]

The influence of the amateur spirit in British public schools and universities was unmistakable during the nineteenth and early twentieth centuries. According to Howard Savage, author of a 1927 Carnegie Foundation report on sport in British schools and universities, sport was taken very seriously by British students, but it had to be kept in balance with other facets of university life.[13] One official intimately concerned with British education reported to Savage that the aim of English education is to turn out "all round-round men, who may or may not be scholars, who can play games, but not too well, and who are not one-sided" (78). The amateur's casualness and dislike for professional drill were very much in evidence among athletes at British schools.

Referring to American oarsmen at the turn of the century who trained year-round by using indoor tanks for stationary rowing, an American observer of British sport commented that "Englishmen would never dream of taking such pains. They have a vague feeling that such action is unsportsman-like"(78). This should not be interpreted to mean that British athletes did not place importance on winning nor that they lacked a competitive spirit. The Harvard–Oxford rowing meet in 1869, which was won by Oxford before a crowd of nearly one million people, illustrates that the British took winning very seriously. What the gentleman-amateur opposed was any methodical drill and overemphasis that might transform sport from recreation into a full-time occupation.

Sport at schools such as Oxford and Cambridge was (and is today) organized by and for the recreation of the players themselves. To quote Savage, "To the undergraduate, sport is not an exhibition to be watched; it is a recreation to be indulged in actively. The spectators at a contest are players who for the nonce [time being] are taking a respite from their own matches to see the others play"(78). This player-centered approach to sport goes to the heart of the amateur ideal. Sport in British schools was not professional entertainment for the masses. Rather, it was a vital part of the liberal education of a well-rounded gentleman.

Not surprisingly, the British universities and public schools have never seriously considered subsidizing students on the basis of athletic ability. Offering inducements to athletes, while not unheard of at the time of Savage's report, did not constitute a serious problem (78). Consistent with amateur conventions, a student who attended Oxford or Cambridge primarily to play sports, whether compensated or not, would have been met with considerable social opprobrium. British universities were perceived by the majority of students to be intellectual agencies, and sport was never conceived by faculty and administrators as a recruiting tool or as a form of commercial entertainment. Even if athletes who played sports for a living had not been viewed as social inferiors (a perception in accordance with the gentleman-amateur's code of conduct), British universities would still have had no reason or inclination to recruit and subsidize them.

AMATEURS, GENTLEMEN-AMATEURS, AND OPEN PROFESSIONALS

When viewed within the context of the British university, the amateur ideal of sport was in many ways supportive of the best academic traditions of the liberal arts. Outside this closed educational system, however, the class bias inherent in the aristocratic view of amateurism created controversy, resentment, and hypocrisy that have lasted into the late twentieth century. Nowhere was this class bias more blatant than in the early definitions of amateurism, none of which included mechanics, artisans, and laborers in this amateur competition even if they had never accepted financial compensation for their athletic involvement. The language that excluded this class of laborers came to be known as the "mechanics clause."

One of the first definitions of an amateur ever published by an athletic organization included the mechanics clause. According to the definition issued by the Amateur Athletic Club of England in 1866, an amateur was "any gentleman who has never competed in an open competition, or for any public money, or for admission money, or with professionals for a prize, public money, or admission money, and who has never in any period of his life taught or assisted in the pursuit of athletic exercises as a means of livelihood; nor as a mechanic, artisan, or labourer."[14]

The usual justification for exclusion of manual laborers from amateur competition, aside from their alleged immorality, was that their strenuous daily occupations gave them an unfair physical advantage over athletes who were employed in more genteel pursuits. There is probably some merit to the argument that watermen, who made a living transporting produce along the Thames by rowing, had an advantage over athletes for whom rowing was a pastime. Excluding other manual laborers, however, had far more to do with social status than with physical advantage. Like India's Brahmans, who avoided shadows cast by untouchables for fear of defilement, Britain's aristocrats used their amateur code to avoid social contamination.

In 1879 the stewards of the Henley Regatta, who are a major governing body of British rowing, issued their classic definition of an "amateur," which included the mechanics clause. Three years later the Amateur Rowing Association did the same.[15] But the exclusion of the working classes did not go unchallenged. As rowing gained in popularity throughout the late 1800s, increasing numbers of working-class athletes became involved with the sport. When these working-class rowers were unable to get the Amateur Rowing Association to remove the mechanics clause, they formed their own organization, called the National Amateur Rowing Association.[16] It took several more decades, but eventually the mechanics clause began to disappear from the definitions of "amateur" according to Britain's sport-governing bodies. In 1938 the Amateur Rowing Association and the Henley Regatta Stewards dropped their references to manual labor, thereby recognizing a class of amateurs who were, strictly speaking, not gentlemen.

Although the disappearance of the mechanics clause reflected movement toward democratization in British amateur sport, the amateur ethos continued to work against the interests of lower-class athletes throughout the world in ways that while perhaps less obvious were far more profound in their consequences. Throughout the late nineteenth and early twentieth centuries, sport in many nations moved rapidly beyond the realm of personal recreation into the arena of international competition and mass commercial entertainment. With the prestige of one's nation and millions of dollars at stake, sport promoters were unlikely to trust their fortunes to amateur athletes who trained in their spare time and viewed sport as a mere avocation.

Not surprisingly, a market began to develop for a class of openly professional athletes who could make a comfortable living playing sport. The aristocratic notion that sport for sport's sake was somehow "purer" or more worthy than playing sport for material gain continued to stigmatize professional athletes, but otherwise, amateurism ceased to exercise an influence on their lives. The situation was quite different for world-class athletes who were supposed to be competing as amateurs. Winning a gold medal in the Olympics, for instance, required methodical training and an expenditure of time and effort that exceeded the demands of most full-time jobs. Sonja Henie, a gold medal winner in figure-skating in 1928, 1932, and 1936, is said to have trained eight hours a day from the age of seven.[17] The amateur requirement that athletes continue working at regular jobs to pay living expenses while pursuing sport as an avocation ignored practical realities.

The question was how a world-class athlete from a lower-class background was supposed to train, travel, and still find time to work at a regular job. The only realistic solution was to compensate athletes for work time missed because of the demands of training.[18] In other words, world-class athletes from lower-class backgrounds needed some form of financial compensation in order to compete successfully. Rather than face this reality squarely, amateur sport-governing bodies continued to insist (as some still do) that one can become the finest athlete in the world in one's spare time. Predictably, the Olympic rules were violated with impunity. In the United States, colleges and universities invented their own special brand of hypocrisy.[19]

SPORT IN AMERICAN COLLEGES BEFORE THE CIVIL WAR

David Young, in his classic book *The Olympic Myth of Greek Amateur Athletes*, argues that amateur traditions were relatively unknown in the United States until the late nineteenth century, when they were suddenly "invented."[20]

This claim seems highly unlikely, given the fact that America had been a British colony. Very few of the colonists were transplanted aristocrats, but as soon as their material circumstances would allow it, they imitated the fashion and lifestyle of the British landed gentry.[21] Among the settlers in New England by 1640 were 130 alumni of British universities; students at Harvard College, founded in 1636, studied the same classical curriculum as students at Oxford.[22] In architectural style, Harvard and most other American colleges were rustic imitations of Oxford and Cambridge.

Colonial Americans with wealth, including both prosperous merchants of the larger cities and the large plantation owners of the South, engaged in many of the same forms of sporting activity as the leisure classes in England. By 1776 there were twenty-seven American-based English sports.[23] The American gentry, though less formal than their British counterparts, tended to approach sport with the spirit of the gentleman-amateur. In 1674 a common tailor "scandalized" the gentry of York County, Virginia, by entering his horse in a race against a horse owned by a Southern aristocrat. The county court fined the tailor 200 pounds of tobacco and asserted that horse racing was "a sport for gentlemen only."[24] It would appear that American gentlemen had imported British aristocratic sporting etiquette along with British saddle horses, pedigreed dogs, racing boats, and other sporting equipment.

British sports and pastimes were a part of campus life at American colleges in the pre-Revolutionary War period, often much to the consternation of college officials.[25] At Harvard college in the early 1800s, interclass football contests pitting freshmen against sophomores became traditional yearly events. Similar games were played at English public schools, and in both America and England they were part of the hazing of underclassmen. Before the American Civil War, sports on college campuses were informal affairs that like their British counterparts were organized by students and pursued for recreation and diversion.

The first intercollegiate contest between American teams was a rowing match between Yale and Harvard on Lake Winnipesaukee, New Hampshire, in 1852. Although the race was promoted by the Boston, Concord, and Montreal railways as a commercial enterprise, the tone of the event was decidedly amateur. There had been no special training for the race. In preparation, "the bottoms of the boats were blackened and abstinence from pastry was observed."[26] One participant described the event as a "frolic without sequel."[27] Commenting on a crew meet in 1858, Charles Eliot, one of Harvard's future presidents, stated, "I had rather win than not, but it is mighty little matter whether we beat or are beaten—rowing is not my profession. . . .

It is only recreation, fun and health."[28] It would be difficult to find any clearer illustration of the British amateur ideal.

Between 1852 and 1880, intercollegiate competition began in baseball, cricket, soccer, rugby, American football, track and field, and other sports, most of which had British roots. According to a report on American college sport commissioned by the Carnegie Foundation, the usages and customs of this period were (consciously or unconsciously) similar to those at Oxford and Cambridge.[29] Management was totally in the hands of undergraduates. Participants generally paid their own expenses. Sport club subscriptions were sometimes used to pay for travel. The practice of recruiting and subsidizing students because of their athletic abilities was as rare as it was at Oxford and Cambridge.

On college campuses before the Civil War, the notion that college sport was recreation for participants rather than a form of commercial entertainment was pretty much taken for granted, thus making rules excluding professionals unnecessary. Furthermore, the privileged backgrounds of most students probably reinforced negative evaluations of athletic professionalism. Outside of universities, however, rules to ensure a clear demarcation between the amateur and the professional were beginning to be formulated as early as the 1830s. In 1834 the Castle Garden Boat Club Association of New York, composed of young men from prominent families, published a constitution that did not permit members to "row for money, or take part in a regatta or races with any club or clubs independent of those belonging to the association."[30] As was the case in England, regulations in America governing amateurs were being used by the upper classes to insulate themselves from their social "inferiors."

The rapid industrialization in America that followed the Civil War transformed sport at colleges and universities in ways that few people in the 1850s could have imagined. Sport promoters early in the 1800s were aware of the potential of sport as commercial entertainment. Boxing, pedestrianism, horse racing, and rowing—these and other sports had attracted large crowds and considerable revenue. The foundations for the growth of organized professional sport had been laid early in the nineteenth century. It was not until after the Civil War, however, that sport became a major business capable of supporting a class of well-paid professional athletes.

The promise of jobs in America's booming industrial sector attracted millions of Americans and immigrants from around the world to U.S. cities. From 1860 to 1910 the number of cities with populations of over 100,000 increased from nine to fifty.[31] Urban growth, coupled with the increase in leisure time and expendable income that the new industrial order ultimately provided, created an ideal market for the sport entrepreneur. Cut off from the rural pastimes of preindustrial America and seeking to escape the tedium of industrial work, urban dwellers turned to spectator sport in larger and larger numbers. Advances in technology in the areas of transportation and communications also contributed to the growth of organized spectator sport.

The railroads made intersectional rivalries possible, allowing sports teams to become the focus of community pride and solidarity. Newspapers and the telegraph fueled fan interest by providing current information on team performance. The media also created sports heroes, with whom fans could identify and whose name recognition could sell products and fill a stadium. In 1869 the Cincinnati Red Stockings, the first avowedly all-professional baseball team, crossed the United States on the newly completed transcontinental railroad and played games before over 200,000 fans in total.[32] In that same year, a group of Princeton students boarded a train for New Brunswick, New Jersey, to play Rutgers in the first intercollegiate football game.

A MARKET EMERGES FOR PROFESSIONAL COLLEGE ATHLETES

The fact that professional sport in the post–Civil War period became a major force in American popular culture does not explain why American colleges and universities also became staging grounds for mass athletic spectacles. The growing popularity of professional sport in mainstream society may have been a necessary condition for professional sport in colleges, but it did not guarantee it. To understand why universities began constructing giant stadiums and recruiting and subsidizing skilled athletes, one must focus on factors peculiar to American higher education and the values of those who controlled it.

Funding for American colleges in the nineteenth century was never as secure or as predictable as at such British schools as Oxford and Cambridge.[33] A number of universities had the financial support of wealthy benefactors such as John D. Rockefeller and Leland Stanford. More typically, funding was unreliable and competition for students intense. The passage of the Morrill Land Grant College Act in 1862 encouraged the rapid expansion of educational institutions into states whose sparse populations could barely support them. In the late 1800s state universities, land grant colleges, technical institutes, and the older liberal arts colleges were all competing in the student market.

Curricular reforms that allowed a greater emphasis on practical skills and vocational training helped to "sell" the universities to the increasingly business-minded public. Attracting students and institutional support, however, also required public relations and advertising techniques that, before the Civil War would have seemed unimaginable. The University of Chicago was just one of the schools that employed advertising with sophistication. Before market segmentation had become a common marketing term, Chicago was producing brochures and pamphlets targeted to specific markets such as businessmen and their sons. The University of Chicago's dean Albion Small advised president William Harper that "We must obey the first and last law of advertising—keep everlastingly at it."[34]

Starved for students and dependent on a broad variety of external constituencies for financial support, college presidents developed a "battle-scarred sensitivity to the subject of public opinion."[35] What they needed more than anything was a bridge that could link the high culture of the university with the mass culture of the broader society, which, of course, provided both their students and their resources. In the late 1800s few campus activities could better meet that need than intercollegiate sport. Nothing could better attract the attention of mass media, and nothing had a greater appeal to the practical-minded business leaders who provided financial support and who increasingly came to dominate academe's governing boards.

The need for public visibility, and (to a lesser degree) gate receipts, undoubtedly spurred on the early professionalization of college sport. Paying-spectators were unlikely to stream onto college campuses in large numbers to watch amateurs engaging in friendly recreation. An additional contributing factor, however, was the changing composition in colleges and universities of their governing boards. Academic trustees had once been clergymen. In the late nineteenth century, they were increasingly made up of businessmen, who were often highly skeptical of the value of a liberal education. Wealthy industrialists tended to support a practical curriculum, one that prepared students for careers in commerce or industry. Many were not entirely convinced that college was even necessary.

For such men, the highly skilled athlete testing his courage, endurance, and native intelligence on a playing field was learning more about life than the poet and the scholar. Richard Hofstadter, in his musings on anti-intellectualism in America, distinguished between two qualities of mind, one being intellect and the other intelligence.[36] There is little doubt that the business class much preferred the latter. Intelligence, as they conceived it, was practical and geared toward no-nonsense problem solving. It operated within a narrow range and had no patience for any thought that did not get right to the point.

In the minds of many late-nineteenth-century businessmen, intellect was associated with wasteful theorizing, physical weakness, overemotionalism, and effeminacy. Games like football embodied masculinity, practicality, and dedication to professional drill. That the demands of college sport should interfere with the cultivation of the life of the mind was unlikely to bother men whose wealth often derived from a no-holds-barred struggle for economic survival. Not surprisingly, they often ignored or even abetted professionalism in college sport. The social climate of the late nineteenth century was hostile toward the amateur spirit. And that hostility was as much anti-intellectual and antifemale as it was antielitist.

The University of Chicago provides a clear illustration of how far college sport had drifted since Yale's first rowing meet with Harvard in 1852. William Rainey Harper, Chicago's newly elected president in 1892, was no anti-intellectual, but his philosophy of higher education had a decidedly utilitarian cast. As the first president of this newly founded institution, Harper consciously integrated sport into the university's marketing plan. One of his first faculty appointments was Amos Alonzo Stagg, a former football star at Yale. Harper's instructions to his new coach were to "develop teams which we can send around the country and knock out all the colleges. We will give them a palace car and a vacation too."[37] Commenting on Harper's sometimes unorthodox methods for promoting the university, one of its professors quipped that Harper was "the P. T. Barnum of Higher Education."[38]

This marketing strategy appears to have worked. Between 1896 and 1909, the university's enrollment increased from 1,815 to 5,500 students. Harper's university had risen to considerable prominence in a fairly short period of time, and winning football teams, in addition to generous support from John D. Rockefeller, had contributed to that rise. Success in football also produced some negative fallout. As early as 1895, Stagg was charged with employing professional athletes and overemphasizing winning.[39] Although Harper reprimanded Stagg for some of his tactics, this did not prevent Stagg from becoming one of the highest-paid members of the university.

Compared with sport at Oxford and Cambridge at the time, the University of Chicago's approach to college football was undeniably professional. An article in *Colliers* written by Edward Jordan in 1905 entitled "Buying Football Victories" sheds light on some of the methods of recruiting and subsidizing athletes common at the time.[40] According to Jordan, Stagg was allowed to use an $80,000 trust fund, originally set aside for "needy students," to subsidize talented athletes. Jordan also claimed that athletes received remission of tuition for campus jobs but actually did no work. An argument often made in defense of this practice was that athletes could not realistically be expected to attend classes, endure the regimen of big-time college football, and at the same time hold down a campus job.

Jordan alleged that Walter Eckersall had "received free tuition during his entire course, with no return except in kicking and tackling ability" (19). Eckersall, one of Chicago's greatest athletes, was twice disqualified from Chicago for academic deficiencies, but never during the playing season. Another athlete mentioned in the article turned down offers from Northwestern and Wisconsin to attend the university after a Chicago real estate broker had supplemented an offer already put forth by Stagg. A high school student named Leo Detray allegedly turned down an offer of room, board, tuition, and full support for himself and a companion to attend California College. He chose Chicago instead, because he got a better offer (20).

What the University of Chicago case demonstrates is that winning athletic teams, especially those in football, were perceived to be playing a significant promotional role in universities. Gate receipts were also becoming an important source of revenue. Given football's strategic importance, it had to be brought under a university's control, and highly talented athletes had to be recruited and subsidized in a fairly systematic fashion. Alumni played a vital role in athletic subsidization and recruitment, but universities themselves were finding innovative ways to use financial aid funds to procure athletes. Although both Harper and Stagg swore allegiance to the time-honored amateur ideal, the demands of the university as they saw them required high-performance spectator sport. Hypocrisy became rampant.

PROFESSIONALISM SPINS OUT OF CONTROL

Participants in British sport were regular students who chose to pursue sport in their leisure time. The demands of sport in American universities increasingly required a class of skilled athletes, many of whom might never have considered going to college if they had not been paid in some way for their athletic services. The subsidization and recruitment of college athletes took a variety of forms throughout the latter nineteenth century. College alumni were often at the center of nationwide efforts to procure athletic talent; cash payments, jobs, and loans that were invariably forgiven were just a few of the inducements. Alumni often operated independently to procure talent for their alma maters. At other times, they worked closely with coaches and college administrators.

At Harvard, according to Samuel Eliot Morison, "of the numerous law students on the Harvard baseball teams in the eighties, a number were professionals, whose tuition fees as law students were paid by patriotic old grads."[41] According to an academic dean at Brown University during this period, "There is not an Eastern college, important in athletics, which does not make a more or less systematic canvass of the [secondary] schools."[42] He went on to assert that students and alumni were heavily involved in recruitment and subsidization. In many instances, athletes who would not have been able to afford college otherwise were receiving financial support from alumni, and it was not uncommon for college and university personnel to arrange these deals.

At Yale, Henry P. Wright, dean of the Yale College faculty, wrote a letter to Walter Camp, a famous Yale football coach, asking: "Has anything been done for [the player] Daly? I understand that some grad could be found from whom he might borrow $100 occasionally, giving his note, to be paid after graduation. He is pretty hard up and is getting rather restless. I do not see how he can come back after this term unless he is able to raise something somewhere."[43] An example of a more creative approach to financing was an attempt by William and Mary's baseball team in the 1890s to get the college to waive tuition for a star pitcher while the team offered to pick up expenses at a local hotel.[44] During these early years, team captains and managers often openly solicited skilled athletes, and townspeople, alumni, and local businessmen raised money to pay their expenses. In small towns, winning sport teams could help to promote local businesses and improve the community's public image. Citizens not formally related to the colleges became "boosters" of college sport and were not adverse to helping to subsidize a talented player.

No approach to subsidizing college athletes has created more sustained controversy than the use of college and university financial aid to attract talented athletes. Before the Civil War, college students were drawn primarily from the privileged classes, and "impecunious" students, even those with considerable academic promise, were often excluded. As enrollments began to dip in the 1840s and 1850s, however, colleges became increasingly sensitive to charges that they were elitist and exclusionary and therefore not deserving of public support. In order to project a more democratic image, schools began to develop funds that could be a source of financial aid for the poor. At first, these were called charity funds. Later, the name was changed to scholarship funds.[45]

Few college faculty saw any problem with offering financial aid to academically qualified students of modest means, including those who were fine athletes. However, it did not take long for coaches, with the help of the admission's staff, to begin funneling financial aid money to young athletes who possessed little academic interest or ability. Financial aid was also awarded to athletes who were not particularly needy. Awarding athletic scholarships was becoming commonplace as early as the 1880s. This is evinced by the fact that Princeton amended its eligibility rules in 1882 to exclude all students whose college expenses were paid because they participated in athletics.[46] By 1905 the chancellor of Allegheny College would comment, "We go out after men for the sake of baseball and football, offering all sorts of inducements. . . . Scholarships are offered to promising players. Professionalism is winked at."[47]

By the turn of the century, athletes were receiving scholarships, sinecure jobs, gifts from alumni and citizens, and a hundred other types of financial compensation. In 1905 *McCure's* magazine reported that James Hogan, a Yale football player, enjoyed free tuition, a free suite in Vanderbilt Hall, and a $100 scholarship. He had also taken a ten-day vacation to Cuba, paid for by the Yale Athletic Association, and had a monopoly on the sale of scorecards at games and the exclusive commission for handling the products of the American Tobacco company on the Yale campus.[48] Football not only paid for Hogan's living and educational expenses; it allowed him to prosper.

In the late nineteenth century, big-time college sport was evolving into an unrelated business of the university, and athletes were being relegated to the periphery of academic life. Recruited by different academic standards than those for other students and subsidized primarily for their academic abilities, college athletes were becoming "outsiders." Alexander Meiklejohn, a dean of Brown University in 1905, who condemned practices ranging from athletic recruiting to the "outright hiring of players," lamented "that thousands of dollars are expended annually in the work of securing for the teams men who have no right to play on them whatever."[49] In Meiklejohn's view, college athletes should be students, not professional athletes masquerading as college students.

UNDER FIRE, THE ACADEMICS TAKE A STAND

The social and economic conditions in the nineteenth century were not conducive to the growth of amateur sport. But on many college campuses there were pockets of resistance to rampant professionalism. Among those most vocal in their support of amateur sport were faculty and others with a commitment to what Hofstadter has called "the life of the mind." Additional support came from elitist anglophiles whose concerns stemmed as much from class prejudices as from an interest in preserving academic integrity. Separating elitism from intellectualism was not always easy.

Among faculty and college presidents in the late 1900s, there were many who supported the British approach to amateur sport. Charles W. Eliot, the president of Harvard from 1869 to 1909, is a classic example. It is not surprising that Eliot, a member of one of Boston's most patrician families, would embrace the amateur spirit. A descendant of wealthy Bostonian merchants, Eliot's views of education, sport, and life in general were shaped by the "old wealth" of New England's colonial period. The banking and mercantile background that had produced Eliot set him apart from the ministerial tradition that had influenced earlier college presidents. His secular outlook and utilitarian values were tempered, however, by patrician origins that set him apart also from the nouveau riche industrialists of the period.[50]

Eliot was an avid sportsman and had rowed at Harvard in the 1850s. His views on sport, as reflected in his inaugural address upon assuming the Harvard presidency, could have been written by Lord Wellington himself. "There is an aristocracy to which sons of Harvard have belonged," said Eliot, "and let us hope will ever aspire to belong—the aristocracy which excels in manly sports. . . ."[51] Like the British gentleman-amateur, Eliot believed in winning and in excellence in sport. What he opposed was many of the methods used in American colleges and universities to achieve success. Eliot wanted winning teams, but not if winning meant recruiting a class of professional athletes for whom education was an afterthought.

In his public statements, Eliot roundly condemned the commercialization of college sport. In his 1882–1883 presidential report, he flatly stated that the authorities at Harvard are "opposed to all money making at intercollegiate contests and . . . to all exhibitions or contests which are deliberately planned to attract a multitude and thereby increase gate money."[52] Like the British, Eliot distinguished clearly between sport as a profession and sport as a form of recreation. From his perspective, only the latter had a place on college campuses. He consistently condemned what he considered to be extravagant expenditures on athletics both by athletic teams themselves and by spectators.[53] Eliot's view of college sport was a blend of aristocratic elitism and a genuine concern for academic standards.

During Eliot's presidency, Harvard faculty played a significant role in molding athletic policy. In the 1880s, when the athletic committee at Harvard was first formed, it was composed entirely of faculty. Later, the committee was expanded to include students and alumni. The Harvard faculty, like Eliot, opposed professional coaches, athletic practices that interfered with serious academic work, and financial inducements to attract athletes to college. Students and alumni, on the other hand, resented the intrusion of faculty into their games and supported policies that would lead to athletic victories and greater public recognition.[54] With the support of Eliot and a governing board composed primarily of Bostonian Patricians, the Harvard faculty slowed the advance of athletic professionalism but saw its influence in athletic matters decline as the nineteenth century came to a close.

It is undeniable that some Harvard faculty involved in the formation of athletic policy shared elitist views not unlike those of Britain's gentleman-amateurs, who supported the infamous mechanics clause. Their opposition to

games between Harvard teams and professionals probably had more to do with
maintaining status distinctions than with defending academic standards. The
same can be said of the athletic committee's decision to build a fence around
the athletic field so as "to exclude objectionable persons."[55] But stripped of this
elitist baggage, Eliot's defense of the amateur ideal also supported a system of
athletics that placed academic excellence above the athletic needs of the newly
evolving college sport industry. This "educational model" also encouraged
regular students to be active participants on college teams rather than relegating
them to the role of spectators.

Eliot was not the only college president who took a stand against professional college sport. Most college presidents held an official position that was
"iron clad" in its opposition to professionalism.[56] Stanford's president David
Starr Jordan, for instance, saw the use of money to recruit players as an agency
of demoralization. Jordan, a contemporary of Eliot's, argued in *Colliers* in
1904 that "no man should receive money, from any source, in consideration
of his playing."[57] Jordan opposed athletic scholarships, under-the-table payments from alumni and boosters, jobs provided for athletes that entailed little
or no work, and any other form of compensation that was given in consideration for athletic ability. Of course, it was one thing to make pronounce-
ments such as this to the press. It was quite another to translate these views
into enforceable university policy.

The case of University of Michigan President James G. Angell illustrates the
political realities that presidents faced in the area of athletics. Angell was a major
proponent of Western Conference rule changes that would have restricted
recruiting tactics used by Michigan's high-powered football coach Fielding
Yost. The faculty approved the rule changes, but students and alumni, fearing
that the rules would destroy Michigan's football dynasty, protested. The
university's regents responded by abolishing the faculty committee on athletics
and substituting a Board of Athletics, which would be solely under the control
of and responsible to the regents.[58] Angell may have been president of the
university, but the regents controlled college sport. Unlike Eliot, whose board
was somewhat sympathetic to amateur principles, Angell had to bow to the
power of commercial interests in football.

It is clear that as early as the late 1800s, faculty often found themselves at
odds with students, alumni, and governing boards when it came to athletic
policy. College presidents were often caught in the middle as they tried to
reconcile the academic integrity of their institutions with the athletic demands
of powerful external constituencies. A number of conferences and athletic
associations also came into existence during the late nineteenth century. They,
too, attempted to hold firm to amateur ideals, but like faculty and college

presidents, they found it impossible to enforce rules that would lessen the spectator appeal of commercial college sport. Although amateur rules were difficult to enforce, there was no shortage of rule-making bodies to promulgate them.

In 1882 the six Eastern colleges that made up the College Baseball Association amended their eligibility rules to exclude all students whose college expenses were paid because they participated in athletics.[59] A few years later, the Intercollegiate Association of Amateur Athletics of America made it illegal to compete for monetary prizes or to sell trophies for money and developed eligibility rules that excluded persons from college teams who were not bona fide students. The Intercollegiate Conference of Faculty Representatives, later to be known as the Western Conference and still later as the Big Ten, was founded in 1895. Included in its rules was the provision that "no person shall be admitted to any intercollegiate contest who receives any gift, remuneration, or pay for his services on the college team."[60] This rule expressly prohibited the practice of awarding financial aid to students on the basis of their athletic abilities. By the end of the century, all of these association and conference rules were being violated with impunity.

At the very close of the century, 1898, a major effort was made by seven of the eight schools that today comprise the Ivy League to establish interinstitutional control over college sport. Colleges from all of the Ivy group, with the exception of Yale, sent faculty, student, and alumni representatives to Providence, Rhode Island, to attend a conference on college athletic reform sponsored by Brown University.[61] Among the major agenda items were athletic scholarships, eligibility of undergraduate and graduate students, summer baseball for pay, commercialism, and the role of faculty in athletic governance. No final decisions were made at the conference, but a subcommittee composed of seven faculty members was charged with writing a report and developing concrete recommendations.

The resulting document presented a model for amateur sport that its authors hoped would be adopted at all colleges and universities. The Brown Conference report contained eligibility rules that are in many ways similar to those of the current NCAA except for their unequivocal opposition to any form of financial compensation for participation in intercollegiate sport. According to the report's authors, "no student should be paid for his athletics. The practice of assisting men through college in order that they may strengthen the athletic teams is degrading to amateur sport" (9). Their report did not recommend that students from poor backgrounds, including those who play college sport, be denied financial aid to attend college. What these authors opposed was financial aid awarded for athletic ability. According to rule 3(b) of the document, any student is disqualified from college sport "who receives from any source whatever a pecuniary gain or emolument or position of profit, direct or indirect, in order to render it possible for him to participate in university athletics" (11).

Furthermore, their rules required that a student engaged in athletic competition be in good academic standing; they also limited the number of years of athletic eligibility, outlawed participation in summer baseball for pay, and generally laid out guidelines that the authors felt would facilitate fair competition among a variety of different colleges. The main purpose of these rules, according to their subcommittee, was to encourage rational amateur sport that would complement rather than interfere with the mental and moral development of students. The British influence on the proposed rules was unmistakable. "No student," said the subcommittee, "should be permitted to make athletics the principal occupation of his college life. We are not engaged in making athletes" (5). Another proposal was that gate-money and other commercial interests be totally eliminated from the college games.

The Brown Conference report stands as a manifesto to amateur college sport and its role in a liberal education. Although the participants in the Brown Conference never took collective action on the rule proposals, some athletic committees did adopt a number of the proposals as their own. Also, the report sketched in a general way some of the main principles that are at the heart of the educational model of college sport to this very day. The subcommittee's unequivocal stand against athletic scholarships foreshadowed a similar position taken by the NCAA for the first four decades of its existence. In 1945 the entire Ivy Group finally eliminated athletic scholarships. Furthermore, the Brown Conference report's athletic philosophy is not unlike that of the NCAA's current Division III. The subcommittee's suggestion that there be yearly meetings to discuss eligibility rules also anticipated a policy ultimately adopted by the NCAA. The Brown report was in some ways ahead of its time.

In other ways, however, the subcommittee seemed out of touch with then-current realities, as if the faculty who wrote the report had never read a sports page or heard of Amos Alonzo Stagg. At the time of the Brown Conference, the rationalization and professionalization of college sport had already progressed to the point where on many college campuses there was no going back to the original amateur model. A chasm was beginning to open between those who supported athletic competition as a complement to the university's academic mission, and those who recognized the vital role that professional college sport could play both in the area of fiscal policy development and public relations and also as a profit center. The framers of the Brown Conference report seemed totally oblivious to the monetary concerns of the latter group and to the tremendous power that this group was beginning to wield in academic and athletic policy matters.

A NOTE ON WHAT IT MEANS TO BE COMPETITIVE

During the last decades of the nineteenth century, what it meant to have a competitive collegiate athletic program took on a very distinctive meaning. Lord Wellington obviously thought of the amateur games played on the "playing fields of Eton" as being highly competitive. It is unlikely that he would have credited Eton's games directly with preparing British officers for one of the bloodiest military engagements in history if Eton's young athletes had cared little for winning. The fact is that amateur sport leaves room for fierce competition. What the amateur team often lacks is high-quality players who can devote their lives to training. Amateur teams must "make do" with the material on hand, but this need not make their games less competitive.

As college sport evolved into a form of commercial entertainment, being competitive acquired a meaning that was synonymous with athletic professionalism. Being competitive in the sense of producing winning teams at the regional, national, and international levels required more than athletes with mere determination. What was needed was the admission to college of an athletic elite. Being competitive came to mean paying college athletes in some fashion, lowering academic standards in many cases, and subjecting athletes to a regimen that was almost guaranteed to interfere with normal academic progress. It also meant expending large sums of money on athletic facilities, coaches' salaries, skilled athletic administrators, training rooms, athletic equipment, and all the other items on the budget of a successful athletic program. On many college campuses, this meant the creation of a large auxiliary enterprise that had little to do with the life of the mind but that performed functions that were as indispensable as many academic programs.

2
The NCAA Turns Professional: 1906–1956

The primary impetus for recruiting and subsidizing college athletes in the early years of college sport was probably the prestige derived from being associated with a winning sports team. Colleges and universities needed the publicity, and successful sports teams gave students, alumni, trustees, and local fans something to be proud of. When "old Siwash" won, everyone associated with the institution shared vicariously in the victory. With the growth of mass media, college sports heroes became national heroes, and winning teams could raise a college from relative obscurity into national prominence.[1] If the price to be paid for sharing in the prestige of a winning sports team was the subsidization of talented college athletes, there was no shortage of people to come forth with the money.

The success of college sport as a commercial enterprise in the first half of the twentieth century further increased the pressure on colleges and universities to recruit and to provide compensation for college athletes. Harvard spent $300,000 in 1903 to build the nation's first permanent football stadium. Yale followed in 1914 by constructing a stadium with a seating capacity of 75,000, making it the country's largest. As the market spread westward, huge stadiums became a common feature on college campuses. In 1923 the University of California at Berkeley built a stadium to seat 76,000 spectators. Throughout the first half of the twentieth century, gate receipts at college games increased dramatically.[2] The 1952 Pennsylvania–Notre Dame game was played at Franklin Field before 80,000 paying spectators. In that year, Pennsylvania's football team generated over $500,000 for its university.[3] With these kinds of revenues and massive investments in infrastructure, it made absolutely no business sense to trust the industry's fortunes to amateur student athletes pursuing sports in their spare time.

Not surprisingly, the first decades of the twentieth century witnessed a relentless professionalization of collegiate sport. In open defiance of amateur rules promulgated by one governing body after another, universities found ways to subsidize talented athletes. The National Collegiate Athletic Association, which was founded in 1906 in part to restore amateur standards, was unable to reverse this trend. Many of that organization's actions, especially after 1948, can best be understood as rearguard accommodations to professionalism rather than efforts to preserve amateur ideals. By 1957, when the dust had settled from a battle over what was then referred to as the "Sanity Code," the NCAA's amateur code had been gutted of most of its substance, and the shell that remained served primarily as ideological camouflage for the newly emerging NCAA cartel.

THE NCAA AND ITS EARLY DEFENSE OF THE AMATEUR IDEAL

The game of football, as it evolved in American schools and universities, was a fairly rough-and-tumble affair at the turn of the century. Players wore little or no equipment and used mass formations, which encouraged collisions of considerable force. Broken limbs and noses appear to have been fairly commonplace, and there were more than enough deaths attributed to the game to raise public concern. During the 1904 season, 21 players were killed and over 200 injured.[4] Muckraking newspapers at the time focused on the brutality and alleged corruption of the game, and editorials began to appear demanding athletic reform.[5] In addition to the issue of violence in college sport, reformers attacked its growing professionalism and its apparent transformation into a form of commercial entertainment.

By 1905 public outrage over violence in football prompted President Theodore Roosevelt to use the prestige of his office to bring about reform. Roosevelt, an avid outdoorsman and advocate of the "strenuous life," admired football as a game and therefore preferred reform rather than the often-suggested remedy of abolishing the game altogether. In 1905 he invited football leaders, including representatives from Yale, Harvard, and Princeton, to the White House to discuss the future of college football. This meeting brought assurances from the existing American Football Rules Committee, headed by Walter Camp at Yale, that efforts would be made to transform football into a more open and safer game. Yet, even with prodding from the president, the

December meeting of the football rules committee produced minimal changes.[6]

Perceived inaction by the football rules committee and growing public criticism during the fall of 1905 led Henry M. MacCracken, then-chancellor of New York University, to call a special meeting of football-playing colleges to address the crisis in college sport. This meeting, attended by representatives from only thirteen colleges, was followed by another in late December that attracted delegates from sixty-two schools. Acting without the sanction of the American Football Rules Committee, this assembly created a formal organization to be called the Intercollegiate Athletic Association of the United States (IAAUS). This organization, renamed the National Collegiate Athletic Association (NCAA) in 1912, created its own football rules committee, which joined with the original committee to create rules far more palatable to the general public.[7]

Football violence was the catalyst that brought the NCAA into existence, but problems relating to amateurism and eligibility rules received as much, if not more, attention at the first NCAA Annual Meeting in 1906. As college sport grew as a commercial spectacle, so did fan interest in competition beyond regional lines. To exploit this newly emerging national market, a national sport-governing body was needed. Playing rules had to be standardized, as did rules regarding recruitment and subsidization. Such rules would assure fair competition on the playing field while at the same time giving institutions an equal opportunity to share the profits of this new industry. In 1906 the NCAA was a fledgling organization with little power and few influential universities in its membership. Over the next five decades, it would evolve into a national economic sports cartel.

The NCAA's position on amateurism, as it appears in Articles VI and VII of its 1906 bylaws, is unequivocal, uncompromising, and virtually indistinguishable from the position taken by British universities such as Oxford and Cambridge. According to Article VI, each member institution was to enforce measures to prevent violations of amateur principles. Included among these violations was "the offering of inducements to players to enter colleges or universities because of their athletic abilities or supporting or maintaining players while students on account of their athletic abilities, either by athletic organizations, individual alumni, or otherwise, directly or indirectly."[8] This principle clearly forbade scholarships or financial aid based on athletic rather than academic ability. In true British fashion, the enforcement of this principle was left to each institution, the assumption being that gentlemen do not need outside agencies to enforce a code of honor.

In 1906 the NCAA stood firmly behind the amateur notion that athletes should be selected from students on campus rather than recruited from the outside with offers of "money or financial concession, or emolument" (34). Financial inducements from any source, including faculty or university financial aid committees, were not allowed. Singling out prominent athletic students from preparatory schools was a violation of the amateur code, as was playing those who were not bona fide students. Article VII required candidates for positions on athletic teams to fill out an eligibility card, answering on their honor "as gentlemen" questions regarding compensation, inducements, scholarships, and academic work completed. Consistent with the NCAA's early commitment to the notion of institutional autonomy, these cards were turned in to the respective schools, not to the NCAA (35–36).

The NCAA's first president, Palmer Pierce of West Point, addressed the issue of amateurism in his speech to the 1907 convention. According to Pierce, "This organization wages no war against the professional athlete, but does object to such a one posing and playing as an amateur." What the NCAA frowns on, said Pierce, is the "more skillful professional who parading under college colors is receiving pay in some form or other for his athletic prowess."[9] Pierce simply wanted college sport returned to college students. The problem of how to accomplish that was far more complex. With high stakes (including national prestige and large amounts of money) riding on athletic victories, violations of the amateur code were inevitable. Leaving enforcement in the hands of individual colleges and universities was quixotic even in the early twentieth century.

The Western Conference, later to become the Big Ten, had its first organizational meeting in 1895.[10] Over the next fifty years, the Big Ten pioneered in their development of eligibility rules, the prohibition of subsidies to athletes, and faculty control of athletics. Many of these rules were later copied by other conferences and by the NCAA.[11] In 1927, in response to a growing concern that amateur rules were being widely ignored, the Big Ten reaffirmed its position on recruitment and subsidization in a report prepared by what was called the "Committee of Sixty." The report stated that "no scholarships, loans or remissions of tuition were to be awarded on the basis of athletic skill."[12] In addition, no financial aid was to be given to students for the purpose of promoting the athletic success of a particular team. Similar carefully worded provisions would eventually appear in the rules of the NCAA.

The 1906 bylaws of the NCAA discussed a number of actions that constituted violations of amateur principles, but it was not until 1916 that an "amateur athlete" was actually defined. According to Article VI(b) of the bylaws, an amateur is "one who participates in competitive physical sports only for the pleasure, and the physical, mental, moral, and social benefits directly derived therefrom."[13] Of course, professional athletes, especially those who love their jobs, may derive similar benefits from sport. The point was, however, that amateurs, unlike professionals, competed *only* for symbolic or intrinsic benefits. Amateur sport, according to the NCAA, as a form of leisure activity, was free from such practical concerns as earning one's room and board.

An amended version of the NCAA's definition appeared in 1922. According to the 1922 version, "An amateur sportsman is one who engages in sport solely for the physical, mental, or social benefits he derives therefrom, and to whom the sport is *nothing more than an avocation*"[14] (emphasis added). An avocation, according to standard dictionary definition, is a "diversion or a hobby." It is usually pursued during free or discretionary time as an escape from the practical concerns of one's job. In the early twentieth century, college sport became more than a hobby for many young men whose room, board, and a variety of other kinds of financial remunerations depended on it. Athletes were putting in long hours of intensive and specialized training to meet the entertainment needs of thousands of discriminating fans. Universities, or those acting on their behalf, were often willing to pick up the bill for services rendered. NCAA rules were unequivocally opposed to such practices.

THE UNDERGROUND ECONOMY OF COLLEGE SPORT IN THE 1920S AND THE 1930S

The enforcement of the NCAA's amateur code presented a dilemma not unlike the one posed by the Eighteenth Amendment of the U.S. Constitution where in it prohibited the manufacture and sale of alcoholic beverages. In both cases, rules were passed that were not embraced with equal fervor by all segments of the American public. Most Americans opposed open professionalism in college sport. But many fans, alumni, students, and even college officials probably saw nothing morally reprehensible about helping to defray the expenses of a student who also happened to be an excellent athlete. More important, the millions of Americans who were in favor of commercialized college sport were unlikely to support strict enforcement of rules that could possibly lower the quality of play. For many Americans, major college teams without high-performance athletes were as inconceivable as a nation without alcoholic beverages.

The NCAA's amateur code, like the Eighteenth Amendment, proved almost impossible to enforce. First of all, the NCAA had no effective enforcement powers until 1948 and depended on individual schools and conferences to police themselves. Secondly, many of the people who were supposed to keep the recruitment and subsidization of athletes under control were among the industry's biggest fans. College presidents, for instance, often railed against the evils of professionalism in the press, but they were inwardly ecstatic about the vitality and excitement that commercial college sport brought to their campuses. Prohibition spawned more than 200,000 illegal speakeasies supplied by a network of gangsters.[15] Amateurism created an underground network of illegal payments to athletes supplied by alumni, boosters, townspeople, and college officials.

Determining the extent in college sports of this under-the-table system of payments is not easy. Journalists in the 1920s and the 1930s, just as today, profited from sensationalized accounts of athletic corruption and often reported allegations as if guilt were a foregone conclusion. While the press reported widespread abuses, image-conscious college administrators often argued that the problems of college sport were overstated and that if there were problems they were to be found at institutions other than their own. Even with the difficulty of finding unbiased data, an overview of newspaper reports, conference and NCAA proceedings, investigations by various committees and foundations, and other archival material from these years gives us some idea of the dimensions of recruitment and subsidization in these two decades.

One of the most rigorous and systematic studies of college sport ever undertaken was sponsored by the Carnegie Foundation for the Advancement of Teaching and was published in 1929.[16] Although this study addressed a wide variety of issues relevant to college athletics, one whole section was devoted to recruiting and subsidizing. To gather data, Howard J. Savage, the director of the study, and his four research assistants made personal visits to a total of one-hundred thirty schools, colleges, and universities, spending from two to six days at each location. They interviewed students, athletes, alumni, faculty, and administrators; gathered statistical data; and examined a variety of documents. They had considered but then abandoned the idea of using mailed questionnaires because of the sensitivity of the questions they were asking. The study, which took three years to complete, became a center of controversy for decades following its publication.

According to their study, subsidization of athletes in some form or degree took place at 81 of the 112 colleges and universities studied.[17] By subsidization, Savage meant the provision of financial or other assistance to students based on their athletic ability. Financial assistance unrelated to athletic ability, even if received by an athlete, was not considered a subsidy or a violation of the amateur ethic. The report identified four broad methods of providing under-the-table financial compensation to athletes, including jobs and employment, loans, athletic scholarships, money, and other tangible considerations. The study provided the numbers of schools violating rules in these areas and listed them by name. One of the major criticisms of the study was that officials who were honest in their responses to research questions found their institutions listed among the transgressors while those that lied escaped public ostracism.[18]

During this period, according to the study, it was not uncommon for colleges and universities to provide jobs to students to help them offset educational expenses. The concern of the Carnegie researchers was that in many cases athletes were getting preferential treatment in the assignment of such jobs. At some schools, athletes were assigned jobs outside the usual procedures and managed to procure high-paying positions not available to other students. Another abuse documented by the report was the assignment of "sinecure" jobs to athletes, which required little or no work. Often it was alumni and local businessmen that provided jobs for athletes, and these job offers became a major bargaining chip in the competitive bidding for blue-chip athletes.[19]

Alumni were also involved in providing loans to athletes that often went unpaid. Alumni funds (slush finds) were established at some universities to provide financial assistance to athletes. At one school, alumni and businessmen made contributions of $10 to $1000 annually to a fund aggregating from $25,000 to $50,000 a year.[20] In other universities, for example, Stanford, alumni funneled money into the university financial aid office with the stipulation that the awards would go to athletes.[21] The Carnegie report revealed that many colleges and universities were using scholarship money to recruit talented athletes. At some schools such as Colgate, Fordham, Penn State, and Syracuse, no attempt was made to hide this practice even though it clearly violated the principles of amateurism laid out in the NCAA bylaws.[22] The findings of the Carnegie report suggest that during the 1920s payments to athletes were as common as the American public's consumption of bootleg liquor.

The Carnegie report outlined the broad dimensions of athletic recruitment and subsidization, but news articles and data from other sources provide richer insights regarding specific violations. For instance, a *New York Herald* article in 1922 reported that eight football stars from Washington and Oregon had been offered salaries of $100 a month to play football at Purdue University.[23] These violations had been reported by Professor Leslie Ayers, then-chairman of the Faculty Athletic Committee at the University of Washington and Pacific Coast Representative of the NCAA. As a result, President H. W. Marshall of Purdue fired Coach William Dietz, saying that "Purdue would not countenance such action."[24] The athletes were not allowed to enter Purdue.

Also in 1922 Joseph K. Hart, a member of the editorial staff of a journal called *The Survey*, published an article that shed some light on college recruiting at the time. In his article, Hart included excerpts from letters received by a West Virginian high school teacher who was corresponding with college recruiters (mostly former players turned coaches after graduation) on behalf of his younger brother, who was about to enter college. One recruiter from a large state institution in the East stated that "we were very glad to hear about your brother and would appreciate more information, in particular as to his height and weight. If you will note on page 420 of the college catalogue, we hold a number of athletic scholarships . . . which will include college incidental fees and room rent at one of our college dormitories. Any athlete may be a candidate for these scholarships."[25] A middle-Southern college recruiter responded, "I am prepared to offer a scholarship, which provides room, board and tuition, if your brother cares to come to (name withheld) and can make the first twenty two men" (304). Another graduate manager from a large eastern university said, "There is no financial assistance here that the athletic authorities can render, but alumni and others are always glad to do all in their power to find remunerating work" (304).

These quotes reveal that by 1922 schools were bartering fairly openly for athletic talent and that scholarships and jobs awarded on the basis of athletic ability were part of the negotiations. Hart showed considerable prescience regarding the impact of the wave of stadium building on college campuses during the 1920s. "These huge investments in stadiums, demanding huge returns in gate receipts, will shortly make the amateur pretension impossible on these stadium grounds," said Hart, adding that "the vested interests in control of the stadiums will control the game that is played . . . and will select the players who play the game" (309). Hart, whose article was based on interviews and correspondence with officials at a number of northeastern universities, concluded that the matter of professionalism had passed from under educational auspices into the hands of alumni and business-oriented boards of regents. College sport had become "theatrical" in the business sense, and the public "has a vested right to a team that will win" (303).

Insight into how athletic scholarships were funded at some universities can be gained from a transcript found in the Harvard University Archives.[26] The author, whose twenty years as a graduate manager gave him extensive knowledge of how colleges often administered financial aid, described what might be called a system of athletic money laundering. First, according to his account, the surplus from football receipts was offered to the college president under the condition that the university would return a similar amount for athletic scholarships. Then a scholarship committee, appointed by the president and therefore well represented by individuals sympathetic to athletics, solicited letters from influential community leaders to recommend certain athletes. One president allegedly remarked about the system:

At first it troubled me considerably, and then it got so that it didn't worry me at all. My only alternative would have been to have taken a stand which would have brought down upon me the enmity, not only of coaches, managers, and undergraduates, but, I am sure, the Board of Regents as well. I happened to know that the Board of Regents had found our athletic prestige a valuable asset in getting appropriations from the legislature, and I knew they would not support me in any activity which threatened our football success.[27]

Although violations of the principles of amateurism were often ignored by college officials, there were risks if such activities became public. In 1929 the Big Ten handed out its first suspension when the University of Iowa violated a number of conference rules. The violations included the operation of a businessmen's slush fund for the subsidization of athletes, tuition refunds, and the improper use of scholarships for athletes.[28] Two other Big Ten schools were also under suspicion of rule violations, but conclusive evidence could only be found in the Iowa case. Bitter countercharges were made. Iowa accused other Big Ten programs of making similar financial arrangements with athletes. Iowa's suspension lasted only nine months.

The very next year, 1930, the University of Kansas was ousted from the Big Six, then composed of Nebraska, Kansas, Iowa State, Missouri, Oklahoma, and Kansas Aggie. An Iowa slush fund was involved in the suspension, and University of Kansas running back James "Jarring Jim" Bausch was discovered to be taking $75 a month from an insurance company representative.[29] As was often the case following a suspension, there were a number of countercharges. An article in the *New York Telegram* reported that a player named Ross Marshall had been offered $300 in cash by an alumnus if he would enroll in the University of Missouri.[30] Nothing came of these latter charges.

The decade of the 1930s saw a continued rash of charges and countercharges concerning illegal payments. An NCAA committee report in 1934 concluded that there were abuses in the areas of recruitment and subsidization, and it claimed that "they have grown to such a universal extent that they constitute the major problem of American athletics today."[31] In 1935 a total of eleven of thirteen colleges in the Southeast Conference voted to recognize athletic ability in determining financial assistance for football players, thus ignoring the NCAA amateur code on recruiting and subsidizing athletes that had been reaffirmed at the 1934 NCAA Convention.[32] The Southern Conference, comprising schools in Maryland, Virginia, and the Carolinas, voted in 1938 to allow athletic ability to be considered in awarding financial aid.[33] As the decade of the 1940s approached, under-the-table payments flourished and the violation of basic amateur principles was becoming formal policy in some schools and conferences.

SETTING THE STAGE FOR THE SANITY CODE DEBATE

In the nineteenth century, the award of scholarships (at first called charity funds) to impecunious students had created a loophole for the evasion of amateur rules. There was no question that taking athletic ability into consideration in the award of financial aid violated basic amateur principles. Because it was often difficult to assess the motives of financial aid officers or to insulate them from pressures exerted by athletic interests, it became a common practice to earmark financial aid for students whose only claim to such aid was exceptional athletic ability. In some cases, efforts to preserve amateurism actually led to discrimination against lower-class students who excelled in both sports and academics, the assumption being that financial aid for athletes was always based on their athletic skills.

Various influential sport-governing bodies made valiant efforts to plug this loophole and to preserve amateur college sport. In 1935 a group of college presidents from the Southern Conference, led by Frank Graham, then-president of the University of North Carolina, made recommendations that they hoped would be adopted by all Southern schools and conferences. Among those recommendations were that there be no remuneration for athletic ability and that all financial aid be awarded through a faculty committee. It was also recommended that "no athlete use his name for commercial advertising, sell game tickets for profit, hold a sinecure job, receive more for a job than the regular rate, or accept counterfeit bets."[34] Finally, to show that they meant business, the drafters of what became known as the Graham Plan recommended that a certified public accountant examine all athletic accounts and publish the results. Any school that violated these regulations would by a majority vote be dropped from the conference for two years.[35]

Graham had earlier taken stands against professionalism that had brought him into conflict with athletic interests. In 1933 he became embroiled in a dispute with the University of North Carolina's (UNC) football coach over financial inducements to players. On that occasion a publisher in Greensboro, North Carolina, wrote a letter to Graham that noted that some "alumni are calling for your resignation because you will not permit the student loan fund to be invaded for the purpose of hiring players."[36] This earlier skirmish, however, had not prepared Graham for attacks that were to follow his involvement in drafting the Graham Plan.

In December 1935, one of Graham's friends wrote to him, warning that "If your policy is adopted and as a result of same the University of North Carolina has a third and fourth rate football team when its competitors, such as Georgia and Tennessee, have first rate teams, the alumni are going to rise up in their wrath."[37] In January 1936 the Montgomery County Alumni Association of UNC did just that. At one of its meetings, the association resolved that if the Graham Plan "is adopted we shall withdraw all our support from the University until such injustice is corrected."[38] By proposing legislation that would put UNC at a competitive disadvantage on the athletic field, especially the provision that would eliminate the subsidization of athletes, Graham had struck a nerve that ran deeper than he had ever dreamed. And, much to his dismay, the support that he thought he would receive from other college presidents throughout the South never materialized.

When the plan was presented at a meeting of the National Association of State Universities, Graham found himself virtually without support. In December 1935 Graham wrote to Howard Savage, the author of the famous Carnegie Foundation report on college athletics published in 1929, expressing his frustration and disappointment at the outcome of the conference. "I am shocked to find," wrote Graham, "that college presidents for this reason and that reason do not want to stand [in] back of the proposed regulations."[39] He added a cautionary note that "this part with regard to the college presidents is of course confidential."[40] He went on to tell Savage that he believed the regulations in the Graham Plan were an attempt to make operational the ideas developed in Savage's 1929 report, and he requested a letter from Savage in support of the Southern Conference initiatives.

President Graham had written to Savage for moral support. But Savage's response fell short of a Knute Rockne–style half-time speech. With a note of cynicism, undoubtedly acquired from his own futile battles on behalf of amateur ideals, Savage told Graham that "the proposed regulations cut too deeply into entrenched practices [for them] to be adopted."[41] He did go on, however, to tell Graham that the fight should still be made. The Graham Plan was ultimately adopted by the Southern Conference in 1936. However, its stringent regulations were liberalized over the next two years. In 1938 the Southern Conference totally abandoned the plan and joined the other colleges and universities in the South that had already begun awarding athletic scholarships. Capitulation on the athletic scholarship issue by Southern schools created a rift within the NCAA that in ten years would lead to college sports' version of the "War between the States," better known as the Sanity Code debate.

Between 1906 and 1947 the NCAA's various wordings of principles regarding amateurism underwent considerable change and refinement. But the association remained formally opposed to athletic scholarships. The constitution of the NCAA, adopted in 1941, is especially informative because it contains informal notes explaining the logic used by the association when it adopted various principles. A section regarding aid for the athlete stated that "Athletic participation should not be a condition for such aid."[42] It also specified that the agency for awarding aid should be independent of the athletic department and that awards of financial aid to athletes should be based on the same need-based criteria used to award aid to other students.

The guiding theme running through Article III of the 1941 constitution was that in the award of student aid, "an athlete shall neither be favored nor discriminated against" (143). Just as athletic ability could not be considered in the awarding of financial aid, such aid could not be withheld if awarded by the same criteria that applied to other students. The constitution also stated that no athlete should lose a scholarship or other aid "because of failure to compete in intercollegiate athletics" (144). In explaining its position, the NCAA noted that at some institutions, athletes were losing their scholarships if they gave up sports and that this practice had a "direct professionalizing influence" (144). This statement hints that the NCAA in 1941 was well aware that making athletic performance a condition for continued financial aid blurred the distinction between a scholarship and an employment contract.

Elite northeastern universities, including Yale, Harvard, and Princeton, had created the nation's first big-time athletic programs. However, in 1945 the Ivy Group changed course and began to deemphasize sport as commercial entertainment. In an agreement adopted in 1945, the Ivy Group reaffirmed its disapproval of athletic scholarships, eliminated spring practice, and condemned the endorsement of commercial products by athletic staff members. Consistent with principles adopted by the NCAA, the Ivy Group took the position that "players themselves shall be truly representative of the student body and not composed of a group of special recruited and trained athletes."[43] The Ivy agreement clearly stated the Ivy Group's intention to bring intercollegiate sport into harmony again with the essential educational mission of the universities.

The Big Ten, a conference composed of faculty representatives, shared many of the views of the Ivy Group regarding amateurism and athletic scholarships. In 1945 the Big Ten published a conference manual to help its member institutions distinguish between permissible and prohibitive financial aid and recruiting practices. According to this manual, it was not permissible "to offer or promise scholarships or loans or remission of tuition to prospective athletes."[44] On the other hand, financial aid could not be withheld from athletes who demonstrated the same academic promise and financial need as other students. In actual practice, it was extremely difficult to prevent general scholarship money from being earmarked for athletes. Given the pressure often exerted on admissions and financial aid officers on behalf of talented athletes, abuses were not uncommon.

As the mid-twentieth century approached, financial aid policies for athletes varied from one conference to the next and from one section of the country to another. Following the rejection of the Graham Plan, many universities, especially those in the South, adopted athletic scholarships as standard operating procedure. The Big Ten and many northeastern schools, on the other hand, shared the NCAA position that all athletically related financial assistance violated the amateur principle. Therefore, unless it could establish some uniform national policy regarding the award of financial aid to college athletes, the NCAA could never hope to become the unified "voice of college sport" in America. In the late 1940s the NCAA was thus forced to address this issue.

THE SANITY CODE AND THE RISE OF NCAA-SPONSORED PROFESSIONALISM

In July 1946 a meeting of NCAA and conference officials was held in Chicago to propose recommendations for how to restore sanity in college sport. Most of the delegates at this "Conference of Conferences" were well aware that the NCAA's policy of leaving the enforcement of amateur rules in the hands of individual schools and conferences was not working.[45] The NCAA's laissez-faire approach to the payment issue had spawned a variety of questionable financial aid practices. Although offering college athletes financial inducements helped to ensure a steady supply of talented athletes for the industry, the hypocrisy and corruption of this system had become a national embarrassment. It is safe to say that most college officials wanted some kind of reform.

The central issue addressed at this Chicago conference was the subsidization of college athletes. Out of the Conference of Conferences evolved a document entitled "Principles for the Conduct of Intercollegiate Athletics," later known as the "Sanity Code."[46] The Sanity Code was a tortured yet in some ways brilliant effort to reconcile a number of disparate interests and athletic philosophies. The committee that had drafted the proposed rules represented conferences from all over the country, and an initial code was then widely circulated among NCAA members to elicit feedback. An official draft of the Sanity Code was presented for discussion at the NCAA convention in 1947. In 1948 a version of the document that incorporated revisions suggested over the previous year was approved by the NCAA and was substituted in the NCAA constitution in place of the existing Article III.

The Sanity Code was an attempt to fashion a compromise between two schools of thought: advocates, mostly in the South, of full athletic scholarships, and their opponents such as Yale, Harvard, and Princeton that insisted that athletes be treated no differently than other students. To placate the former, the Sanity Code abandoned the NCAA's forty-two-year-old commitment to amateur principles and allowed financial aid to be awarded on the basis of athletic ability.[47] This accommodation to professionalism was softened somewhat by the requirement that this aid be tied to need and limited to the amount of tuition and incidental expenses. In essence, the Sanity Code allowed schools to seek out skilled athletes and to pay their tuition, provided that they qualified for need. Aid exceeding tuition and unrelated to need could be granted if based on superior academic scholarship.

To counter the argument that financial awards specifically earmarked for athletes constituted "pay" for services rendered, the Sanity Code retained a clause that had appeared in earlier NCAA constitutions stating that "No athlete shall be deprived of financial aids . . . because of failure to participate in intercollegiate athletics."[48] The Sanity Code allowed universities to offer substantial financial inducements to attract talented athletes, thereby violating long-established principles of amateurism. But by not allowing these inducements to be withdrawn from athletes who decided not to play, the code, arguably, avoided some of the legal problems that may have been associated with pay for play. What the Sanity Code sanctioned was "gifts" to athletes, not pay.

The Sanity Code allowed the payment of tuition for exceptional athletes, but in its earlier drafts it took a tough stand against recruiting. The draft of the Sanity Code presented at the 1947 NCAA Convention stated that coaches and other athletic interests could not go off campus to recruit; nor could they offer financial aid or other inducements to prospective students.[49] Such a stand would certainly have appealed to those faculty and amateur aristocrats who favored recruiting athletic teams from the regular student body. However, this strongly worded statement on recruiting did not survive the political infighting leading up to the 1948 convention. Fearing that this clause might hurt the code's chances of being approved, committee members amended the principle governing recruiting to allow off-campus recruiting as long as coaches made no offer of financial aid. The final version also stated that while a coach could make no offer of financial aid, "giving information regarding aid" was permitted.[50]

While crumbling on the issue of amateurism, the Sanity Code at least provided the NCAA with its first effective enforcement mechanism. An

executive regulation issued in conjunction with the code created a Constitutional Compliance Committee as well as a Fact-Finding Committee, each
consisting of three members. The Compliance Committee was authorized to
make rulings regarding interpretations of constitutional language and to
answer inquiries regarding whether or not stated practices are forbidden by the
constitution. These rulings were to be deemed "final and authoritative, subject
only to reversal by vote of the Association in convention assembled."[51] Failure
to comply with rules could lead to termination of membership by a two-thirds
vote.

No sooner had the first Constitutional Compliance Committee been
formed than critics began to argue that the Sanity Code was unenforceable.
There seemed to be a general belief that limiting financial aid to the cost of
tuition would simply lead athletes to find financial subterfuges to pay for their
room and board. According to one observer, "the biggest impediment to the
enforcement of the Sanity Code is the alumni. The only way it ever can work
is to strangle every alumnus on graduation day."[52] Journalist Tim Cohane took
the position that the Sanity Code would favor rich schools because their rich
alumni could provide more jobs and under-the-table payments.[53] Colgate
Darden, Jr., then-president of the University of Virginia, stated publicly that
his school would not abide by the Sanity Code. Said Darden: "It cannot be
properly enforced."[54]

Nowhere was opposition to the Sanity Code greater than in the South. The
Southern, Southeastern, and Southwestern Conferences had been giving full
athletic scholarships since the 1930s. For them there was no going back. The
first signs of a possible "Southern Revolt" against the Sanity Code appeared at
the 1949 NCAA National Convention in San Francisco. At this convention,
three Southern Conferences (the Southern, Southeastern, and Southwestern)
decided to organize a meeting in May to discuss the Sanity Code and to find
ways to liberalize it.[55] Blake Van Leer, then president of Georgia Tech, was
chosen to head this "Three-Conference" conference, to be held in Atlanta, and
to work with representatives from the other Conferences to develop an agenda.

At the resulting joint meeting in May, a number of proposals were discussed
for augmenting financial inducements allowed by the Sanity Code.[56] Other
items on the agenda addressed the issue of outright secession from the NCAA
and raised a number of questions not unlike those that must have been
considered before South Carolina's attack on Fort Sumter. For instance, would
it be possible for one of the Southern Conferences to withdraw and still
conduct an athletic program? If all three Conferences withdrew, could they
combine and still have among themselves a viable athletics program? What
kind of governance structure could be set up in place of the NCAA's format?
These and other questions raised at the conference suggested that the NCAA's

claim to being the "voice of college sport" was now on the line in the Sanity Code debate.

The Sanity Code crisis gained momentum when the chairman of the NCAA Constitutional Compliance Committee announced early in 1949 that twenty institutions were not in compliance with the Sanity Code and that they would face suspension if corrective action were not taken.[57] By July 1949, a total of thirteen of the twenty had come into compliance, leaving seven to face expulsion at the January 1950 NCAA Convention. The seven included Boston College, the Citadel, Villanova, Virginia Military Institute, Virginia Polytechnic Institute, the University of Maryland, and the University of Virginia. As the convention neared, a prediction was reported in the *New York Times* that the major Southern Conferences would secede from the NCAA if these seven schools were actually expelled.[58]

Before the vote to expel was taken at the 1950 NCAA Convention, representatives of the accused institutions were allowed to defend themselves. Speakers for the military institutions argued eloquently that it was not possible for an athlete in financial need to follow a rigorous schedule of classes, military drills, and sports yet still have time left to work at a job to pay for room and board.[59] Several other speakers felt that there was hypocrisy inherent in the code itself. Stated a representative from the Citadel: "The Code defines the word amateur and then promptly authorizes students to participate . . . who do not meet the requirements of the definition.[60] President Francis McGuire of Villanova saw another form of hypocrisy. Stated McGuire: "Do you mean to tell me that there are only seven schools in America which don't live up to the N.C.A.A. code?"[61]

According to the NCAA constitution, a two-thirds vote was necessary for a motion to expel to carry. When the vote was taken, 111 voted yes and 93 voted no. NCAA president Karl Lieb announced that the vote had carried, but then "cries of no" came from the college officials who realized that the tally of "yes" votes had fallen slightly short of the two thirds necessary. President Lieb smiled and said, "You're right, the motion is not carried."[62] With these words, the Sanity Code died after only two turbulent years of existence. The South had finally had its day.

PICKING UP THE PIECES

The adoption of the Sanity Code in 1948 had been an accommodation to interests that supported the subsidization of college athletes. However, the 1950 vote of no-confidence for that code threw the door open to unbridled professionalism. In 1951 the section of the NCAA constitution that had contained the Sanity Code was dropped altogether. In 1952 the principles governing financial aid that reappeared in Article III, Section 4, gave individual institutions freedom to set their own financial aid policies for athletes, the only requirement being that such aid be administered by each athlete's institution.[63]

Over the next five years, with Walter Byers as the NCAA's new executive director, rules governing financial aid to athletes were tightened up considerably. The 1956 legislation extended the amount of allowable financial aid to cover commonly accepted educational expenses, and it eliminated need as a requirement. In 1957 an "Official Interpretation" specifically defined educational expenses to include tuition and fees, room and board, books, and $15 per month for laundry.[64] Like the Sanity Code, the 1957 legislation contained provisions to counter the argument that athletic scholarships constituted pay. For instance, financial aid could not be reduced (gradated) or canceled on the basis of an athlete's contribution to a team's success or of his decision not to participate.[65]

Few of the people who attended the NCAA's first convention in 1906 could have conceived that by 1957, NCAA rules would allow a university to pay the room, board, tuition, and fees of an athlete in order to induce him to participate in sports. In fact, they probably would have been astounded to find that these payments could be made on behalf of athletes with absolutely no financial need or remarkable academic ability. What some may have found even more disturbing was the hypocrisy of labeling this new approach to college sport "amateurism." By allowing universities to pay the day-to-day living and educational expenses of athletes, the 1957 constitution had clearly violated the amateur principle. Within a half century, the concept of amateurism had become a convenient label that the NCAA could arbitrarily define to suit its needs.

There is evidence that the NCAA leadership at the time knew quite well that the 1957 rules on financial aid were replacing the concept of amateurism with a counterfeit version. Walter Byers, the executive director of the NCAA from 1951 to 1987, has recently characterized the awarding of athletic scholarships in 1957 as the beginning of "a nationwide money-laundering scheme."[66] According to Byers as he and other key NCAA personnel had envisioned it, the purpose of full grants-in-aid was to eliminate illegal benefits to athletes. Under this new system, however, alumni and boosters who had formerly given money directly to athletes or their parents could still funnel money to athletes but now through legitimate university channels. In other words, by 1957 the NCAA had formally incorporated practices into its constitution that it had previously condemned as professionalism.

Byers also suggests that besides sidestepping the long-established amateur principle, the NCAA also engaged in a public relations campaign to hide this fact from the federal government and the general public (69). As the awarding of full athletic grants-in-aid became commonplace, colleges began to fear that NCAA athletes might be identified as employees by state industrial commissions and the courts. To meet this threat, Byers remarks that "We crafted the term student-athlete, and soon it was embedded in all NCAA rules and interpretations as a mandated substitute for such words as players and athletes. We told college publicists to speak of 'college teams,' not football or basketball 'clubs,' a word common to the pros" (69). According to Byers, every effort was made by the NCAA to avoid the appearance that an athletic grant-in-aid was a contract for hire. Rules preventing universities from withdrawing financial aid from injured athletes or from athletes who decided not to participate were as much an effort to protect universities from workers' compensation cases as an effort to protect the education and safety of athletes (75).

After the repeal of the Sanity Code in 1950, major athletic powers went on a spending spree to buy winning teams. In just the 1955–1956 season, Auburn awarded 107 full grants-in-aid in football; the football programs at Florida and Georgia Tech awarded 114 and 123 respectively[67]; and at Kentucky, which had built a basketball dynasty under the legendary Adolph Rupp, there were 20 athletic scholarships in basketball alone.[68] Many smaller schools viewed athletic scholarships as a way to break into the big-time, and some saw little difference between hiring athletes and hiring other university personnel. The *Track and Field News* ran the following advertisement in 1957:

FOUR TRACK SCHOLARSHIPS. Available effective Jan. 29, 1957. Covering all necessary school expenses for sprinter, hurdler, middle distance and weightman. If interested, send complete details of self with photograph to: L. J. Olson, Track Coach, McNeese State College, Lake Charles, La.[69]

By the late 1950s, the outlines of what would become corporate college sport began to emerge. Football and basketball in the Big Ten and other major conferences had become important profit centers. By 1957, there were 40 million television sets bringing college sport into people's living rooms.[70] This new technology, combined with the NCAA's newly acquired powers of enforcement and regulation, led in the 1950s to a series of lucrative television agreements between college sport and NBC.[71] Acting as an industry-wide cartel, the NCAA not only set limits on the number of television appearances that any one school could make but also decided how schools' revenues would be distributed. Television provided college sport with opportunities for commercial growth unimaginable in the 1940s.

A high level of commercialism is a defining characteristic of the so-called corporate model of college sport, but this model is incomplete without factoring in professionalism. College sport as an industry can realize its full potential only if it has access to a pool of high-performance athletes. It also has to control the distribution of these athletes among the competing teams. The athletic scholarship system that emerged during the 1950s, in conjunction with the NCAA's new power to enforce eligibility rules, helped to rationalize the recruitment, distribution, and subsidization of player talent. NCAA rules set a "cap" on financial inducements to athletes by universities, developed transfer rules to limit player mobility, and imposed penalties on schools and athletes involved in under-the-table payments. This athletic scholarship system, together with rampant commercialism, thus laid the foundation for today's corporate college sport.

Not all colleges and universities gave up on amateurism. In 1954, during the same period in which the NCAA was formally turning professional, the Ivy Group signed an agreement that reaffirmed its previous stand against athletic scholarships. "Athletes," according to the agreement, "shall be admitted as students and awarded financial aid only on the basis of the same academic standards and economic need as are applied to all other students."[72] Their agreement also prohibited spring football practice, post-season games, and product endorsements by coaches. The best indicator of the Ivy Group's success in implementing its amateur model is the dramatic drop of such schools as the University of Pennsylvania and Yale from national athletic prominence. Never again would the University of Pennsylvania have the quality of players that had allowed it to play Notre Dame to a 7–7 tie as it had in 1952.

The Ivy League's success in implementing an amateur model of college sport belied the conventional wisdom that amateur rules were unenforceable. If amateur rules were abandoned in other schools and conferences, it was most likely because presidents and regents at those schools were not committed to enforcing them. The 1954 Ivy Agreement had the unanimous support of the Ivy Group presidents and governing boards, which had decided to compete only against schools that shared their educational and athletic philosophy. The Ivy League Conference, formally established in 1956, did not eliminate all athletic abuses, but it was able to implement an athletic system not unlike the one envisioned by the NCAA's founders at their 1906 convention.

Another approach to college sport that was separating itself from the others during the 1950s was the "educational model." Those programs that offered no financial aid on the basis of athletic ability and for whom college sport was

HICKSVILLE PUBLIC LIBRARY
HICKSVILLE, N.Y.

recreation, rather than a form of commercial entertainment, fit this model. These programs would eventually become the NCAA's Division III. Many of these schools were philosophically committed to amateur sport because it seemed most consistent with the educational needs of student athletes. Another group that adopted the educational model was women. Although starved for resources and denied equal access to athletic opportunities, women struggled to develop a model of collegiate sport that would be free from the hypocrisy so characteristic of the corporate model. In the years ahead, the concerns of these women were to move to the very center of the debates regarding college sport.

3

Physical Education and the Genesis of Women's Collegiate Sport

The previous chapters examined the cultural and social conditions that had transformed college sport into a form of mass commercial entertainment in the late nineteenth and early twentieth centuries. They also traced the evolution of amateurism into an exploitative ideology. These developments, while important, were only a part of the overall story of college sport.

At the same time that men in academe were creating a model of sport that bore little relationship to the stated goals of higher education, women faced the more fundamental challenge of establishing a place for themselves within colleges and universities. Excluded on the basis of perceived female physical and intellectual inferiority, women found it necessary to explain why they should even be allowed to attend college, let alone participate in sport. Physical education, a precursor to present-day women's college sport, would eventually become a centerpiece for the arguments used to create a presence for women on college and university campuses. Physical education also provided the philosophical foundation for intercollegiate athletics for women.

THE RISE OF WOMEN'S EDUCATION IN THE 1800s

During the late 1800s, American society evolved from an agricultural to an industrial economy. Social and economic centers relocated from family-owned farms and small rural communities to more populated urban settings. As the distance between workplace and home became more pronounced, so too did the requirement for a division of labor between public wage earning and private homemaking. These separate spheres, as they were called, became the respective domains of men and women. Although some women did venture into the public workforce as educators and factory workers, jobs held outside the home were regarded as secondary considerations in comparison to women's obligations to their families and their responsibilities as wives and mothers.[1]

Given these narrowly defined roles for females, an acceptable argument for the education of women forged a link between school and the home.[2] A growing public awareness that middle- and upper-middle-class women needed to be educated in order to raise virtuous and moral children and citizens started to build. A leading activist named Mary Ashton Rice Livermore spoke passionately about the necessity for young women, destined to become mothers, to be informed on matters of government so as to retain the respect of their sons once those sons passed into adulthood. She wrote:

For them [mothers] to be willingly, yes, gladly, indifferent and ignorant, when their own affairs are the subject of legislation, and laws are passed concerning their property and their children without their advice in the matter being asked, or their approval being sought, is to justify the category in which women are frequently mentioned— "women, children, and *idiots.*"[3]

The expansion into the westernmost parts of the United States and the subsequent Christianizing of the Western nations provided further support for educating women who would function in the roles of teachers and religious leaders. Barbara Miller Solomon notes that "Educating women to be teachers became a respected element in the good works and goals of all religious groups."[4]

Fashioning a female education that adhered to the precepts of womanhood as defined by the Republic, Christianity, and the Victorian ideal—which uniformly called for passivity, piety, purity, and obedience—while affording female students the freedom and choices attendant to a quality education was no mean feat. Prominent educators such as Mary Lyon, who founded Mt. Holyoke College in 1837 as the first women's college in the United States, constantly were called upon to respond to the public's concerns that education might spoil women for family duties by "rendering them manly, indelicate, and unsexed."[5]

Nowhere was the shortfall between women's experience while in school and the requirements of their future roles seen more dramatically than at commencement. Women's colleges participated in the common practice of inviting the most outstanding students to write commencement addresses. Despite the encouragement that female students received to craft those speeches, societal prohibitions preventing women from speaking in public during most of the 1800s were very much in evidence on commencement day. On the occasion of commencement, it would be male officiants who would read the words written by these very women. Even Oberlin College, well known for its liberal stance in admitting both women and blacks in 1833, did not allow a woman to speak at commencement until 1857.[6]

Concerns about the negative effects of education on women were reported by several leading educators of the day. Renowned Harvard medical school professor Dr. Edward H. Clarke reported in his clinical observations of female undergraduates that brainwork apparently exacted a serious toll on women's health. Clarke identified the acquisition of neuralgia, dyspepsia, hysteria, and other derangements of the nervous system as the "sad results" of modern education for women.[7]

Similarly, Harvard president Charles Eliot expressed grave concern that educated women would fall prey to "impracticable theories" that led them to believe that they could support themselves and therefore remain unmarried, a condition that Eliot found completely unacceptable. Eliot wrote:

If brain education is what woman now seeks . . . she must only sink to a lower level. We all blunder, and we all sin and suffer through ignorance, and woman more than man, because she is weaker and can bear less.[8]

Although many female educators agreed with Eliot's notion of "natural differentiation" and "complementary functions" of men and women whereby the natural weakness of women was thought to complement the natural strength of men, there were several women who as educators vocally and publicly took exception to the assumption of male supremacy. While she was president of Bryn Mawr College, the indomitable M. Carey Thomas gained national publicity by suggesting that President Eliot might have had "sunspots" on his brain when it came to women's education. Thomas vehemently maintained that women could not only compete on an equal plane with men intellectually; they could surpass men in that domain if given the chance. She called for a life of "intellectual renunciation" and "sex solidarity" (i.e., an exclusively female, single-sex education) so that women could have the opportunity to fulfill their promise, undeterred by the social conventions of the day.[9]

As the number of females enrolling in colleges and universities rose from 11,000 in 1870 to 85,000 in 1900, the issue of coeducation came to the fore. In September of 1870, Jenny Spencer sought and gained admittance to Cornell University. Other prominent universities followed suit.[10] Harvard started slowly in 1882 with the Harvard Annex. Wesleyan University, on the other hand, went through stages: at first all male, then going coed, then reverting to all male in 1912, and then finally making a commitment to coeducation in 1917.[11]

As college and university campuses became the shared territory of men and women as students, baffling contradictions to theories of male superiority and female inferiority surfaced. Contrary to prevailing expectations at the time, women soon outperformed their male peers in certain academic realms. As more women were admitted into coeducational institutions, not only did they accrue more academic honors than their male peers, they received the more prestigious academic honors as well. By 1902 women were yearly receiving 56.3 percent of Phi Beta Kappa honors.[12]

In attempts to rationalize the unanticipated success of female students, male academics turned to theories that pinpointed women as an inhibiting factor in male academic performance. President Charles Van Hise from the University of California put forward his "sex repulsion theory" to explain why certain subject areas, such as philosophy, had become more popular among women than men. This theory held that the rising number of women in those courses contaminated an otherwise desirable subject area for men, thus accounting for the decline in male academic performance.

The eminent scholar G. Stanley Hall developed an alternative thesis, the "sex attraction theory." Hall hypothesized that because males were essentially magnetically drawn to women, female presence in the classroom was distracting. Men, in effect, found it too difficult to concentrate when in the company of women. As Solomon concludes, "Women, charged with sex repulsion and sex attraction, both which interfered with the . . . process of educating future leaders [males] of the country, simply could not win."[13]

Female educators and their supporters knew that dismantling the mythology of female inferiority while avoiding manifestations of female weakness was absolutely essential to their success. As a result, women's education added to its focus not only the intellectual development of women but worthy consideration of their physical development. This merging of the intellectual and physical interests of women through the physical education curriculum forms the structural foundation upon which college sport for women was built, a very different origin from that of men's collegiate athletics.

WOMEN'S PHYSICAL EDUCATION AND BASKET BALL: THE EARLY BEGINNINGS OF WOMEN'S COLLEGE SPORT

Under the watchful eye of an inquisitive public, which expected that women would collapse from the strain of intellectual work, presidents and founders of women's colleges and proponents of women's education saw physical education as a vehicle to ensure women's health and by extension to guarantee the success of the women's education experiment. Countering the misassumptions that education would disturb women's apparently delicate emotional and mental balance as well as cause disruption to their reproductive capacity, educators sought to identify and champion valid contradictory medical philosophies that *supported* women's education.

In reporting on the emerging thinking of the day, Livermore applauded the work of female physicians who "have sought to change the conditions and habits of women, which at one time threatened to make womanhood and invalidism interchangeable terms." For instance, Elizabeth Blackwell, who had earned the distinction of becoming the first female doctor in the United States by graduating from the Geneva Medical College in 1850, argued for the systematic development of exercises that would benefit women's health.[14]

In 1865, the founding year of Vassar College, its board of trustees identified physical training as "the branch of education, if not as first, intrinsically considered . . . as fundamental to all the rest. Good health is, in the first place, essential to success in study."[15] Similarly, L. Clarke Seelye, the first president of Smith College, commented on women's health in his inaugural address in 1875:

We admit it would be an insuperable objection to the higher education of women, if it seriously endangered her health. . . . With gymnastic training wisely adapted to their peculiar organization, we see no reason why young ladies cannot pursue study as safely as they do ordinary employments.[16]

By 1900 fully 40 percent of American college students were women. As the acceptability of women's education grew, so too did the demand for women as physical educators. In response to that need, physical culture specialists at the Sargent School and the Boston Normal School of Gymnastics began to train women as instructors in physical education.[17] Courses in physiology, hygiene, and medical gymnastics were mainstays of almost every women's college curriculum from the very beginning, although they were rarely found in men's colleges in the late 1800s.[18]

The physical education classes taught to women communicated mixed messages that resulted from immersion in both an enterprise devoted to discovering women's potential abilities and a larger culture that would have preferred that those possibilities go unrecognized. Thus, physical education curricula included a wide range of activities intended to strengthen the vulnerable female body. Health exams, lectures on parenthood training, and posture inspections as well as the reporting and regulating of diet, weight, sleep habits, dress, exercise behavior, and menstrual cycles were all viewed as legitimate components of physical education for female students.[19]

Along with this concentrated focus on physical education, which consisted of gymnastics and other regulated exercises, sports soon occupied a significant portion of the women's physical education curriculum. Between 1833 and 1890, fourteen sports, from long-distance walking to field hockey, had been incorporated into physical education programs at institutions as diverse as private women's colleges, private coed colleges, state universities, and state normal schools.[20]

The existence of sport in women's physical education is further substantiated by Harriett Isabel Ballintine in her written history of physical education and sport at Vassar College. She pointed out that "contrary to popular opinion, competitive sport has been an integral part of the college scene since the 1860s when baseball teams organized at Vassar College and match games were played on Saturday afternoons."[21] Sports held an appeal for women that gymnastics and regulated exercise did not.

As women's physical education took root as an academic discipline and became a vehicle for the systematic training of growing numbers of women, the issue of fashionable dress during sports became more problematic. The existing standard for feminine attire, which restricted and constrained movement, was antithetical to the purposes of women's physical education.

From head to toe, women in the 1800s were outfitted in layers and styles of clothing that inhibited movement, making almost every activity—from walking to eating to breathing—difficult and at times impossible. Literally weighted down by the "gospel of good clothes," the fashionable woman typically wore up to fifteen layers of petticoats and crinolines under floor-length skirts. In the late 1800s bodices described in fashion magazines as all the rage had tight, stiff collars that were two to four inches high and made of "absolutely unbendable aluminum-plated watchspring steel collar supports." These were worn over starched camisoles and undershirts.[22] It was not uncommon for a fully dressed woman to carry as much as twenty pounds of clothing, including contraptions such as bustles and hoops on her person.

A truly dangerous aspect of women's fashion was a contrivance called the corset, worn for the purpose of achieving an hourglass figure: a tiny waist (20 inches or smaller) and an accentuated chest. Social critic Thorstein Veblen noted, "The corset is, in economic theory, substantially a mutilation, undergone for the purpose of lowering the subject's vitality and rendering her permanently and obviously unfit for work."[23]

One of the challenges facing women as physical educators in the latter 1800s was extricating female students from the cloth and metal ties that had bound them to a life of passivity and ill health. Working along with the dress reform movement, female physical educators were eventually successful in devising uniforms patterned after the very freeing bloomer concept, a garment that consisted usually of a tunic worn over a set of voluminous pantaloons.[24]

By the time that Senda Berenson introduced a new sport called basket ball into the physical education curriculum at Smith College in 1892, women in college appeared ready for a game that allowed them to express the freedom they were slowly beginning to realize through their education. Between 1880 and 1900, as the second generation of college women appeared on the scene and as the New Woman emerged to offer a more healthful and active alternative to the Victorian ideal, basket ball seemed just the sport to ignite interest and enthusiasm on women's college campuses.[25]

Never far from the probing eyes of a public that expected its standards of womanliness upheld, Senda Berenson and later Clara Baer at Sophie Newcomb College in Louisiana were careful in their directed efforts to make the sport different from the original game designed by James Naismith for sportsmen at the Young Men's Christian Association (YMCA). Conventional wisdom taught that women tired easily, were unable to deal emotionally or physically with the rigors of competitive team sport, and needed to have guidelines in terms of womanly court behavior to protect against trauma to the reproductive organs. By dividing the court into three sections, Berenson satisfactorily built in safeguards to overexertion. Through restrictions on the number of dribbles and the length of time allowed to hold the ball and with a prohibition against aggressive play, the game became customized for the woman of the 1890s.

Encountering even more stringent standards of womanly behavior in the South, Clara Baer developed a department of physical education at Sophie Newcomb College, a place where students in 1891 were driven to the college in carriages, accompanied by their mammy nurses, who waited outside while they attended classes.[26] Responding to the culture of the times, Baer adjusted the game of basket ball to a much greater degree than did Berenson so as to make it even more accessible to her female students. In Basquette, the court was divided into nine or eleven sections. As many as eighteen or twenty women occupied the court at any one time. Rules such as no dribbling, no guarding, no falling down (a sign of overexertion), and no talking (an activity thought to produce overexcitement) were deemed by Baer to be necessary in order to make the game palatable to New Orleans society.[27]

Although women's basket ball replicated what had gone before by accommodating belief in the naturalness of female inferiority, it was revolutionary in the liberating effect it had on students. For the first time, civil rivalries in a refined atmosphere became commonplace among women. Similar to men's sport, women's games served as a rallying point for exuberant students. Extensive interclass basket ball programs established at schools such as the one at Smith College bear testament to the significant change that had occurred for women's sport on college campuses. Sport historian Reet Howell conveys a sense of the excitement generated by these events in this account:

Inside the gymnasium all was turmoil and excitement. Crowds blocked the hallways and stairs. Girls here, girls there, everywhere, talking, laughing, shouting, and singing their class songs. In the balconies . . . there were almost 1,100 young ladies anxiously watching the entrance from the dressing room on either side of the stage. Both balconies were splendidly decorated with class colors."[28]

In the sport of basket ball, women's athletics had something it had not had before: an entity that demanded regulation at a national level. This is salient because as women's physical education explored avenues to ensure a place for this exciting addition to their curricula, educators encountered problems on a large scale that they had not faced before.

In the rush to bring the sport to women on college campuses, Berenson and other leading female physical educators were confronted with evaluating the possibility and potential for competition. Having a team presupposed that there should be an opponent. By 1896 the first women's intercollegiate basket ball game, which was the first women's intercollegiate athletic event, took place between Stanford and the University of California at Berkeley.[29]

In response to the question of what form of competition was appropriate for women, female physical educators weighed the educational interests of their charges as well as the intercollegiate sport model that had become a hallmark of men's athletics in the late 1890s. Although schools such as Berkeley and Stanford had sporadically organized interschool athletic events for women, female physical educators began to articulate a formal position that opposed the rough and seemingly unchecked sporting practices associated with college football and other men's sports.

Believing that sport "should *never* overemphasize winning" because such an element would likely "bring out 'unwomanly' behavior," Senda Berenson, among others, promoted physical and moral health as the sole purposes of women's sport on college campuses.[30] This group of women scorned men's intercollegiate athletics as unnecessary and hinting of professionalism.

In a meeting at the 1899 Physical Training Conference in Springfield, Massachusetts, female physical educators made two decisions that would have a lasting impact on the organization and development of women's collegiate sport. Through the establishment of a basket ball committee, women's college athletics found its first governing body, which would eventually become part of the American Physical Education Association (APEA) in 1905.[31] This sport-governing body officially codified the structural connections between college sport and college curricula for women through physical education, a tie that male college athletics did not share. By adopting a governing principle that placed the health and well-being of female students above all other concerns, the seeds for an enduring philosophy of women's college sport had been sown.

The void created by the need for competition among women's teams was filled when female physical educators embraced the notion of intramural sport. Charged with devising a sport system that improved women's opportunities for physical activities while adhering to gender norms, intramurals appealed to women as physical educators for a variety of reasons. First, by conducting contests within the boundaries of their individual campuses, women could more easily control and regulate games played by female students. Second, intercollegiate contests would have meant the introduction of a public aspect into the relatively private area of women's education and women's college sport. From all indications, these physical educators were not prepared to violate that norm.

The intramural program, however, gave form to extensive and intensely competitive interclass rivalries. As interest in competitive athletics for women on college campuses increased, greater organization of activities was warranted. Coalitions of female students and faculty came together in Women's Athletic Associations (WAAs), which were usually run under the direction of the women's physical education department. The first WAA, which was started at Bryn Mawr in 1891, was soon copied by others. Within twenty years, over 80 percent of large colleges had WAAs that exerted considerable influence over the sporting activities of college women.[32]

By the end of the nineteenth century, sport for women on college campuses had undergone an enormous transformation from mere gymnastics exercises, designed to protect and not imperil women's health, to interclass contests that allowed for somewhat more vigorous expression. As the twentieth century approached, a foundation for women's college sport that was deeply grounded in an educational philosophy calling for a rational, curricularly based, and balanced approach to athletics had been firmly established.

VICTORIAN IDEALS AND MEN'S COLLEGE SPORT

An analysis of the nineteenth-century origins of college sport itself would be incomplete without a discussion of the impact that Victorian ideals had on both men's and women's experiences in higher education. Whereas this chapter's discussion thus far has focused on women's education and women's sport, Victorian beliefs about the so-called male sphere and the preparation of men for public life also served as subjects for educators, physicians, politicians, clergy, and parents to argue about as well.[33]

Although by virtue of birth and social position, upper- and middle-class men from European backgrounds had uncontested access to education, a circumstance very different from that which existed for women, men's relationship to higher education was open to debate. The source of the debate centered around the intellectual traditions of the academy, which, ironically, were very much at odds with the dictates of Victorian notions of masculinity.

When observed from a distance, intellectual life seemed more aligned with qualities considered feminine than with those categorized as masculine. Scholarly work, for instance, although mentally rigorous, was not overtly active; it required periods of solitude and quiet; and it occurred in such places as libraries, which could hardly have been thought of as part of the public domain.

While reservations circulated that education was thought to have a masculinizing effect on women, anti-intellectual attitudes that warned against too much education for men also were rather commonplace. In his work *Anti-Intellectualism in American Life*, Richard Hofstadter wrote that at the heart of American anti-intellectualism is a deeply rooted sense that intellectual life, and intellectuals "are pretentious, conceited, effeminate, and snobbish; and very likely immoral, dangerous, and subversive."[34]

Just as medical doctors had formulated practices to protect women's health in accordance with the views of the day, so too did they offer opinions about the connections between men's health, their education, and appropriate sexual and social behavior. The level of passivity and restraint thought appropriate for women was perceived to be dangerous to men's health.

Whereas involuntary passivity was prescribed for women so that their valuable energy could be directed toward the reproductive function, rigorous activity was believed to be important in facilitating virility in men. Sport was seen as a means of reining in unbridled sexual passion. Sexual activity outside the bounds of marriage or engaged in for purposes other than procreation was considered to be a misuse of the limited energy that men had so as to fulfill their roles as fathers. With the concept of "spermatic economy," sport came to be viewed as an acceptable and reasonable outlet for male sexual energy and an overt expression of masculinity.[35]

Unlike women, who had a seemingly limited and unrecoverable reserve, men were thought to have the capacity to regenerate energy through an active life. Because scholarly activity was thought of as passive, there was a palpable sense that a conscientious effort had to be made to balance study with physical activity.

A failure to provide accordingly had the potential to produce a class of men described by one nineteenth-century physician as "those who live in-doors and use the mind much and the muscle very little" and who exhibited tendencies similar to "the hysterical, the sensitive, the nervous." And, of course, society knew that *the* hysterical, *the* sensitive, *the* nervous were, for the most part, women.[36]

Apprehension about the untoward feminizing effects of education on men is seen in the manner in which studious males became the targets of jokes and innuendos. Sociologist Todd Crosset reported in his work on masculinity, sexuality, and the development of early modern sport that bookish boys and weaker boys were commonly referred to as "saps" or "wankers," expressions rife with derogatory sexual overtones.[37]

At such schools as the University of Notre Dame, where legendary football coach Knute Rockne was said to have "fought any intrusion against masculine habits and outlook," intellectuals met with swift and humbling ridicule if they trespassed even remotely in athletic territory. In 1922, following a suggestion made by the Notre Dame debating coach that his team be awarded varsity letters, Rockne and his press aide, Frances Wallace, published a story recommending that the debaters dress in "ruffles and lace and go after each other in fierce formations." As writer and researcher Murray Sperber related, "students laughed the debating coach's idea into oblivion."[38]

An understanding of the gender factor regarding the anti-intellectual climate both in the mainstream culture and on its college campuses provides important insight into how men's college sport evolved in the late 1800s and serves to highlight the distinctions between men's and women's athletics. Not only did men's college sport emerge as a manifestation of student interest and a declaration of student independence, it also came to symbolize tests of manhood and displays of masculinity that lent a much needed air of acceptability to men's presence in academic institutions. Headmasters and college presidents used college sport as a way of connecting upper-class elite education with the masses while assuring the public that a requisite level of masculinity was in force to temper the feared feminizing effects of intellectual work.[39]

A HISTORY OF DIFFERENCE

It becomes clear that when examined within the framework of Victorian attitudes and beliefs, men's and women's college sport evolved as distinct entities rising up out of the separate public and private spheres designated as male and female domains. The trademark characteristics of men's college sport (including its emphasis on rough and aggressive play), the generation of gate receipts, the forays into professionalism, and the adoption of men's sport as a public relations vehicle for institutions were all consistent with male gender role expectations. In turn, the refined and restrained nature of women's sport, so intimately connected to women's education models, replicated the standards of womanly behavior.

Despite the negotiations that occurred in order to facilitate women's entrance into college life in general and to allow for women to play and compete on college campuses, the model of women's college sport that finally emerged in the late 1800s was very similar in its rhetoric to that espoused by men's sport leaders, who believed in an amateur ideal. The women's sport model designed by Senda Berenson and Clara Baer embraced educationally sound, balanced forms of competition that taught teamwork, thinking skills, and cooperation. Unlike men's college sport programs, which predominantly allowed for the recruitment and subsidization of male athletes for the purposes of providing mass commercial entertainment, women's physical education programs offered no separation between athletes and the remainder of the student body; women preferred instead to conceptualize athletics as something to which all students should have access. Ironically, then, it is women, not men, who came closer to acting on the lofty principles professed by the National Collegiate Athletic Association. But women were also much less likely than men to be given the ideological credibility and financial resources to implement their programs.

4
A Sport-for-Women Philosophy

THE EMERGENCE OF THE FEMALE ATHLETE: 1900–1920

During the first half of the twentieth century, while men's college sport acquired the customs, practices, and traditions that would eventually distinguish it as a professional and commercial enterprise, women's sport was undergoing a profound metamorphosis of its own. Within the vibrantly optimistic and forward-thinking atmosphere of the early 1900s, the New Women of the new age streamed into the paid workforce, reform movements, education, and athletics in numbers never before realized.

As some of the Victorian attitudes about inherent female weakness were pushed into the background, sport became one of an array of endeavors wherein women sought to discover their physical, social, and political potential. Out of this context of shifting expectations for women, the magnetic Eleanora Sears, considered to be the first true American sportswoman, burst onto the scene in 1905 with both daring and panache.[1]

Born into Boston's elite society and boasting a direct family tie to Thomas Jefferson, Sears's love of sport set her apart from other socialites. Blessed with social standing, financial means, and physical skill, Sears challenged notions that women would supposedly "fall apart nervously" if they engaged in strenuous sport. With ease, Sears distinguished herself in a variety of sports including tennis, golf, swimming, polo, squash racquets, and long-distance walking. As a figure of controversy in her time, Sears's reputation as an athlete was matched only by her utter disregard for convention and flare for taking on the establishment.[2]

The relatively new entity of the athletic woman was not only shaped by famous and infamous women like Eleanora Sears but by many ordinary women who wished simply to experience the joys of sport. Just as the recently formed National Collegiate Athletic Association labored through its infancy struggling to define what intercollegiate athletics was and ought to be for men, so too did individuals involved with women's athletics work to articulate a vision of women's sport that would be responsive to the views of the day and the needs of women. And just as the achievement of consensus in men's intercollegiate athletics proved to be a daunting undertaking, so too was there considerable disagreement about the appropriate conditions under which women should play and compete.

Reflecting this growing interest in female athletic competition, women began to participate in a limited number of intercollege contests at select colleges and universities around the country. In the early 1900s female students at such institutions as the University of California at Berkeley, Radcliffe College, and the University of Washington traveled off campus to play games in basketball and hockey with other schools in their vicinities.[3]

Higher levels of participation and the beginning of inter-school competition led these physical educators to develop professional organizations that would enable them to address women's athletic issues with credibility. In 1917 the Women's Basketball Rules Committee of the American Physical Education Association, established to write rules and standards for basketball, was re-named the Committee on Women's Athletics (CWA).[4] The CWA expanded its jurisdiction to include field hockey, swimming, soccer, and track and field. (The Committee on Women's Athletics would undergo several other transformations throughout the twentieth century, eventually becoming the National Association for Girls and Women in Sport [NAGWS]. The Association of Intercollegiate Athletics for Women [AIAW], which would become the female counterpart to the NCAA, was originally formed as a subcommittee of NAGWS.)[5]

The mission of the CWA and its membership was the design and implementation of a system of athletics that "demonstrated the need for a set of standards which should be based on the limitations, abilities, and needs of the [female] sex."[6] Part and parcel of the vision outlined for women's athletics by the leadership of the CWA was a preference for moderate forms of competition that took place within rather than between schools.

Although various sport-governing bodies such as the CWA had begun to address women's athletics by 1920, there was as yet no unified position on the subject and no single voice or organization that had enough power or authority to present a national position on women's sport. As the public profile of female athletes became more prominent—particularly due to the exposure they had received through elite and international competition—two competing views of athletic womanhood emerged.

On the one hand, the freedom afforded women through sport was seen by women in physical education as something to be encouraged and fostered. However, their philosophical support for women's sport rested also on a desire to improve the conditions of women's lives, to ensure that women were playing and competing within a morally acceptable climate, to recognize and respect differences between men and women, and to protect women's health and welfare.

In contrast, several male sport promoters and coaches within both amateur and industrial leagues outside of academe perceived women's athleticism to be a marketable commodity. Speculating that a socially acceptable form of femininity could be established in the minds of audiences through the use of sexual illusion, thus assuring a degree of heterosexual appeal with the suggestion of marriageability, male promoters and writers often referred to female athletes as graceful and statuesque goddesses, mermaids, and modern-day Junos (Juno in mythology was Jupiter's wife).[7]

Although aware of the liberating effects of sport participation, female physical educators observed with unease the charges of masculinization that some highly publicized female athletes were inspiring as well as the level of sexploitation to which other female athletes were subjected at the hands of male sport profiteers. With their faith in the viability of an integrated system of sport shaken, female physical educators believed that it was now their duty to devise a framework for women's sport totally apart from that in existence for men. They hoped the idea of a separate sphere for women's sport, untainted by the corrupting influences of money and exploitation, would be adopted not just on college campuses but at every level of sport in which women participated.

STRUGGLES FOR CONTROL OVER WOMEN'S ATHLETICS

The catalyst that ultimately enabled the widespread adoption of a separate sport-for-women philosophy in colleges and universities was a controversy that occurred beyond academe's confines: in the international track and field realm. Following a refusal by the International Olympic Committee (IOC) in 1920 to recognize women's track and field as an Olympic event, advocates of the sport set out to create an alternative venue for international competition.[8]

In 1922, under the aegis of the newly formed Federation Sportive Feminine Internationale (FSFI) and led by French sportswoman Alice Milliat, various national track and field sport federations organized their own event in Paris. The FSFI chose, aptly, to call the event the Women's Olympics. An American delegation, formed under the direction of Harry Stewart, a coach and physiologist from New Haven, Connecticut, competed in the Women's Olympics despite the fact that the American Athletic Union (AAU) would not sanction this team.[9]

The reality of women competing in a separate international arena appeared to threaten the amateur sport-governing bodies, all of which in 1922 were led exclusively by men. As one historian writes, "Previously content to ignore women's track, male athletic officials developed a sudden interest in the sport after the conclusion of the 1922 Women's Olympics."[10] In a domino effect, first the IOC, then the AAU, and finally the International Amateur Athletic Federation (IAAF) all resolved to assume control over women's track because of the alleged excesses that they believed had occurred during this women's meet.

Male sport leaders were not the only ones perturbed about the situation. Female physical educators regarded the actions of the Women's Olympics delegations and the subsequent decisions by the IOC and the AAU to constitute direct threats to their authority.[11] According to sport historian Ellen Gerber, "The women were challenged by the AAU's blatant statement that henceforth they would control girls' athletics."[12] Thus, women in physical education worked to establish a coalition that would assert more forcefully their philosophy of athletic moderation. They worked with and through the Committee on Women's Athletics and other organizations such as the National Association of Physical Education for College Women.[13]

In 1922 their cause was delivered a fortuitous assist in the form of the National Amateur Athletic Federation (NAAF). Initiated by the U.S. War Department, the NAAF brought together leaders from the military and men's intercollegiate sport. As a result of the high number of draftees rejected for physical reasons during World War I, the military was searching for ways to engender a national commitment to the physical training of boys and men. Alternatively, in the wake of scandals surrounding intercollegiate sport and the AAU's domination of amateur athletics, college administrators sought to position themselves to play an influential role in the NAAF's formulation of national sport policy.[14]

At the time of the NAAF's founding, Secretary of War John W. Weeks and Secretary of the Navy Edwin Denby met with Lou Henry Hoover, President Herbert Hoover's wife, to discuss ways of establishing physical fitness standards for girls and women. After consulting physical educators, Mrs. Hoover concluded that a separate organization for that purpose was most appropriate, a decision that resulted in the formation of the Women's Division of the National Amateur Athletic Federation.[15]

Using this opportunity to formalize their beliefs about women's sport, the leaders on the Women's Division Board, many of whom were involved with the Committee on Women's Athletics, approved a package of sixteen resolutions in 1923, which was then distributed under the name of the Women's Division Platform.[16]

THE WOMEN'S DIVISION PLATFORM

The Women's Division Platform emphasized that sport for women should be inclusive and based on democratic and educational principles; in balance with other aspects of life; and unmotivated by profit, spectator, or commercial interests. Furthermore, in keeping with the idea of a totally separate and distinct form of sport for women, there was a belief that women's sport should be coached, administered, and officiated by women.[17]

The Platform's advocacy of a supposedly saner and more controlled form of sport as compared to men's intercollegiate and amateur athletics spoke to the very heart of the organization of sport in the United States. The Platform expressed in quite vivid prose the inappropriateness of marketing athletic contests as commercial entertainment, its detrimental outcome being the elevation of the interests of spectators or institutions above those of athletes. Contributors to the Platform were persuaded on educational grounds that commercial/professional elements had no place within a sport-for-women model. Although pronounced, the Platform's stance against the commercialization and professionalization of sport eluded its detractors, many of whom focused instead on the attempts also made within the document to regulate and define competition within a separate sphere of women's sport.

When considered in context, the idea of moderate forms of competition espoused by female physical educators was consistent with their efforts to avoid the excesses that inevitably accompanied commercial/professional forms of sport competition. Women as physical educators engaged in a delicate philosophical balancing act by attempting to develop a form of athletics that allowed for competition while avoiding the mine fields of overemphasis, student exploitation, and the abandonment of sound educational practice.

The end result was a form of competition that did not look like the contests in which men participated. Efforts to contain costs and prevent conflicts with academic work while providing competitive experiences produced such unique events as telegraphic meets. In contrast to regular meets, where athletes from various schools would gather to compete on one campus, telegraphic meets allowed athletes and teams to remain on their own home campuses; athletic meets were scored by telegraphing results between the schools involved.

The perceived necessity to regulate competition in this way and the belief that athletics should be accessible to all students gave the appearance that winning was unimportant and performance secondary. As a result, many believed and continue to believe, wrongly, that the Platform and its creators were opposed to the idea of competition and winning itself rather than commercialism and professionalism.[18]

Delivered in an era when competitive college sport in the American mind had already become synonymous with highly commercialized, varsity-level competition, the novelty of the Women's Division's attempts to develop a model of sport that centered on an educational, rather than a commercial and professional framework, invited distortions and fed the belief that female physical educators were against competition. Indicative of the intellectual chasm that existed on college campuses between physical educators and coaches in the 1920s, Knute Rockne, the legendary football coach from Notre Dame, observed about physical educators that "they are not interested in mass competitive games [but in recreation]. . . . Their stock in trade is kinesiology, anthropometry, and group-consciousness. Remove their vocabulary and they have nothing left."[19] The dismissiveness of Rockne's comment exemplifies the difficult task that female physical educators faced in trying to rally support and understanding for their concept of a saner form of athletics.

The notion that women in physical education were against competition lingers still. This feeds suspicion that the present-day obstacles encountered in the development of women's sport are attributable to certain archaic and odd perspectives of misguided women involved in this controversy. For example, in 1995 as the former executive director of the National Collegiate Athletic Association Walter Byers discussed the evolution of women's sport, he pointed out that "The men and the NCAA, itself, didn't discriminate against women. Women's athletic leaders discriminated against themselves through the years by refusing to accept competitive athletics as a proper pursuit for teenage women."[20] Several noted sport studies scholars have drawn similar conclusions. Consistent with Byers's viewpoint, sport historian Allen Guttman interpreted female physical educators' endorsement of an inclusive model of sport to mean that they "abjured competition."[21]

Regardless of how its stand on competition has been perceived through the years, the Platform was more than a statement about competition. It was a sophisticated commentary on the value of sport in American life and in higher education and on women's place within those institutions because it addressed four major concerns:

- the mutual objectives of academic education and physical education,
- negative aspects of contemporary men's intercollegiate sports competition,
- special needs of females, and
- absence of women in the formulation of sport governance and sport policy.

An examination of the Platform provides insight into the factors that shaped women's intercollegiate athletics as a separate and distinct entity on college campuses. It also reveals the particular set of expectations and societal values to which women were expected to adhere while also exposing the difficulties associated with advancing such a philosophy within higher education at a time when men's big-time sport dominated the landscape.

THE PLATFORM OF THE WOMEN'S DIVISION: AN EDUCATIONAL STATEMENT

By 1920, with the successful graduation of three generations of college women, the mythology that women were patently too weak to engage in intellectual endeavors, although not completely expunged from the American viewpoint, had been arrested considerably. As a consequence, physical education and sport moved beyond the pragmatic roles of remediation or preparation for education to become a substantive part of the overall educational process.

In considering how best to provide athletic opportunities for women, the writers of the Platform relied on democratic ideals and principles of equity to guide their thinking. It is telling that the Platform begins with a pledge to "promote programs for all members of a given social group."[22] As reflected in the Women's Division's motto, "A Game for Every Girl and Every Girl in a Game," women as physical educators maintained a deep and abiding commitment to a concept they called "sport for the masses."[23]

The democratic ideal of education that suffuses the Platform reflects the integrity that physical educators found in the work of John Dewey and the enormous impact that Dewey's philosophy exerted on the profession of physical education.[24] Dewey held that one of the goals of education should be the preparation of students to strive for an ideal society. According to Dewey, as citizens work to build such a society, they should not "simply repeat the traits which are actually found" in the present one. Rather, the creation of a new ideal requires a critical examination of the existing society along with a willingness to eliminate undesirable features and make improvements where possible.[25]

When it came to devising an ideal for women's sport, a critical examination of the existing model was precisely the strategy that female physical educators chose to take. In their view, the highly specialized, commercialized, spectator-oriented model of men's athletics could not help those individuals who were less skilled or unskilled in sport and thus who were "most in need of the benefits which athletics can give."[26] In effect, the democratic premises of equalizing opportunity and facilitating the greatest good for the greatest number could not accommodate a sport system that excluded the less skilled. As Agnes Wayman, the executive director of the Women's Division of the NAAF at the time explained, "We must make them realize that our games and sports are not Roman spectacles, that they are not an end in and of themselves, but a means to an end—a finer, better equipped citizenry."[27]

NEGATIVE ASPECTS OF MEN'S INTERCOLLEGIATE SPORT

Female physical educators, influenced substantially by the educational incongruities and obvious hypocrisy at the core of the problems that faced intercollegiate athletics, were intent on designing a model of athletics that adhered to educational principles and avoided the compromises that had occurred when the commercial and professional elements of sport took precedence over student welfare. In a poignant speech delivered in 1924 at the University of Chicago (with Amos Alonzo Stagg sitting at the dais), Agnes Wayman spoke of the failure of men's systems of sport. Recalling that during World War I over a third of men examined had been found unfit for service, she observed: "Too many sat in the great stand. And we considered ourselves a nation of athletes."[28] She also cautioned that women's physical education was in trouble. Wayman remarked that, "Our ideals have been set by men. What is sauce for the goose is not sauce for the gander."[29]

In the thinking of female physical educators at the time, sauce for the goose clearly did not include gate receipts, programs that relied on revenue generation, and the exploitation of athletes through sensational publicity and reliance on student performances for institutional gain. Although they most often attributed problems associated with men's intercollegiate sport to commercialism, women's sport leaders also decried increasing professionalism—such as subsidization of athletes, the hiring of coaches rather than educators for athletic programs, and the subsequent production of mass spectacles.

Mabel Lee observed that "educational experts" had become "business managers," who perceived that they had to develop highly specialized teams in order to produce spectacles worth paying for or betting on when gate receipts became the primary focus of athletic programs.[30] Those female physical educators who saw men's intercollegiate sport as both commercial and professional were not alone in their assessment.

In expressing his support for the work of the Women's Division, the religious leader and educator John M. Cooper leveled at members an indictment of what he called the "traditionally athletic sex"; he wrote that "We have winked at professionalism until some of us are [just] about disgusted with the whole business, its jockeying, its underhandedness, its pretense, its sham, its bunk."[31] Another ally was sportswriter John Tunis, who observed that one result of the commercialism creeping into amateur games was the creation of "an organized class of men, professionally dependent upon sport."[32]

THE "SPECIAL NEEDS OF WOMEN"

By the 1930s, enormous progress had been made in the lives of American women. Having negotiated a place for themselves in the public spheres of work, politics, education, and sport, women as a group experienced more freedom than they had known before. Despite the progress made, women continued to be viewed as the weaker sex, who had "special needs."

Faced with that belief, women in physical education turned to the sciences and medicine for support of their theories on women's involvement in physical activity, just as their predecessors had done generations earlier. Science, as it turned out, offered less-than-definitive answers. Studies such as one that showed "conclusively that with previous medical examinations and careful supervision girls might not only safely indulge in such sports [track] but that their hearts were greatly improved by them" helped provide at least some reason to grant permission for women to play vigorous sports.

However, the absence of substantive information about the exact moment when "physical training" turned into "physical straining" was a difficult obstacle for educators to overcome.[33] Furthermore, the work of Ernst Herman Arnold, who had reported that sportswomen ran the risk of developing a condition that he called an "infantile uterus" (which supposedly resulted in reduction in fertility) offered a sobering realization that female physical educators could not overlook this issue without appearing to be negligent.[34]

Because athletic participation for women remained a relatively uncharted territory, fear of the unknown manifest itself in cautionary tales and "what if" speculation. Urging that careful monitoring of competitive athletics be done, commentators speculated that a coach's zeal or a young girl's commitment to her team might provoke one or both parties to risk her health, especially her reproductive health. Blanche Trilling maintained that there is a "tendency which such games breed to disregard physical safeguards, to play during menstrual periods and to play beyond the effort a girl ought to have, for the sake of a championship."[35]

Measures to avoid the potential health risks and dangers of sport for women thus became prominent features of the Platform. The model of sport that they espoused controlled the competitive atmosphere through the elimination of gate receipts and sensationalizing publicity, afforded protection through the provision of "adequate medical examination and medical follow up," and argued in general for the avoidance of circumstances that would "sacrifice" an individual's health for the sake of competition.[36]

THE ABSENCE OF WOMEN IN THE GOVERNANCE OF SPORT

As women's involvement in sport changed during the years between 1900 and 1930, so too did the professional milieu for women as physical educators. Some of these women were entering coeducational settings for the first time.[37] Vying for academic legitimacy with mostly male faculties, these women also faced the problem of establishing their own expertise with male coaches and administrators. When the Amateur Athletic Union moved to take control of girls' and women's sport, it threatened the essence of female physical educators' professional lives and work.

The result was the somewhat defensive tone, separatist rhetoric, and overt protectionism in the Platform, which called for physical activities to be placed under the "immediate leadership" of "well qualified and trained women."[38] It is quite clear that these women had every intention of claiming authority over women's athletics. So strong was the consensus on the merits of the Women's Division philosophy that it was endorsed in its totality by five existing women's educational associations.[39]

One price paid for this unified front was occasional intolerance for alternative viewpoints on the matter of moderate competition. Gladys Palmer, a women's sports advocate from Ohio State University, for instance, was treated with considerable hostility by her female peers in 1936 and 1941 when she campaigned for a national collegiate women's championship in golf.[40]

Similarly, Constance Applebee, the Englishwoman who introduced field hockey to the United States and later became director of Physical Education at Bryn Mawr College, met with disfavor from members of the Women's Division because of her avid support for upper-level competition culminating in international play.[41] Regarding the hockey enthusiasts whom Applebee inspired, Agnes Wayman remarked: "Let's hope they do not ultimately split the ranks of women working in physical education."[42]

Contradictory to their expressed philosophy of student-centered education, female physical educators frequently overlooked or overruled their students' wishes for less restrictive forms of competition. In a poll conducted at Wellesley College in 1924, students voted 237 to 33 in favor of intercollegiate sports. Female undergraduates at Radcliffe, Mount Holyoke, Connecticut College, and Wheaton also expressed majority interest in intercollegiate sports.[43]

Sport historian Ronald Smith has argued that female physical educators of this era were violating their own professed commitment to democratic processes by attempting to exert single-minded and unyielding control over women's sport and physical education. Indeed, it is true that female physical educators could at times be coercive, dismissive, and intolerant in their dealings with each other and with representatives from other sport organizations that posed a threat to the goal they were attempting to achieve. It should be noted, however, that these women had an ever-present political reality in mind. Given the all-male power structure of the day, their views on sport could be, and were, passed over and ignored with regularity. Some female educators acknowledged the value of a less confining and conservative stance. Ethel Perrin, for instance, in an article entitled "More Competitive Athletics for Girls—But of the Right Kind," went as far as to admit that certain views that female physical educators professed were "prudish and old-fashioned."[44]

Nonetheless, the writers of the Platform were constantly reminded that they were in a minority position. With women having obtained the right to vote only two years prior to the AAU's attempt to assume control of women's athletics, women in physical education were endeavoring to outline a vision of women's sport in an America that was not accustomed to affording women a voice in matters of public import.[45]

In higher education during 1920, only 26 percent of all full-time faculty were women.[46] The number of female physical educators within that percentage would have been appreciably less. Similarly, the percentage of women in decision- and policy-making roles within sport-governing bodies outside of education was almost nil. To have chosen a more radical direction for women's sport and opened themselves to charges of tampering with motherhood or female morality would have meant professional extinction. Furthermore, female physical educators were themselves products of a culture that taught them that women were the weaker sex. It is reasonable to suppose that some women even as educators still agreed with that position.

Whatever flaws it may have encompassed, the model of sport set by the Women's Division established the primacy of students' interests, a forum for reconciliation of athletics with the educational mission of colleges, and the right of women to shape their own destinies in sport.

THE IMPACT OF THE WOMEN'S DIVISION PLATFORM ON INTERCOLLEGIATE SPORT FOR WOMEN: 1920–1960

Many of the leading female physical educators at the time believed that an inclusive program of sports could not exist simultaneously with a selective program. Their reasons for such a belief varied. According to author Helen Smith, limitations of time, financial resources, staffing, and facilities argued against support for varsity teams.[47] Mabel Gummings, the director of Physical Education at Wellesley College, observed that "Interscholastic competition will have to be somewhat neglected, for the attention needed to run a girl's physical education program adapted to the strengths and abilities of the individual takes time."[48] Noting that varsity programs typically called for the skills of a coach rather than a physical educator, Mabel Lee argued that budget constraints would not permit hiring staff to support both types of programs.[49]

The most popular form of competition during the 1930s and 1940s was a concept called the "play day," which had the sport-for-all ideal as its raison d'être. Women from several colleges met at a host campus and were placed onto mixed teams through a lottery system. The key aspects of the sport-for-women philosophy—including a provision for all skill levels, a balanced perspective on competition and winning, and a concern for student health and well-being—all came together in the play day.[50] By 1936, due in part to the promotion of the play day format by Women's Division and CWA supporters, over 70 percent of colleges found this form of competition preferable to interschool games.[51]

Because the play day (and its sister competitive form the sports day) departed so intensely from varsity competition, this concept was vulnerable at times to dismissive attitudes that reduced these forms of organized competition to nothing more than quaint social affairs. Marcia Winn, then-director of physical education at William Smith College, recalls:

Once at a "Play Day" an observer remarked, "Isn't it nice to see the dear girls playing without any desire to win." Utter rot—and an injustice to the "dear girls," who, being normal, healthy individuals, presumably had a normal healthy desire to win. The object in any game is to score points while preventing your opponents scoring—in short, to win.

By the late 1930s there was enough turmoil over the issue of high-level competition that the membership base for the Women's Division had diminished considerably. Increasingly, girls and women interested in an outlet for elite competition found it in community-based or high school programs. In an effort to ensure its future, the Women's Division merged with the National Section on Women's Athletics (NSWA, formerly the CWA), a natural liaison, because it was in the colleges and universities where the Platform had exerted the greatest lasting influence.

The profound philosophical dilemma with which female physical educators struggled is revealed in their perception that an educationally sound and responsible form of sport could not exist alongside varsity-level competition. Within the context of the factors they were attempting to mediate out and work within, competition by itself was not the problem, as was shown in their attempts to provide for it. The problem as they saw it, was the intermingling of competition with commercialism and professionalism.

Unfortunately, their commitment to avoid the mistakes of their male counterparts produced a kind of tunnel vision among some female physical educators. Consequently, they failed to recognize and embrace the contribution of a small group of institutions, located primarily in the Northeast, who had constructed an intercollegiate model of athletics for women as early as the 1920s that adhered completely to the Platform's dictates while providing for highly skilled play.

By 1920 a group of institutions in the Philadelphia area, including Beaver College, Bryn Mawr College, Swarthmore College, the University of Pennsylvania, and Ursinus College, were already playing varsity games against one another in field hockey, basketball, and tennis.[52] In a 1923 yearbook entry, one female athlete wrote: "URSINUS COLLEGE—one of the few co-educational institutions which encourage intercollegiate sports for the fair sex. . . . For four years we have had a hockey team which rivals the best ones in this section. Likewise we have a basketball sextette which . . . finally came through with a winning season."[53]

One of the persons responsible for this isolated nest of intercollegiate competition for women was Constance Applebee. Known to history principally as the "grand dame" of field hockey in the United States, Applebee had also developed a vision of how sport for women could be played at all levels.[54] An Englishwoman by birth, Applebee saw no impediments to women competing in upper-level sport within the framework of an amateur ideal. Having been appointed to serve as games mistress at Bryn Mawr College in 1903, "The Apple," as she was called, spent several decades developing a sport system in the Philadelphia area that would teach girls and women to play field hockey through instructional programs and engage them in keen competition at the varsity and club levels.[55]

Participating institutions created tiers of teams that accommodated a broad range of skill levels. As late as 1977 Ursinus College continued to engage in action four field hockey teams, all of which played a competitive schedule. Its first team competed against upper-level elite institutions, and the lower teams played against varsity opponents matched to their own abilities.[56]

Applebee's professional relationships with other leading physical educators of the day were said to have been acrimonious and tense.[57] This misperception was unfortunate because she, perhaps better than anyone, had apprehended that the problems plaguing men's intercollegiate sport reflected the absence of an amateur compass that could lend appropriate direction to its evolution. In an editorial in *The Sportswoman*, a publication owned and edited by Applebee, she wrote:

The very words intercollegiate competition are unpleasant, and we do not wonder that the idea is repugnant to many. It sounds as though the main idea was to set out to win something, for the college, in the name of the college and something that a college doesn't exist for. It is perfectly true that this is what in many cases men's intercollegiates have degenerated into and it is quite possible that in some cases women's might also. But on the whole, women's [games] are more apt to be friendly, and conducive to a better understanding of each other than merely an artificial fight for a trophy.[58]

Whereas women such as Constance Applebee understood that women's intercollegiate sport was possible if it adhered to amateur principles, the vast majority of female physical educators at the time feared that encouraging varsity competition would lead to the corruption prevalent in men's sport. Although, as the years went by, women in physical education would relax their stance on varsity competition for women, they remained grudging in their support for several decades to come.

As late as 1957 the Division for Girls' and Women's Sport (DGWS) policy statement still called for limiting "competitive sports to the few highly skilled" because it "deprived others of the many different kinds of desirable activities which are inherent in well conducted sports programs." Given the year, this is particularly illustrative of the very different evolutionary paths taken by men's and women's intercollegiate athletics. In the same year that the DGWS continued to show apprehension about moving into the highly specialized competitive arena for fear that educational principles would be compromised, the NCAA was adopting financial aid policies that would structurally transform men's intercollegiate sport from an amateur model to a professional model. It would not be until the 1960s, which saw the rise of a new feminism and the women's movement, that the women's leadership in physical education would finally end its ambivalence on the issue of varsity competition and that the development of women's intercollegiate sport would begin in earnest.

Part II

Athletic Scholarships and the Emergence of Corporate College Sport

5

Athletic Scholarships: From Gifts to Employment Contracts

During the first half of the twentieth century, one of the most striking contrasts between the men and women who administered collegiate athletics was their attitude toward commercialism. As indicated in the previous chapter, the Women's Division Platform opposed college sport as a commercial spectacle. This position was in part an accommodation to the prevailing sexism of the time, which viewed any public display by women (including speaking out on public issues) as akin to prostitution.[1] Leaders in women's collegiate sport opposed commercialism also because they felt it would place the needs of spectators above the educational needs of athletic participants.

The men who founded the NCAA, on the other hand, had little quarrel with commercialism. From the time of its founding in 1905, the NCAA has never passed a piece of legislation to limit gate receipts or in any other way impede the growth of college sport as a commercial spectacle. Professionalism, however, was a very different issue. Between 1906 and 1948, the NCAA, just like the CWA and other women's sport-governing bodies, was unequivocal in its opposition to financial inducements for talented athletes. NCAA policy encouraged professionalism by supporting the growth of college sport as a revenue-producing business, but it was not until 1956 that the NCAA incorporated professionalism into its constitution and bylaws.[2] It was at this point that the question was increasingly raised as to how scholarship athletes differed, if at all, from other university employees.

Awarding athletic scholarships as inducements for playing sports violates long-standing amateur principles. Still, for the most part, the scholarships that existed before 1967 did not constitute employment contracts. According to NCAA rules during that time, an athletic scholarship could not be reduced or canceled during the period of its award on the basis of an athlete's contribution to a team's success. Nor could the award be taken away simply because of an injury or if the athlete decided not to participate in sports. At this point in the evolution of athletic subsidization, scholarships were more like gifts used to attract talented athletes than payments for services rendered. There are conditions, however, under which scholarships clearly do become employment contracts; throughout the NCAA's rule changes over the past decades, the line between high-level collegiate sport and employment has largely disappeared.

THE *VAN HORN* CASE: THE NCAA GOES ON ALERT

One of the first court cases to focus directly on the question of whether or not an athletic scholarship constitutes a contract for hire involved Edward Gary Van Horn, a football player at California State Polytechnic College who had been killed in a plane crash while returning from a game in Ohio in 1960.[3] Van Horn had received an athletic scholarship from funds contributed to the college by a group known as the Mustang Booster club. As athletic director of the college, its coach would periodically submit a budget to the booster club, including the names of athletes that he was recommending for financial assistance during the ensuing school year. The funds contributed by the club were then distributed by the college to the students who qualified. This method of distributing financial inducements to athletes had been legitimized by the NCAA's 1956 athletic scholarship decision.

To qualify for this award, a student had to be a potential athlete, maintain a 2.2 grade average while carrying twelve units of college courses, and be recommended by his coach to the scholarship committee. Van Horn's athletic scholarship, which covered tuition, books, and some apartment rental expenses, was awarded for one year only, thus freeing the university from the four-year commitment often made to athletes at other universities during this era. Before the 1958 season, Van Horn had told his father that he had been offered a "pretty good deal to play football."[4] He received similar deals in 1959 and 1960. Because Van Horn was married and had a family to support, he told his father that he could not play football unless he received some kind of financial support.

In court the Industrial Accident Commission and the university argued that this scholarship had been a gift, not a payment for services rendered. To support that claim, they pointed out that the scholarship had been awarded for an entire year and that it was not dependent on any seasonal participation in sports; even if Van Horn had not played a single game, he still would have received the scholarship during that year. The university also argued that his scholarship had been awarded on the basis of scholastic records, rather than on athletic prowess, and that the coach had not been consulted in the application process. In the university's view, Van Horn was not rendering a service by playing football and was therefore not an employee.

In its 1963 decision against the Commission and the university, this California district court of appeals pointed out that because a recipient of athletic scholarships "must be a member of an athletic team," athletic prowess was a factor in the award. The court also noted that previous rulings on this matter had held that one may have the dual capacity of a student and an employee with respect to a collegiate activity. The court agreed that the coach had no power to terminate a scholarship during the one-year period of its award; it contended, nonetheless, that Van Horn had received the scholarship because of his athletic prowess and participation. Because it believed that Van Horn's scholarship was dependent on his athletic participation, the court concluded that his scholarship was an employment contract. As a result of this decision, death benefits were awarded to Van Horn's family.

The legal issues raised in the *Van Horn* case were crucial to the future of college sport. Thus, it is not surprising that the decision sent shock waves through the NCAA. Almost immediately, the NCAA began to develop a strategy to head off future workers' compensation challenges. In June 1964 Walter Byers contacted Marcus Plant, a noted tort expert in the University of Michigan Law School and member of the NCAA Council, to express his concern about the *Van Horn* ruling. Plant, who viewed workers' compensation as one of his subspecialties, offered to prepare a memorandum on the subject for distribution to the NCAA leadership. Plant told Byers that the subject warranted careful consideration, but he added reassuringly, "I do not think the picture is as black as the newspapers have made it out to be."[5]

The memorandum that Plant prepared for Byers laid out the broad strategy that guided the NCAA through the minefield of workers' compensation court cases over the next twenty years. In December 1964 an edited draft of Plant's memo was sent out to faculty representatives, athletic directors, and officers of allied conferences by Robert F. Ray, then-president of the NCAA, and Everett D. Barnes, its secretary-treasurer.[6] The December memorandum urged NCAA institutions to have their attorneys review the wording of their grants-in-aid policies in light of state workers' compensation statutes, and it provided specific recommendations as to what revisions should be made so that language would not suggest an employment relationship. The key to the NCAA's workers' compensation strategy was to avoid the impression that athletes had to participate in sports in order to retain their athletic scholarships.

According to Walter Byers, one-year grants, especially when coaches made oral or written commitments to renew them if athletes continued to participate, were perilously close to being outright employment contracts.[7] To avoid the appearance of employment, therefore, the NCAA memorandum recommended that universities delete such language and instead refer to sections of the NCAA constitution that explicitly state that athletic scholarships do not constitute payment or compensation for participation.[8] In addition, the NCAA offered the assistance of its Kansas City–based attorneys, who would provide suggestions for handling this problem, and encouraged colleges and universities to inform the NCAA immediately of workers' compensation claims made on behalf of an injured athlete.

It is noteworthy that Everett D. Barnes, who was the athletic director at Colgate as well as secretary-treasurer of the NCAA at this time, favored a very different workers' compensation strategy. Before sending out the memo drafted by Plant, Barnes had written to Walter Byers suggesting that the *Van Horn* decision provided good reason for the NCAA to pass legislation that would award financial assistance on the basis of need. Barnes based his opinion on discussions with a New York attorney who advised that if scholarships are not contingent on athletic activity, athletes would not come under workers' compensation as there would be "no penalty to students when and if they cease athletic endeavors."[9] There is no doubt that Barnes's proposal would have instantly eliminated the workers' compensation problem. But it would also have forced coaches to relinquish the control that comes from being able to award or withdraw financial aid. In the end, the NCAA chose to prop up the myth of amateurism rather than pass legislation to restore the real thing.

THE DEATH OF FOUR-YEAR SCHOLARSHIPS

In the decade following the *Van Horn* decision, the NCAA continued to avoid language in its constitution and bylaws that would suggest that scholarships are employment contracts. Yet, it was during this same period that NCAA legislation was passed that actually increased a university's ability to remove scholarships from athletes who decided not to participate in sports or who, because of injury or lack of athletic ability, could no longer contribute to team success. In other words, at the same time that NCAA officials were doing everything in their power to deny that scholarships constituted employment contracts, they were diligently seeking innovative ways to have nonproductive or noncooperative athletes fired.

In the 1960s many athletic directors were concerned that athletes were accepting four-year grants-in-aid and then deciding not to participate. Arizona State's athletic director Clyde B. Smith complained to Walter Byers that "approximately 10 students who accepted their scholarships to compete in our program . . . have decided not to participate." Smith added, "I think it is morally wrong. Regardless of what anyone says, this is a contract and it is a two-way street."[10] When it came to the workers' compensation issue, NCAA officials were virtually unanimous in their position that scholarships were gifts awarded with no obligation whatever to participate. When athletes took that notion seriously, however, those same officials had no problem rediscovering the contractual nature of such relationships.

At the 1967 NCAA convention, two pieces of legislation were proposed that would allow universities to cancel scholarships of athletes who in the colleges' eyes were not living up to their end of the scholarship agreement. The first proposal was to amend the constitution so it would allow reduction or cancellation of a scholarship during the period of its award if the recipient "fraudulently misrepresents any information on his application, letter of intent or tender, or . . . engages in serious misconduct warranting substantial disciplinary penalty."[11] This proposal, which was passed by a vote of 214 to 13, allowed a coach to refer an athlete who engaged in such action to appropriate authorities on campus for disciplinary action leading to loss of a scholarship.

According to the new legislation, if a scholarship athlete made only token appearances at practice or did not show up at all, such action would be considered a fraudulent misrepresentation of information on the student's admissions application, letter of intent, or tender and would constitute grounds for the immediate termination of financial aid.[12] Serious misconduct included refusal to "meet the normal good conduct obligations required of all team members, and *defiance of the normal and necessary directions of departmental staff members*" (emphasis added).[13] This amendment was passed in 1967 and became part of the same NCAA constitution that had stated that athletic scholarships could not be canceled during the period of their award for failure to participate. The NCAA could now have it both ways.

This new amendment allowed a university to immediately terminate scholarships for perceived insubordination or failure to take sports seriously. But schools with four-year scholarships still had no way to cancel awards of players who had sustained injuries early in their college careers or who had turned out to lack athletic abilities necessary to compete in high-performance college sport. Such athletes ended up getting four-year grants even though they made minimal or no athletic contributions. To give themselves the option to discontinue the grants of such athletes, many schools had already begun to limit athletic scholarships to one year or less. At the 1967 NCAA convention, a proposal was made to make this one-year limitation the athletic policy at all NCAA institutions.

One of the motives for this legislation, as Walter Byers has pointed out, was to limit the recruiting advantage of programs that were offering athletes a four-year "ride."[14] The floor debates at the convention, however, revealed that many delegates believed that four-year grants encouraged some athletes to try to get "something for nothing." A representative of the Big Eight Conference argued in favor of the proposal to limit the period of the award, saying that "it compels the boy to meet his moral obligation to the university and to athletics."[15] The real issue, therefore, was one of control. With one-year grants, coaches could cut financial support for athletes who in their eyes were not making an honest effort. Another argument made in favor of one-year grants was that it was a better way of getting rid of "dead wood" than the practice of "running off" athletes by subjecting them to dehumanizing drills.[16]

Although the 1967 effort to eliminate four-year grants fell short of the two-thirds majority needed for passage, the momentum for the change was growing rapidly. At the 1973 NCAA convention, the one-year limit on athletic grants was approved in less than 90 seconds by a show of hands.[17] At that same convention, the membership soundly defeated a proposal to go to a need-based system of awarding financial aid to athletes. Such a system, if adopted by all institutions, would undoubtedly have reduced athletic expenses. More important, need-based aid would have allowed athletes to place educational priorities over those of sports without fear of losing financial aid. By rejecting this proposal, the NCAA was committing itself to continuation of professional college sport. The separation of the amateurs from the professionals was formalized in 1973 by the creation of Divisions I, II, and III. Division III continued the amateur tradition of awarding no athletic scholarships.

Between 1963, the year of the *Van Horn* decision, and 1973, the NCAA had rewritten financial aid policy to fit the needs of the rapidly expanding college sport industry. Four-year scholarships were dropped in favor of one-year awards, thus giving coaches more power to remove athletes who had been "recruiting mistakes." A number of changes were also made that allowed immediate cancellation of an award for such reasons as voluntarily withdrawing from sports or refusing to follow directions of athletic staff. The NCAA had given its member institutions far greater control over the college athlete workforce. It was still an open question as to how these new rules would hold up under another round of workers' compensation challenges. Two court decisions in the 1980s shed light on this question.

FRED RENSING: A CASE OF FRAUDULENT MISREPRESENTATION

In 1983 the supreme court of Indiana reached its decision in the case of Fred Rensing, an Indiana State University football player who had been paralyzed in an injury sustained in spring football practice in 1976. The *Rensing* decision is testimony to the effectiveness of the NCAA's conscious campaign to defend its membership from such setbacks in workers' compensation as the *Van Horn* decision of 1963. In denying Rensing workers' compensation benefits, the Indiana court accepted without question the NCAA's unsubstantiated claims that intercollegiate sports are clearly distinguished from the professional sports business, that financial inducements in the form of athletic scholarships do not constitute pay, and that financial aid cannot be conditioned on athletic performance. Once these claims were accepted a priori by the court, Rensing did not have a chance.

The NCAA was involved in the *Rensing* case from the very outset. In 1977 James E. Sullivan, an attorney representing Indiana State University, wrote to George H. Gangwere, an NCAA attorney, requesting help in preparing his defense in the *Rensing* case. Gangwere sent materials to Sullivan, but more important, suggested that Marcus Plant, the Michigan law professor who had helped develop the NCAA's strategy for dealing with such cases, be used as an expert witness.[18] Over the next couple of years, Plant and other NCAA attorneys played an important role in helping Indiana State University prepare its case. Plant appeared as an expert witness, and Gangwere's firm wrote an amicus brief on behalf of the NCAA. Although the Indiana court of appeals ruled in favor of Rensing, the case ultimately went to the Indiana supreme court, where the strategy outlined by Plant twenty years earlier proved to be remarkably effective.

The influence of the NCAA in the Indiana court ruling is unmistakable. To establish whether or not a contract for hire existed, the Indiana court placed a great deal of weight on any evidence that there had been a mutual belief that a contract for hire existed, an approach that was suggested also in the NCAA's amicus brief. In ruling against Rensing, the court argued that the financial aid that Rensing had received was not considered by the parties involved to be pay. The university did not consider the scholarship to be pay, in the court's opinion, since the award was perfectly legal under the rules of the NCAA, an organization that itself strictly prohibits taking pay for sports. As for Rensing, he did not consider his benefits as income because "he did not report them for income tax purposes."[19]

The major problem with this line of reasoning as it applies to the university is that it assumes that the NCAA and Indiana State University actually believed the characterization of athletic grants that appears in the *NCAA constitution*. One could just as easily argue that Indiana State University knew very well that it was paying Rensing but had an interest in sustaining the NCAA mythology that athletic scholarships are merely gifts awarded with no contractual intent. The motive for this fraudulent misrepresentation of the nature of athletic scholarships would obviously be to avoid workers' compensation claims, scrutiny by the Internal Revenue Service (IRS), and antitrust concerns about cartel-imposed controls on the price of athletic labor.

It can be argued that Rensing's failure to pay taxes on his athletic grant-in-aid was yet another manifestation of the NCAA's fraudulent misrepresentation of the true nature of corporate college sport. Walter Byers states that as Executive director of the NCAA, he often told congressional committees that college sport was essentially amateur in order to avoid colleges having to pay the same taxes as those levied against other entertainment businesses.[20] The fact that Rensing did not pay taxes on his scholarship may have more to do with the fact that the IRS has yet to penetrate the NCAA's amateur mythology than with Rensing's belief that his financial aid was not income. Rensing may well have viewed his scholarship to be pay, and he would have paid taxes if asked; the issue just never came up. The court's reasoning with regard to establishing intent was seriously flawed.

Attorney Mark Atkinson has criticized approaches to defining employment that rely primarily on definitions offered by the contesting parties. According to Atkinson, workers' compensation law does not blindly accept characterizations made by employers or employer organizations. For example, "if an employer calls himself an independent contractor in an attempt to evade workmen's compensation liability, the courts will look past mere titles to realities."[21] Had the Rensing court followed this logic, it would have looked beyond NCAA or its member institutions' definitions of pay to assess the intentions of the contesting parties. A close examination of what Indiana State University actually required Rensing to do as a condition for continued financial aid would have yielded far better inferences as to contractual intent than taking at face value the self-serving definitions of pay provided by the NCAA.

The *Rensing* decision, a major victory for the college sport industry, demonstrated the effectiveness of the NCAA in responding to legal challenges. In response to the *Van Horn* decision in 1963, the NCAA helped its member institutions incorporate language into their financial aid agreements that would mask their contractual intent and crafted legislation that gave the impression that scholarships could not be canceled during the period of their award for failure to participate. The NCAA also encouraged member institutions to seek the advice and support of its legal staff when confronted with a workers' compensation challenge. All of these strategies helped Indiana State University win the *Rensing* case. In addition, the economic and cultural significance of college sport in the state of Indiana undoubtedly weighed heavily against Rensing, as did fears that recognizing college athletes as employees would burden college sport with many of the labor problems so common in professional leagues.

COLEMAN v. WESTERN MICHIGAN UNIVERSITY: A FRAMEWORK FOR ANALYSIS

A few months after the *Rensing* decision, a Michigan appeals court rendered a workers' compensation decision in the case of Willie Coleman, a football player at Western Michigan University. Coleman had sustained a serious injury in football practice in 1974 that prevented him from continuing on the team. Although the NCAA does not appear to have been as directly involved in this case as in the *Rensing* proceedings, its amateur ideology undoubtedly shaped this outcome. Regardless of whether or not one agrees with the court's decision against Coleman, his case provides a helpful framework for working one's way through this complex issue.

The State of Michigan requires application of a so-called economic realities test for determining the existence of an employment relationship. This test, based on criteria developed in *Askew v. Macomber* (1976), sets forth certain factors that Michigan courts must consider in determining whether or not there exists an expressed or implied contract for hire.[22] These factors include: (1) the proposed employer's right to control or dictate the activities of the proposed employee; (2) the proposed employer's right to discipline or fire the proposed employee; (3) the payment of wages and, particularly, the extent to which the proposed employee is dependent upon the payment of wages or other benefits for his daily living expenses; and (4) whether or not the task performed by the proposed employee was an integral part of the proposed employer's business.

Regarding the first factor (i.e., the right of the proposed employer to control or dictate the activities of the proposed employee), the Michigan court stated that the control that coaches had over Coleman "applied to the sports activity whether or not an athlete had the benefit of a scholarship."[23] In the court's view, there seemed to be no difference in the amounts of control exercised by the Western Michigan coach and a coach at a school such as Amherst College—even though the latter awarded no athletic scholarships. By taking this position, the court gave no weight to the fact that if Willie Coleman had challenged his coach's authority by regularly showing up late for practice, for instance, he risked the loss of his grant-in-aid.

It is difficult to overstate the kinds of demands that legitimately can be made on scholarship athletes as a condition for their continuing to receive scholarships. As an athletic trainer has noted, "the managers of sport ask the athlete to change diet. They ask the athlete to change patterns of weight gain and loss. They ask the athlete to run anaerobic training patterns. They ask the athlete to play with injury. They ask the athlete to think certain kinds of things, to behave in certain ways."[24] It should be added that in some sports, athletes are asked to risk serious injury almost every day. It is undeniable that many athletes regularly subject themselves to this kind of intense training voluntarily. The fact remains, however, that coaches who have significant control over financial awards have considerable power to dictate such activities.

On the second factor in the State of Michigan's economic realities test (i.e., the proposed employer's right to discipline or fire the proposed employee), the court in the *Coleman* case ruled that the evidence weighed against Coleman because his grant could not be canceled during the one-year award period because of his performance. This argument would be a convincing one if in 1967 the NCAA had not added a number of conditions under which grants *could* be reduced or canceled during the award period. As mentioned earlier, athletes deemed to have "refused to meet the normal good-conduct obligations required of all team members" or who "defied the normal and necessary directions of departmental staff members" could lose their grants. These are exactly the reasons why workers are often "fired" in other industries. College sport after 1967 was no different.

The 1967 rule changes also allowed a university to cancel a grant during the award period for so-called fraudulent misrepresentation of information on athletes' letters of intent and other documents. An athlete who skipped practice, loafed during practice, or quit the team could have his grant withdrawn immediately because the NCAA would classify this as a case of "fraudulent misrepresentation." The Michigan court made no mention of these crucial rule changes and how they were being interpreted by the NCAA.[25] It is a fact, however, that athletes in Coleman's era could be disciplined by threats to terminate the financial support they needed for housing, food, and educational expenses. And their "firing" could take place during the period of the award.

The third factor in the economic realities test is the extent to which the proposed employee is dependent on the payment of wages or other benefits for daily living expenses. Given the court's position on the first two factors, it is surprising that it found that the payment-of-wages factor weighed in favor of the finding of an employment relationship. Citing *Morgan v. Win Schuler's*

Restaurant (1975), the court defined wages as "items of compensation which are measurable in money or which confer an economic gain upon the employee."[26] The court argued that in return for his services as a football player, Coleman had received room, board, tuition, and books and that he was therefore dependent on his scholarship to pay his daily living expenses. The court was clearly suggesting that the athletic scholarship took the form of a quid pro quo when it came to the issue of the payment of wages.

The fourth factor in the economic realities test was whether or not the task performed by the proposed employee was an integral part of the proposed employer's business. The court placed considerable weight on this final factor in its ultimate decision to deny Coleman workers' compensation. According to the court, Western Michigan University may have had some very limited rights to its control and discipline of Coleman's activities, and even though his scholarship had constituted a wage, there was still no way that college football was an integral part of the university's business. "The primary function of the defendant university," said the court, "was to provide academic education rather than conduct a football program."[27] And in the court's opinion, Coleman's football playing was not essential to the university's primary educational task of education and research.

One can argue that the real issue is whether or not athletes perform a function that is at least as integral to the business of the university as other jobs performed by nonacademic personnel. As a college football player, Coleman had participated in what has long been perceived to be one of higher education's most effective public relations activities. It is precisely college sport's capacity to attract media attention and revenue that led American universities to recruit and subsidize talented athletes like Coleman in the first place. The evolution of college football as a form of commercial entertainment is well documented, and the other vital economic functions it performs in universities and in surrounding communities is undeniable. So important has college football become as a commercial venture that schools have gone to the U.S. Supreme Court to defend their property right to the sale of football broadcasts to television.[28]

Despite arguments such as these, the Michigan court of appeals ruled that the four economic reality factors taken together did not support the finding of an employment relationship. In making its ruling, the court reaffirmed the position of the workers' compensation board that Western Michigan University had no more of a pecuniary interest in the football program than it had in the accomplishments of other scholarship recipients—even though the latter fill no stadiums and attract little public attention. The board characterized Coleman's sport involvement as recreation and argued that the college had received no direct benefit from Coleman's activities as a football player. One can only speculate as to whether a Michigan court applying this same economic realities test in the 1990s to a University of Michigan football player would reach the same conclusion. It seems highly unlikely.

Although the Michigan court's view of modern college sport as recreation is open to debate, it provided a fairly straight-forward method for defining employment. Armed with the logic of this four-factor economic realities test and our foregoing exposure to the history of collegiate sport, one can easily assess the degree to which scholarship athletes indeed resemble other employees in a wide variety of industries. Because Western Michigan University's athletics program was relatively small-time, factor four of the economic realities test left some room for honest debate. Nonetheless, when this test is applied to multimillion-dollar corporate-sponsored football and basketball programs in the 1990s, the criterion of a scholarship athlete's sport performance being an integral part of the proposed employer's business seems easily satisfied, thus allowing athletes on such teams to meet all four factors outlined by the Michigan court.

Regardless of what courts may rule in the future regarding college athletes' right to workers' compensation benefits, it is undeniable that universities in the 1990s condition athletic scholarships on participation and can use athletic ability as a criterion for the renewal of an award. In 1996 Kate McEwen, a University of Nebraska basketball player, was informed by her coach that her athletic scholarship would not be continued. The reason given by her coach was McEwen's apparent lack of basketball productivity. The coach pointed out that this was "a business decision" necessitated by Nebraska's preparation to join the expanded and more athletically competitive "big 12" conference.[29] McEwen had been on the Big Eight Conference academic honor role the previous season, but it was athletic ability that had gotten her this scholarship.

In the fall, just prior to the 1996 basketball season, McEwen had been physically assaulted by University of Nebraska running back Lawrence Phillips. Phillips was suspended for six games but did not lose his scholarship, an action that would have been perfectly consistent with NCAA rules passed in 1967 regarding serious misconduct. The university, which apparently did not con-sider physical assault on a former girlfriend a serious-enough offense to merit removal of financial aid, reinstated Phillips in time for him to run in total 165 yards and score three touchdowns in the Fiesta Bowl, thus helping Nebraska win its second straight national championship. Nebraska's coach, Tom Osborne cited Phillips's need for the structure of an athletic team to give him stability during a period of personal turmoil as justification for letting him continue to compete. It took a national public outcry over McEwen's treatment for

Nebraska to reverse its decision and to restore her grant. Nebraska had violated no NCAA rules.

The Nebraska case places in sharp relief some of the key features of NCAA financial aid policies approved since 1956. Athletic scholarships pay for the services of the finest athletes in the country, many of whom, like Lawrence Phillips, view college sport as valuable preparation for professional sports. Renewal or nonrenewal of athletic grants is based primarily on athletic ability, with personal character and academic performance often counting for very little. Athletes are contractually obligated to meet rigorous athletic standards, and universities, as in the case of Kate McEwen, have the option to discontinue grants for poor athletic performance. Athletic scholarships have become employment contracts.

THE COSTS OF PROFESSIONAL COLLEGE SPORT

There are genuine educational, economic, and moral reasons for opposing the NCAA rules that have transformed college athletes into university employees. The educational costs of conditioning grants on athletic participation and ability will be discussed in detail in Chapter 6. Suffice it to say here that it takes an exceptional scholar-athlete to give education top priority when room, board, and tuition depend on meeting the athletic demands of one's coaches. Many college students work while they are attending college. But few jobs are as demanding or as distracting as revenue-producing college sports. An added problem for college athletes is that the myth of amateurism obscures the fact that what they are doing is virtually full-time employment.

The economic costs of paying college athletes to play sports are substantial. According to one estimate, universities award yearly nearly $514 million in athletic scholarsips to Division I athletes alone.[30] The University of Michigan, for instance, spent about $5,400,000 on athletic scholarships in 1992–1993. Duke and Notre Dame each spent $4 million.[31] Because these grants are unrelated to a recipient's financial need, money is sometimes being spent to subsidize athletes who could afford to pay their own way. Even though football and basketball at a small number of schools can cover expenses for an entire athletic program, it is generally the case that sports programs depend on institutional support to cover their deficits.[32] At the vast majority of Division I and II institutions, athletic scholarships are a financial burden.

Although the transformation of college athletes into professional entertainers has been costly in educational and financial terms, the moral costs of using amateurism as an exploitative ideology are also substantial. There is nothing inherently wrong about paying the expenses of talented college athletes to provide mass commercial entertainment. What can be questioned on moral grounds is the use of the term "amateur" to set a limit on the kind of compensation that athletes can receive. The major task of a university is to challenge falsehood and ideology, not to perpetuate them. The Olympics movement no longer insists that its professional athletes masquerade as amateurs. American universities could probably enhance their moral stature if they too reevaluated the appropriateness of the amateur label.

Additionally, college athletes are not the only students on campus who are paid to participate in extracurricular activities. A relatively small number of students also receive merit scholarships for such activities as playing in the college band. Only athletes, however, are expected to pose as amateurs. A band member who earns money on weekends by playing in a jazz club is free to do so. That same musician can leave school for a year, accept a salaried position with a symphony orchestra, and still return to school on a music scholarship. Even though scholarship athletes as a group generate far more revenue for universities than musicians do, the amateur myth denies them rights that are often taken for granted by other scholarship recipients.

Over the past decades, college sport has matured into a multimillion-dollar industry. Gate receipts and television broadcasts remain major sources of revenue. But universities have moved aggressively also to exploit new markets; many have licensing agreements with manufacturers who pay handsomely to use the institutions' logos on merchandise ranging from T-shirts to macaroni. It is estimated that the University of Kentucky will earn as much as $5 million a year from its licensed merchandising for the next several years as a result of its victory in the 1996 NCAA basketball tournament.[33] The University of Michigan has reported annual revenues of $6 million in each of the past two years from its trademark licensing.[34] Little of this revenue will find its way back to the athletes whose performances have given these schools name recognition.

Universities also enter into lucrative corporate sponsorship agreements. For instance, eleven colleges, including Florida State, Penn State, and Alabama, have across-the-board contracts with Nike. Reebok has similar deals with UCLA and the Universities of Texas and Wisconsin. These companies provide shoes and uniforms for all sports and annually pay the universities millions of dollars. In exchange, Nike and Reebok get worldwide marketing rights to each university's athletic merchandise.[35] Corporations such as Tostitos and Frito-Lay now sponsor many bowl games; in 1995 McDonalds offered Georgia Tech $5.5 million to display its golden arches on the playing floor and exterior of the basketball arena.[36] Many college coaches enter "personal service contracts" with such companies as Nike and vigorously endorse their athletic products. The athletes wear the sneakers; the coaches reap the substantial benefits.[37]

Some college administrators and sport officials feel strongly that an athletic scholarship is more than enough compensation for the services that athletes provide.[38] Nonetheless, in a free enterprise system that allows college coaches and their families to be shown visiting famous resorts and sipping fancy champagne in horse-drawn carriages, all at Nike's expense, it is hard to justify why the income of young athletes should be capped at only room, board, tuition, and related fees.[39] At Notre Dame, an athletic scholarship is worth about $25,000 a year. Although this seems like a princely sum to parents struggling to pay a child's educational expenses, it cannot compare to the financial benefits derived by other major stakeholders in the college sport industry.

Few questions elicit more heated debate in athletic circles than whether or not college athletes should be paid. The major thesis of this chapter has been that scholarship athletes are already being paid in the form of room, board, tuition, and the like. If this thesis were true, a more appropriate question for college administrators and faculty to address would then be whether the pay that athletes are currently receiving now needs to be either adjusted upward to meet the realities of modern college sport or eliminated altogether to bring college sport into line with its supposed commitment to amateur principles. One can only conclude that the ethical questions raised when the term "amateur" is applied to athletes who receive substantial financial inducements to play college sports deserve far more attention than they have received to date.

6

Athletic Scholarships as Failed Academic Policy

The commercialization of collegiate sport invariably creates pressures to win that can easily compromise academic standards. When professionalism is added to the mix, education is relegated even further to the background. The granting of athletic scholarships subverts educational values in two fundamental ways. First, when students are recruited and paid to attend college primarily because of their athletic skills, it is very likely that some of them will have neither the motivation nor the aptitude to perform college-level work. Setting minimal academic standards for athletic eligibility has been tried to ensure that athletes are bona fide students. However, the effectiveness of such measures as the NCAA's Proposition 48 is highly debatable.

A second problem with athletic grants is that they give coaches inordinate control over the lives of athletes. When faced with the conflicting demands of sports and the classroom, athletes are likely to feel pressure to meet the demands of coaches who make key decisions about the renewal of financial aid. Although athletes with marginal academic skills are most likely to experience role conflict, even the best of students are likely to find themselves making academic compromises to accommodate the demands of sports. In an athletic scholarship system, there is far less of an incentive for coaches to accommodate to the academic needs of athletes than is the case when athletes are true amateurs.

COLLEGE ATHLETES AS ACADEMIC OUTSIDERS

It would be difficult, if not impossible, to find a major athletic program in the country that does not lower admissions standards for athletes, especially in the revenue-producing sports of football and basketball. Full-time students at the University of Notre Dame have average combined Scholastic Aptitude Test (SAT) scores in the 1,260 range, and 94 percent of freshman in 1995 were in the top fifth of their high school graduating class. Yet, the SAT average for their football team was about 890. Similar disparities can be found at other academically competitive institutions such as Stanford, Northwestern, and Michigan. The differences are not as pronounced at academically less competitive universities, but they exist nonetheless. Entering freshmen at Saint John's University in 1995–96, for instance, had average SAT scores of 950. The men's basketball team averaged 784.[1]

A recent study based in part on NCAA data found that the average athlete on a top college football or men's basketball team enters college in the bottom quarter of his class.[2] These findings were based on a comparison of the high school grade point averages (GPAs) and median scores on college entrance examinations of football and men's basketball players on teams that had finished in the top twenty-five in 1996–1997 with those of freshmen who had entered the same institutions in September 1996. At Miami and the University of Florida, according to this study, the grade point average of the typical freshman football player was more than a full point lower than that of other students accepted for admission in 1996.

The practice of lowering admissions standards for talented athletes was, of course, quite common long before the advent of athletic scholarships. However, if universities began paying the room, board, tuition, and related fees of athletes who could barely read or whose chances of graduating were extremely slim, it would become increasingly difficult to argue that athletes were an integral part of the student body and that college sport was substantially related to education. With an athletic scholarship system in place, it became absolutely imperative for the NCAA to establish a minimum academic level for awarding scholarships. To not do so would have fueled public cynicism that already surrounded professionalized college sport.

After several years of study and considerable debate, the NCAA in the 1960s adopted what was known at the time as the "1.6 rule," limiting athletic scholarships and freshman eligibility to those predicted to be capable of earning a freshman-year grade point average of 1.6 (the equivalent of C–). Eligibility for aid in subsequent years required the maintenance of at least a 1.6 average. In schools that did not award athletically related aid, failure to meet the 1.6 standard simply meant that an athlete would be barred from freshman eligibility.[3]

The 1.6 rule became applicable in 1966, at the height of the civil rights movement, and was immediately met with a barrage of criticism. Because the

1.6 rule relied on standardized test scores whose validity and reliability were increasingly being called into question, it was alleged to discriminate against minority athletes.[4] Black institutions were strongly opposed to the legislation, and Walter Byers fully expected them to take legal action against the NCAA. Said Byers: "While I do not believe a lawsuit is a wise course for the historically black institutions to follow, I suppose we will face one."[5] A separate concern voiced by some schools was that by setting nationwide academic standards for eligibility, the NCAA was violating its member institutions' autonomy.

Ivy League schools also opposed the 1.6 rule but based their criticism on a commitment to amateur principles. In a memo to the president and the council of the NCAA, the Ivy Group policy committee explained that "Ivy Group institutions do not award athletic scholarships or subscribe to the concept of the 'student athlete.'"[6] From the Ivy League's perspective, admitting and awarding need-based aid to athletes by the same criteria that apply to other students was the key to maintaining athletes as an integral part of the student body. The Ivy Group urged the immediate repeal of the 1.6 rule and recommended that the NCAA Council "place on record . . . that the 1.6 rule is inapplicable to those institutions which award financial aid on the basis of need."[7]

In 1973, one year after a historic decision to allow athletes in all sports to compete as freshmen, the NCAA rescinded the 1.6 rule. By a vote of 204 to 187, the membership decided that each institution could decide for itself what kinds of standards should be applied when awarding scholarships.[8] At that same convention, four-year scholarships were replaced by athletic grants that could be discontinued after one year if an athlete were injured or found lacking in ability. In a flurry of legislative action over a two-year period, the NCAA had passed measures that tended to obscure the distinction between college athletes and paid professionals. For the most part, these changes went unnoticed by those who are supposed to be the guardians of academic standards in the nation's universities.

PROPOSITION 48: A MASTERPIECE IN PUBLIC RELATIONS

In the decade following the repeal of the 1.6 rule, television revenues from college sport continued to spiral upward. The television contract signed by the NCAA with ABC in 1977 was for four years and averaged about $30 million a year.[9] As the financial stakes increased, so did the competition for talented athletes who could help produce winning teams. The result was the virtual abandonment of academic standards in many major athletic programs. Newspaper and television exposés made college sport a national embarrassment. For instance, Kevin Ross, a Creighton University basketball player, was reported to have completed four years of college literally not knowing how to read or write. Systematic research by scholars, educational foundations, and even the NCAA supported claims that athletes woefully underprepared academically were being admitted to college.[10] As the decade between 1973 and 1983 wore on, calls for athletic reform increased from both inside and outside of academe.

In 1983 the NCAA responded to this erosion of public confidence by supporting Proposition 48, a proposal not unlike the 1.6 rule, which had been rescinded a decade earlier. This new proposal, developed by a committee of the American Council on Education, required a minimum combined SAT score of 700 or an ACT (American College Testing) exam score of 15 in order to be eligible for freshman competition and athletically related financial aid. The rule also specified eleven core high school courses that had to be completed with a 2.0 grade point average.[11] Proposition 48 applied only to Division I schools when it went into effect in 1986. It was later extended to include Division II. (Division III schools were excluded because they offered no athletically related financial aid.)

Although Proposition 48 was hailed by many as an effort to impose tough new academic standards on college sport, the legislation's public relations value to the NCAA far outweighed its academic substance. First of all, the minimum standardized test score requirements were embarrassingly low. Scores on the SAT, for instance, typically range from 200 to 800 in each of the two parts of the exam. The maximum possible combined verbal and math score is 1,600. Because test takers start off with a combined score of 400 for merely signing their names and answering one question, a student needs to score only 300 points to meet the Proposition 48 minimum. The U.S. College Board, creator of the exam, indicated that in 1982 between 80 and 85 percent of the men and women who took the SAT would have met the Proposition 48 minimum.[12]

Between 1983 and the present, the rule has undergone a number of modifications, one of which allows poor performance on one of the two criteria to be balanced by a somewhat better performance on the other.[13] Under Proposal 16, the modified version of Proposition 48, Division I eligibility standards include three categories of freshman athletes. "Qualifiers," those who meet minimum criteria on the standardized tests and have a GPA of 2.5 (C+) in thirteen high school core courses, can compete while freshmen and receive athletic aid. Qualifiers who score lower than a 2.5 in the high school core courses can offset their GPAs by scoring higher in the standardized test. This type of indexing system offers greater flexibility than the original Proposition 48 legislation.

Athletes who do not meet the SAT/ACT score minimums but score higher than 2.5 in the high school core grouping are classified as "partial qualifiers." A partial qualifier with a combined SAT score as low as 600 can still practice as a freshman and receive athletic aid if this low SAT score is balanced out by a high school GPA of 2.75. If partial qualifiers demonstrate satisfactory academic progress during their freshman year, they can then join the high-pressure world of big-time college sport by the time they are sophomores. In 1997 the NCAA passed legislation to allow partial qualifiers four years of athletic eligibility.

Athletes whose standardized test scores and high school GPAs are even lower than those of partial qualifiers cannot practice during their freshman year, but they are allowed to receive institutional need-based aid. As sopho-mores, these nonqualifiers can receive scholarships and participate in sports. In effect, the Proposition 48 reform movement's major accomplishment has been to deny athletically related aid and athletic eligibility during the fresh-man year to athletes whose academic preparedness borders on functional illiteracy. The fact that this legislation has been hailed as one of the major reforms instituted by the NCAA's president's commission reveals how resistant professional college sport is to change.

ROLE CONFLICT FOR THE STUDENT ATHLETE

There may be good reasons for admitting athletes to a university who do not fit the academic profile of the general student body. Students with special talents, such as athletic ability, may enhance campus life far more than those who perform well only in standardized tests. And all students, including athletes, can sometimes offset academic deficiencies by demonstrating excep-tional qualities such as leadership and perseverance. Nonetheless, even if there are solid academic reasons for admitting athletes with marginal academic qualifications, one must still question an academic policy that requires students with woefully inadequate academic preparation to engage in high-profile college sport as a condition for receiving financial aid. Athletes who are academically at risk should be able to de-emphasize or withdraw from a sport altogether if it interferes with their academic progress. This is unlikely to happen in schools where athletes are under contract to perform in the collegiate sport industry.

Henry Pritchett, in the preface of the 1929 *Carnegie Report*, poignantly described the central dilemma of corporate college sport. "It takes no tabulation of statistics," said Pritchett, "to prove that the young athlete who gives himself for months, body and soul, to training under a professional coach for a grueling contest, staged to focus the attention of thousands of people, and upon which many thousands of dollars will be staked, will find no time or energy for any serious intellectual effort."[14] Pritchett made this statement before college sport became dependent on television revenues, corporate sponsorships, and one-year–renewable athletic scholarships. Although Pritchett felt his observation needed no "tabulation of statistics for support," a review of empirical research on the conflicting demands of being both a student and scholarship athlete tends to support his claim.

The 1970s and 1980s spawned scores of studies of college sport and student athletes.[15] One of the first national studies to examine the often-conflicting demands of being both a student and collegiate athlete was sponsored by the Center for Athletes' Rights and Education (CARE), an organization funded by the U.S. Department of Education, and was carried out between 1983 and 1985.[16] This survey focused on a national sample of male and female basketball players at Division I, II, and III institutions. The sample was not random, but it did include 644 athletes representing 47 colleges and universities in 35 conferences nationwide. This study remains one of the few to compare the athletic and educational experiences of athletes in all three NCAA divisions.

A number of questions included in the survey addressed the issue of role conflict. In response to the question "Do you feel pressure to be an athlete first and a student second?" 41 percent of Division I athletes, 23 percent of Division II athletes, and only 12 percent of Division III athletes said "yes." When asked if coaches made demands on their time and energy that prevented them from being top students, Division I athletes were again far more likely than athletes in the other divisions to answer yes. In every division, females were somewhat less likely than males to feel pressured by coaches, but among females those in Division I reported far more pressure on their time and energy than those in Division III. The CARE study reported also that Division I athletes were far more likely than athletes from other divisions to say that being an athlete had forced them to take fewer courses a semester, cut classes, take less demanding majors, miss important exams, and to engage in a variety of other academic shortcuts.[17]

During this same time period, Peter and Patricia Adler were engaged in a qualitative research study of role conflict among basketball players at the University of Tulsa.[18] Working anthropologically, the Adlers studied the sub-culture of college basketball by acting as participant observers. Through intimate contact with the team and coaches over a number of years, the Adlers were able to bring life to the dry statistics being compiled by survey researchers. The Adlers found that most athletes in their study had entered the university feeling optimistic about their academic prospects. Their idealism about education lasted until about the end of the first year, when they realized how difficult it was to play sports and still keep up with schoolwork. At about this point, the athlete role began to dominate all facets of their existence, a phenomenon that the Adlers referred to as "role engulfment" (226).

Basketball began to occupy all of the players' waking hours. As one player related, "Many times I'm in class and I'm thinking about who I gotta guard, you know, what play we're gonna run, or tryin', you know, to remember the film. I go through the whole class daydreamin' about a game. And then I go out and I haven't learned a thing" (149). More and more the players' images of self became consumed by one dominating status: that of being an athlete. Instead of developing a broader understanding of themselves and the world in which they live, the players developed a "blinded narrowness to one set of expectations above all else" (228). Players became one-dimensional and specialized, cut off from academic traditions that emphasize personal growth and critical awareness.

As these athletes progressed through school, they began to make a series of pragmatic adjustments in their academic attitudes and goals. Some 75 percent of those who had originally enrolled in professional programs ended up dropping out and taking more manageable majors. Others began to do only the minimum to get by. According to one player, "If I was a student like other students, I could do well, but when you play the caliber of ball we do, you just can't be an above-average student. What I strive for now is just to be an average student" (151). Athletes with inadequate academic backgrounds became frustrated and bored when enrolled in demanding courses. After repeated failures, they often stopped trying, figuring that it was better not to try than to try and not succeed, a response the Adlers called role-distancing.

In both the Adlers' study and the survey carried out by the Center for Athletes' Rights and Education, the athletes were aware that coaches had the power to set priorities. For many of them, college sport had become a job. The dividends were great in terms of extrinsic rewards and recognition; the price to be paid was in the classroom. In an insightful comment concerning the nature of college sport and role conflict, one of the Adlers' players wrote that "in college the coaches be a lot more concerned on winning and the money comin' in. If they don't win, they may get the boot, and so they pass that pressure onto us athaletes. . . . I go to bed every night I be thinkin' 'bout basketball. That's what college athaletics do to you. It take over your mind" (85).

Many of the studies done of college athletes in the 1970s and early 1980s, while full of insights, were plagued by a number of methodological weaknesses. The study sponsored by CARE, for instance, was based on a scientifically inadequate sampling design, as were many of the other studies during this period. The Adlers' work, while an excellent case study of a single institution, could likewise be challenged as not being representative of all big-time programs. In 1987 the president's commission of the NCAA, mindful of the flaws in the extant research, commissioned a multimillion-dollar study of college athletes. The study, which consisted primarily of a survey comparing 4,083 student athletes with students in general, was carried out by the American Institutes for Research (AIR) in Palo Alto, California. The results were published in four separate reports.

The first AIR report found significant differences among the comparison groups. For instance, while 74 percent of the football and basketball players had received a sport/activity scholarship, this was true of 66 percent of the athletes in other sports and only 25 percent of extracurricular students (30). This disparity was even greater regarding full as opposed to partial scholarships. Not one student who was intensely involved in extracurricular activities other than sport received a full scholarship for that activity. Some 60 percent of football and basketball players were currently on full scholarships, as opposed to only 19 percent of the athletes in other sports. The AIR study provided unequivocal evidence that the lion's share of full scholarships go to athletes in revenue-producing sports and that students in the performing arts or who are involved in campus newspaper and radio stations do so primarily as amateurs.

The first AIR report revealed that, whereas big-time college athletes were more heavily recruited and subsidized than other students, they were also more likely to encounter obstacles to getting a quality education.[19] Athletes in the study, especially football and basketball players, were more likely than students participating in other extracurricular activities to say that their sport or main activity made it much harder to keep up in coursework, study for exams, prepare for classes, and to get the grades they thought they were capable of.[32] Athletes typically cut twice as many classes and, not surprisingly, were plagued by far more injuries. Basketball and football players were also far more likely to report pressure to ignore their injuries (52).

In the years following the adoption of Title IX and the takeover of women's athletic programs by the NCAA, increasing numbers of college women had been exposed to the corporate model of college sport. The AIR research provided an excellent opportunity to determine if the same kind of academic problems traditionally associated with college sport for men were also affecting women. The comparison groups in the fourth stage of the AIR research included female basketball players, male basketball players, women with athletic grants in other sports, and women who participate extensively in other extracurricular activities.[20] The results were very similar to those of the earlier study of college basketball players carried out by the Center for Athletes' Rights and Education, except that the slight differences between Division I males and females found in the earlier study had all but disappeared.

When asked if their sport or other extracurricular activity made it easier or harder to keep up in coursework, about 80 percent of both male and female basketball players reported that being an athlete made it "harder" or "much harder." Only 69 percent of the women in other sports and 59 percent of women in other extracurricular activities made this response (38). Basketball players, regardless of gender, also reported that being an athlete made it harder to study for exams, get the kinds of grades they were capable of, and prepare for class. Basketball players also cut more classes than other students. It would seem that by the time of the AIR study, the negative effects of professionalized and commercialized college sport were already being felt in women's programs.

In addition to corroborating the findings of previous research concerning the conflicts inherent in the student athlete role, the AIR study broke new ground by including questions that specifically explored whether or not sport provides opportunities for self-discovery and personal growth. The findings were disturbing. When compared to students intensely involved in other extracurricular activities, Division I athletes found that sport participation made it harder to take on leadership responsibility, develop new abilities and skills, and learn about themselves. Athletes also had problems making their own decisions and speaking their minds (53). In other words, the women and men in the AIR study reported that being an athlete had made it harder to experience the personal growth and self-discovery that an undergraduate education is supposed to encourage.

Partly in response to the American Institutes for Research study, the NCAA has abolished athletic dormitories and attempted to limit the amount of time that athletes can spend in practice. These kinds of changes, although difficult to enforce, reflect a recognition by the NCAA president's commission and its membership that athletes need to be more meaningfully integrated into campus life and into the regular student body. However, as long as coaches can use athletic scholarships to recruit and control the behavior of athletes, the freedom of athletes to expand their educational and social horizons will be severely circumscribed; athletes will remain academic outsiders.

THE COLLEGE SPORT INDUSTRY AND BLACK ATHLETIC LABOR

Throughout U.S. history, sport has often served as an avenue for social mobility for immigrants and minority groups who faced discrimination in other sectors of the economy. This has certainly been the case for many black

Americans. During periods in American history when overt racial discrimination was commonplace, black athletes such as Althea Gibson, Jack Johnson, and Joe Louis were able to rise to national prominence. This belief in black success through sport continues to play such a pivotal role in black culture that some observers have begun to question whether it diverts energies away from other emerging career opportunities that may be far more attainable than professional sport.[21]

At first glance, the dominant role of blacks in collegiate sport would seem to provide further evidence that sport is indeed an elevator to success. A closer look, however, reveals that universities have been far more concerned with exploiting the athletic talent of the black community than with nurturing its academic potential. During the 1970s, universities, responding to initiatives coming from the Civil Rights movement and the U.S. Supreme Court, liberalized their admissions standards in order to attract larger numbers of minority students. Such federal solutions as the Basic Educational Opportunity Grant (BEOG) program (later called the Pell Grant program) were also initiated that would provide financial aid for these students. Once coaches figured out the system, however, these new policies proved to be a bonanza for corporate college sport.

In the decades that followed, the black community became a major source of labor for the burgeoning college sport industry. With the widespread use of Basic Educational Opportunity Grants and other nonathletically related grants-in-aid for minorities, many schools found that they could reach the maximum number of athletes receiving aid without having to use up their athletic scholarship money.[22] Because the NCAA limited athletic scholarships to the value of room, board, tuition and related fees, a poverty-level athlete could not be awarded a full athletic scholarship and then additionally receive a Pell Grant. In the 1970s, what many universities did was use the entire Pell Grant to pay a part of a minority student's athletic scholarship expenses, thereby allowing the athletic department to use its own money to finance other athletes. Over the years, NCAA rules have been changed to allow minority athletes to keep some of the Pell Grant money, but the rest is still used to cut athletic department costs.[23]

Not only did the college sport industry find a way to subsidize its operations through the use of federal funds but it used the rhetoric of social justice to justify the recruitment of talented but academically marginal black athletes. A more reasonable explanation for the astonishing numbers of black athletes in revenue-producing sport is that it has been profitable for the sport business. Cut off from other avenues for social mobility and inspired by a pantheon of black athletic heroes, many young black Americans have dedicated their early lives to sports. It is from this talented pool of highly motivated black athletes that the college sport industry has increasingly drawn its athletic labor. Providing academic opportunities for minorities has had little to do with this pattern of recruitment.

If the influx of black athletes were really a part of a larger effort by universities to increase minority enrollment, one would expect at least as much time and effort to be expended recruiting black nonathletes with academic promise as with scouring the nation for black running backs. This has rarely been the case. Notre Dame's present football team, for instance, is 55 percent black; blacks comprise only 3 percent of the student body.[24] Perhaps Notre Dame's location and its Catholic traditions may be cause for its difficulties attracting African American students. But if Notre Dame applied the same affirmative action strategies to recruiting minority nonathletes that it has used to recruit football players, the demographic mix of the student body could be altered overnight. The same would, of course, be true of the other athletic powers that currently employ disproportionate numbers of blacks in revenue-generating sports.

Affirmative action programs on behalf of minority college students are currently under attack across the nation. Yet, affirmative action programs that give preferential treatment to athletes remain sacrosanct.[25] The message this sends out is that America's colleges and universities are more concerned with producing winning sports teams than with seeking out and educating future black lawyers, doctors, and corporate executives. Tennis star Arthur Ashe once observed, "we [blacks] have been on the same roads—sports and entertainment—too long. We need to pull over, fill up at the library and speed away to Congress, and the Supreme Court, the unions and the business world."[26] Universities are certainly not helping young blacks make this transition when they treat the black community primarily as a source of athletic talent.

Although black students constitute just 6.6 percent of the undergraduates at Division I institutions, they make up 46 percent of the Division I football teams and 60 percent of Division I basketball teams.[27] It is in these high-pressure sports that produce millions of dollars in revenue that graduation rates are lowest for both black and white athletes. Blacks, however, are the least likely to graduate. According to a 1996 study, the graduation rate for Division I black male basketball players was 39 percent, the lowest for any group in the study.[28] It is little wonder that universities are often accused of exploiting the labors of black student athletes.

DEFENDING THE MYTH OF THE AMATEUR STUDENT ATHLETE

Despite substantial evidence to the contrary, the NCAA continues to argue that corporate college sport is education rather than business and that scholarship athletes are merely amateurs playing sport during their free time. Not everyone accepts these claims, but the higher-education establishment, through the NCAA, has rallied around the myth of the amateur student athlete and expended substantial legal and financial resources to keep it secure. The NCAA is not merely a rule-making body. It is also a highly effective lobby whose influence reaches into the halls of Congress. The NCAA has recently hired a full-time lobbyist to represent its interests in Washington. In previous years the law firm of Squire, Sanders, and Dempsey kept the NCAA abreast of developments on Capital Hill.[29]

There are many instances in which the NCAA has had to mobilize to defend its business interests. A classic illustration of the NCAA lobby in action occurred in 1977 when the Dallas office of the Internal Revenue Service threatened to tax television and radio broadcast revenues from college football and basketball as "unrelated business income." The IRS contended that these revenues resulted from activities that were not substantially related to the tax-exempt purpose of higher education. The Texas institutions under scrutiny were Texas Christian University and Southern Methodist University, but an unfavorable IRS ruling could have affected schools and conferences across the country. The IRS was also threatening to tax broadcast revenue from the Cotton Bowl. If the IRS position were upheld, the taxation would be retroactive for three years and would cost the universities millions of dollars in interest and back taxes.[30]

The universities acted immediately to bring pressure to bear on the Dallas office of the IRS. On May 12 James M. Moudy, chancellor of TCU, wrote to U.S. congressman and house majority leader James Wright of Texas urging him to bring this matter to the attention of Jerome Kurtz, then-commissioner of Internal Revenue in Washington, D.C. Moudy warned in his letter that the IRS action "will undoubtedly curtail and may even terminate many or most college and university intercollegiate athletic programs in this country."[31] He noted also that any reduction of income would seriously jeopardize efforts to comply with federal initiatives in the area of women's athletics. Moudy told Wright that a similar letter was being sent to Senator Lloyd Bentsen and that he believed SMU was contacting several members of Congress among their alumni.

Congressman Wright wasted little time contacting key people in Washington. On May 17, Wright wrote to Jerome Kurtz as well as to Michael Blumenthal, Secretary of the Treasury. Wright told Blumenthal that "were the IRS to prevail, it would obviously mean the death knell of intercollegiate athletics as we now know it."[32] In both letters, he emphasized that taxes on broadcast revenues would contradict efforts to implement Title IX, pertaining to the civil rights of female athletes. Wright assured Blumenthal that he would be hearing from many of his colleagues in both the House and Senate on this matter and urged an "expeditious turn-around of a potentially overzealous ruling."[33] He also recommended that Blumenthal resolve the matter within his department by working with IRS commissioner Kurtz.

The very next day, a Western Union mailgram went out to J. Neils Thompson, president of the NCAA, from the chief executive officers of TCU and SMU. The message urged NCAA institutional leaders to make quick legislative contact on the IRS situation: "Please join us promptly in asking your legislators, as well as members of the House Ways and Means Committee, and the Senate Finance Committee, to inquire of Treasury Secretary W. Michael Blumenthal and IRS Commissioner Jerome Jurtz [sic] as to whether they are aware of the interpretation and direction of the exempt organizations section in the matter."[34] Prompt action was urged in order to reach the secretary and the commissioner before "their minds are made up on this matter."

TCU and SMU had asked seventy of the larger universities in the country to join in their opposition to the tax. The NCAA contacted its membership. Another school that the IRS was targeting was the University of Kansas. In May Charles M. Neinas, the commissioner of the Big Eight, met personally with Senator Robert Dole of Kansas to make his case against the IRS position. In a follow-up letter to Dole, Neinas thanked him for their private meeting and said he would appreciate any suggestions and advice Dole might be able to offer.[35] Meanwhile the Cotton Bowl Athletic Association (CBAA) was coordinating its efforts with the NCAA. In a letter to the NCAA, R. L. Phinney, a CBAA attorney, mentioned that Sheldon Cohen, a former commissioner of and chief counsel for the IRS, had joined the CBAA legal team.[36] A formidable cast of experts and political leaders was lining up on the side of corporate college sport.

In June the NCAA lobbying effort began to gain further momentum. Members of Congress and senators who had been contacted by NCAA institutional leaders were now exerting pressure on the Internal Revenue Service. For example, in Massachusetts, key congressional leaders responded promptly to the Boston College athletic director William Flynn's request for assistance. Thomas (Tip) O'Neill, then-Speaker of the House and congressman from Massachusetts, contacted Al Ullman, chairman of the House Committee on Ways and Means, to inquire about the tax matter. O'Neill mentioned to Flynn that the IRS falls within the jurisdiction of the Ways and Means Committee. Congressman Robert F. Drinan assured Flynn that he had contacted the IRS and was told that there were no changes in either statutes or regulations being proposed. Senator Edward M. Kennedy also responded to Flynn that an inquiry "has been referred to the appropriate agency."[37] One can only assume that similar inquiries were being made by congressional leaders around the country. Given the popularity of college sport in some states, it is hard to believe that any member of Congress would want to appear to be insensitive on this issue.

At the very center of the Texas tax case was the question of whether or not the sale of broadcast rights to college sport was substantially related to the performance of colleges and universities of their tax-exempt, educational function. SMU and TCU argued that broadcast revenue was necessary for financing nonrevenue sports and for funding women's sports. This point was made time and time again in letters to the IRS opposing the tax proposal. However, the fact that an unrelated business activity produces profits that are used to support exempt functions is not relevant under tax law.[38] What is relevant is that the activity itself, in this case the sale of sports broadcasting rights, is substantially related to the exempt function. In other words, the NCAA somehow had to establish that negotiating multimillion-dollar television deals contributes in an important way to educating big-time college athletes.

There is evidence that even the NCAA's own attorneys found it hard to make this important connection. In a letter to assistant executive director of the NCAA Tom Hansen, Attorney Richie Thomas from the NCAA's Washington-based law firm, noted that it was "in this area of defining and documenting the relationship between sales of broadcasting rights and the colleges' exempt status that the parties directly involved are having the greatest difficulty developing their arguments."[39] Thomas, who was trying to draft a memo on the subject, admitted that he too was having trouble making the link, and he expressed his hope that Hansen and Walter Byers would "have further ideas as to ways of tying broadcasts to exempt functions of colleges and universities."[40] He also wanted NCAA legal counsel George Gangwere's views on the subject.

The most obvious argument for an exemption was that college sports, like other extracurricular activities, are integral to the educational experience. However, even if the IRS were willing to accept the premise that corporate college sport is merely another extracurricular activity, it was not clear how marketing the activity to television networks contributed to the tax-exempt function. Football and basketball games, according to the Dallas IRS, would still go on even without broadcast revenues.[41] In fact, such contests had been going on well before the advent of television. Furthermore the argument that the profits from television broadcasts would be used for educational purposes was not relevant under law. If it were, there would be no limit on the kinds of unrelated businesses that universities could operate on a totally tax-free basis as long as the profits were used for education.[42]

In the end, it was probably the lobbying efforts by the NCAA more than the finer points of tax law that persuaded the national IRS office to reverse the stand taken earlier by its Dallas office. At the rehearing of the case, which took place later in the summer, the Washington office of the IRS reaffirmed its traditional position that radio and television income are an integral part of an intercollegiate athletic event and therefore should not be subject to business taxes. Just as in Fred Rensing's workers' compensation case, legal briefs from the NCAA and the other affected parties shaped the IRS decision. The national IRS office accepted without question the claim that college athletes are amateurs and that big-time college sport is an integral part of the education of the athletes who play it.

The myth of amateurism had served the college sport industry well during the 1970s. The Texas tax decision kept the IRS at bay for a while, and the argument that scholarship athletes are amateurs protected the industry from workers' compensation claims and other employee demands. One area where the myth of the amateur student athlete actually left the NCAA vulnerable was on the issue of Title IX. If college sport were really an integral part of the educational experience, as the NCAA argued so forcefully in the IRS and workers' compensation cases, how could the NCAA possibly oppose a piece of legislation that would guarantee women equal opportunity and resources to participate in this important component of college life? What conceivable educational justification could there be for spending more money on men's sport than on women's sport, especially when women had been excluded from this activity for so long?

The fact of the matter was that business concerns rather than education were the source of the college sport industry's opposition to Title IX. When the NCAA fought to avoid income taxes under the unrelated-business ruling or to deny athletes their rightful workers' compensation, it took the position that college sport was first and foremost an educational enterprise. However, when the NCAA went to war against sharing university resources with women's sport, it suddenly found it expedient to treat big-time college sport as an independent revenue-producing business whose profits universities could not live without. If women wanted to be treated as equals in the athletic arena, they too would have to abandon education and transform sport into an unrelated business. Although the hypocrisy of this position is fairly transparent, the college sport industry has used it effectively to deny women equal educational opportunities.

7

Athletic Scholarships for Women: The Complexities of Intercollegiate Athletic Equality

From bloomers to spandex shorts, from Basquette to prime-time basketball, and from three dribbles to powering to the hoop, signs of the remarkable changes wrought in women's sport over the past 100 years can be found in virtually every aspect of American society. For the generation of men and women born in the decades of the 1970s and 1980s who have witnessed the emergence of the American Basketball League, the Colorado Silver Bullets, and the Women's National Basketball Association, the notion that women's professional sport prospects were once largely restricted to tennis and golf seems unbelievable.[1] Perhaps even more remote is the idea that less than 25 years ago athletically gifted girls, could not aspire to earn athletic scholarships because those kinds of scholarships simply did not exist for women.

In 1997, as women comprise 37 percent of college athletes and are the recipients of over $212 million dollars of athletic scholarship money nationally, the absence of athletic scholarships for women appears almost unthinkable.[2] And yet, there was a time not so long ago when the leadership of women's athletics thoroughly opposed such awards because they believed athletic scholarships to be a form of student exploitation and educational irresponsibility. To examine and reflect on the rationale behind their opposition to athletic scholarships and how that opposition fit within the overall evolution of women's intercollegiate athletics on college campuses reveal a great deal about the educational and philosophical dilemmas posed by the effective professionalization of both female and male student athletes.

THE AIAW: AN IDEAL WHOSE TIME HAD NOT YET COME

A critical turning point in the evolution of women's intercollegiate athletics occurred during and following the decade of the 1960s. As the American landscape echoed with the passionate voices of women's liberationists and civil rights activists, a growing realization began to form in the minds of many that women had been held back by unfounded societal attitudes and beliefs. No longer willing to accept educational policies and practices that prohibited women from pursuing careers in law, medicine, engineering, the military, and a variety of other male-dominated professions, the higher-education community finally started, either voluntarily or via legal mandate, to take on the task of educating women completely so that the full range of their intellectual and physical aptitudes could be discovered and demonstrated.[3]

The argument that women both deserved and had an inherent right to fully pursue excellence in all endeavors was sufficiently compelling to overcome the historical reluctance that female physical educators had typically shown toward the concept of full-blown varsity competition. As Katherine Ley, the president of the Division of Girls' and Women's Sport (formerly the Committee on Women's Athletics) reported in a June 1965 address to the all-male National High School Federation, the DGWS was responding to the winds of change by designing basic standards for the conduct of intercollegiate athletics for women.[4]

With women poised on the threshold of a new era of intercollegiate sport, the DGWS recognized the need to create a governance structure for the purpose of conducting national championships. The result of the committee's efforts came to fruition in 1971, when the DGWS approved the creation of the first and only national women's athletic association, known as the Association for Intercollegiate Athletics for Women.[5]

As a sport-governing body, the AIAW maintained a unique position within higher education from 1971 through 1982 alongside such prominent male-only organizations as the National Collegiate Athletic Association and the National Association of Intercollegiate Athletics (NAIA). The uniqueness of the AIAW, however, did not reside solely in its mission to provide national championships for female athletes.

As a governance organization, the AIAW was markedly different from other athletic associations of the day. Its origins as a committee of the Division of Girls' and Women's Sport tied it directly to the National Education Association through the American Association of Health, Physical Education, and Recreation (AAHPER).[6] Consequently, the AIAW was and remains the only intercollegiate sport-governing body to have derived from an educational association.

Furthermore, the factors precipitating the creation of the AIAW emanated largely from the lack of varsity athletic programs that would allow female athletes to achieve their very best. Within intercollegiate athletic circles, the need to provide opportunities where there had been few before contrasted sharply with factors that contributed to the formal organization of the National Collegiate Athletic Association. As mentioned previously, the NCAA emerged onto the American higher-education scene in the early 1900s in response to charges of uncontrolled brutality and incidents of scandal and corruption. So great was the chaos in men's college sport in 1906 that, as earlier stated, it took the stature and influence of President Theodore Roosevelt to restore a semblance of order.[7]

This difference in origin reveals a great deal about the overriding premise from which AIAW leaders proceeded in developing a vision for women's intercollegiate athletics. In conveying a sense for who she and her contemporaries were, former AIAW president Leotus Morrison wrote, "One must remember that the AIAW leaders were educators first, and they were trying to develop a very different model to govern athletics."[8] Not persuaded that existing male models of intercollegiate sport adequately or accurately reflected the educational missions of their institutions because of the professional and commercial aspects of their conduct, certain women set upon a course of discovery and inquiry armed with "the cardinal principle . . . that the focus of intercollegiate athletics should remain on the individual participant in her primary role as a college student and that the justification for such athletic programs is their educational value."[9]

Guided by a student-first mindset, the AIAW was fundamentally committed to a form of athletic governance that protected the rights of student athletes to pursue college life in a manner similar to that available to all students within a given institution. In their policy-making process, the AIAW struggled to establish an appropriate balance among the interests of the association itself, member institutions, and individual student athletes. As former AIAW president Bonnie Slatton reported, there was a belief among AIAW members that "there are certain rights [namely, freedom of education] which belong to a student-athlete" and ought not to be infringed upon by the collective actions of any sport-governing group.[10]

At a structural level, the AIAW's deliberate decision to emphasize the rights of students over institutional rights translated into a vastly different approach to governance than the one in operation for the National Collegiate Athletic Association. Whereas the NCAA chose to assume the role of enforcement agency when member institutions violated NCAA rules, the AIAW insisted on a self-policing form of enforcement. Maintaining that a focus on student welfare rather than on winning at all costs or on revenue generation should guide ethical conduct and decision making, the AIAW squarely placed the burden of accountability on the shoulders of its individual members as a reminder that they were representatives of educational institutions, not remote athletic states unto themselves.[11]

Whereas the NCAA considered itself to be a body that represented the interests of an institutional entity (i.e., members and their collective interests in intercollegiate athletics), the AIAW envisioned its role to be one of representing the interests of individual student athletes. Consequently, the AIAW carved out a place within its governance structure for student-athlete representation. The AIAW's desire to ensure a place for student athletes within the decision-making process was based on the idea that "if the exploitation of student athletes is to be avoided, adequate voice and power must be assured to those who are governed."[12]

Not surprisingly, given the difference in approach taken to athletic governance, many of the AIAW's original positions on intercollegiate athletic policy purposely departed from what was considered to be standard practice within men's college sport. In the area of eligibility, the AIAW hesitated to adopt policies that established minimum grade point requirements. Instead, student athletes were eligible to compete as long as their academic performance met the standard required by their individual institutions for participation in all other campus activities.[13]

In contrast to the system of redshirting (a college athlete being kept out of competition for a year so as to extend eligibility), which was endorsed by the NCAA as a means of regulating the movement of student athletes from one institution to another, the AIAW opted for a liberal transfer rule whereby any student athlete wishing to enroll in another institution could immediately compete. Their argument in support of open transfer was based on the idea that students in general were not precluded from participating in activities of their choice when they transferred to another school. In keeping with that logic, if athletes were in fact members of the general student body, it was believed that transfer policies voted upon by AIAW members ought not to impose a more limiting standard than the ones in place for the average student.[14]

The ideological centerpiece at the core of the AIAW's model of educational sport for women was its original stance on athletic scholarships. Rooted in a philosophical statement made by the DGWS in 1969, the AIAW strictly prohibited athletic scholarships.[15] AIAW leaders perceived that the link between the awarding of athletically related financial aid and what they called "pressure recruiting," as well as the increased possibility of student-athlete exploitation and the greater financial burden that accompanied the "buying of athletic talent," could not be reconciled within a model of amateur/educational athletics.[16]

The circumstances under which student athletes' amateur status could be maintained was if a player had not and did not receive any money tied to her athleticism. Within the AIAW's operating definition of amateurism, the term "student-athlete" was synonymous with "amateur." In effect, AIAW leaders knew that the concept of an athletic scholarship constituted a form of payment for athletic performance. To be the recipient of an athletic scholarship represented a shift in status to that of a professional nonstudent.

Starting in 1972, within only a year of its founding, the AIAW would be challenged repeatedly on every one of its innovative policies, starting with the prohibition against athletic scholarships. These challenges arose from almost every imaginable sector—NCAA officials and supporters, higher-education's decision makers, female student athletes, legal entities, educational associations, and some female coaches and administrators within the ranks of the AIAW itself. During an eleven-year window of time, the AIAW's rendition of an alternative model of intercollegiate athletics would be systematically dismantled piece by piece. In stages, the power of the AIAW would be undermined and weakened by these tests until its final demise in 1982.

In retrospect, perhaps it was an inevitability that the AIAW would suffer such a fate. As a visionary association that delivered a provocative and potentially workable alternative to the existing intercollegiate athletic structure, the AIAW had provided the backdrop against which illusory and problematic questions pertaining to equality played themselves out. The separateness of the AIAW model itself, so very different from that presented by the NCAA, invited speculation about what women actually meant when they made reference to intercollegiate athletics.[17]

The critical question of "What is equal?" inspired no easy answers. For some women, equality meant "the equal right to develop their own programs, but given that men's programs were already long established, the pressure was there to develop identical programs." With the emergence of the AIAW, those within higher education struggled with competing viewpoints. Was equality the right of women to determine for themselves what intercollegiate athletics should be, or was equality the right to access the same type of programs already in place for men?[18]

The presence of a separate and distinct women's model of athletics also invited the question, Could a different model provide equal opportunity? These serious and puzzling issues served to polarize factions that had an investment in the future of women's intercollegiate sport and created fertile ground for a power struggle to ensue.[19]

In summarizing this dilemma, Slatton observed, "While striving for equal opportunity for female athletes, it has often been difficult to maintain steadfast commitment to the philosophical tenets of the AIAW. In an effort to provide immediate quantitative benefits to female athletes similar to those afforded male athletes, some have lost sight of the struggle to establish an alternative model of intercollegiate athletics."[20] Nowhere was this dilemma felt more keenly within the women's athletic community than when the AIAW was named in a Title IX complaint by a small group of female tennis players from several Florida schools.[21]

ONE SMALL STEP FOR WOMEN'S ATHLETICS, ONE GIANT LEAP FOR THE ATHLETIC PATRIARCHY

In the 1970s, the AIAW was one among several agencies campaigning for change on behalf of girls and women. With the passage of Title IX of the Education Amendments Act of 1972, a piece of legislation designed to eliminate discrimination on the basis of sex within educational institutions, the AIAW found both an ally and an adversary in the U.S. Department of Health, Education, and Welfare (HEW) as that office attempted to address the complexities of enforcing the Title IX mandate.

Because Title IX was an instrument designed to facilitate equitable access to education for female and male students, it appeared on the surface as if Title IX ideally aligned with the goals and objectives of the AIAW. In concert with other women's groups such as the National Organization for Women (NOW) and the Women's Equity Action League (WEAL), the AIAW did, in fact, play a prominent role in influencing how this legislation would be applied to athletics.[22]

Rather than promoting uncontested acceptance of the AIAW's vision of intercollegiate athletics, however, the implementation of Title IX proved to have a profoundly ambiguous effect on the work accomplished by the AIAW. Sport historian Joan Hult described Title IX as "a double edged sword" that served as the "single most significant piece of legislation to affect the direction and philosophical tenets of women in sport."[23] Whereas Title IX facilitated the entry of millions of girls and women into sport within educational settings, a goal embraced by the AIAW as well, it did at the same time hamper the ability of the AIAW to forge an alternative intercollegiate athletic model that would be philosophically distinct from men's intercollegiate athletics.

In an ironic twist, Title IX was instrumental in altering positions taken by the AIAW on a variety of athletic issues. In a case that Hult described as "momentous," the AIAW and its parent associations—the NEA, AAHPER, and NAGWS—were identified as defendants in a lawsuit filed in federal court in January 1973.[24] In it a young woman named Kellmeyer, along with several other tennis players from two Florida colleges, alleged they had been denied their rights of equal access to education and championship eligibility because of the AIAW's prohibition on athletic scholarships.[25]

Although opinions from the AAHPER counsel and the legal division of the NEA determined that the suit itself had been poorly prepared and the absence of Title IX case law left the area wide open for argument, several concerns became problematic for the AIAW leadership. Despite a desire for the challenge to be debated in a court of law, the AIAW's parent associations chose not to support the AIAW. The NEA, in particular, balked at the prospect of participating in a lawsuit that had the potential to generate a public impression that the NEA did not support the right of students to demand equal access to education. The NEA's position, in conjunction with a report from legal counsel that more suits would follow, convinced the AIAW Executive Board to place before their membership a resolution to liberalize their existing policy on athletic scholarships by allowing institutions to offer them.[26]

Whereas the final vote on the matter was characterized as overwhelmingly in favor of a change in the athletic scholarship policy, an examination of the reaction to the voting process itself is worth considering. Accompanying many of the ballots returned to the AIAW's executive offices were statements written by members in attempts to qualify their votes. For example, in a letter to Dr. Carole Oglesby, president of the AIAW at that time, from Linda Estes, the director of women's athletics at the University of New Mexico, Estes wrote that "The latest AIAW mailing regarding the modification of the scholarship statement was of great interest to me. I sincerely hope the voting members have the sense to vote in favor of the resolution."[27] Given the strength of the vote itself, one might expect that many such statements of support for athletic scholarships would have been voiced.

However, a portion of the women casting a positive vote made mention of the fact that they did so only because they believed they had no other alternative. Despite casting a "yes" vote, Roberta Howells from Western Connecticut State College wondered, "Do we want to move in the direction this may lead? Should we let the U.S. courts define *amateur* and *educational*?" Similarly, athletic administrator Doris Soladay from Syracuse University wrote that "It is with deep regret that we vote 'yes' on this issue. I was sure it was coming but hoped not so soon."[28]

In letter after letter, whether members voted for or against the change in policy, the rhetoric of disappointment, sadness, and anger over being asked to relinquish a sound, defensible, and meritorious position resonated over and over again. Not surprisingly, some of the most compelling arguments to fight in court rather than acquiesce before the battle had been engaged came from those voting "no."

In a final attempt to articulate the profound loss that women's athletics would suffer by taking this giant step toward a male athletic model through the avenue of offering athletic scholarships, Donna Mae Miller and Mary Pavlich Roby observed:

The earmarks of bad athletics, whether they involve men or women, have been well documented historically and have always centered around such practices as scholarships and recruitment. Even though women have no athletic history in the annals of their kind, we are at this moment preparing to write history which may, in fact, indicate that we have resigned ourselves to pale replicas of men's programs. If we are really talking about the "rights of women" . . . the question of whether women have the same access to "talent" scholarships as men do appears to be a miniscule point when it is contrasted to the greater question of whether women have the same right that men do to determine their own rules and regulations in their own athletic contests.[29]

It is notable that even after the AIAW unwillingly reversed its position on the awarding of athletic aid, their membership continued in their attempts to present alternatives to the concept of a "full-ride" scholarship. In 1976, three years after their decision to offer athletic scholarships, the AIAW approved a recommendation intended to be shared with the NCAA that athletic scholarships for men and women be limited to tuition and fees only. Initiated by Christine Grant, director of women's athletics at the University of Iowa, the rationale that developed to support limitations on the awarding of athletic scholarships was based on the belief that, nationally, institutions could not afford to duplicate a full-ride system of athletic scholarships for women; that men's programs did not have the resources to sustain full-ride scholarships in their own programs; and that a more moderate approach to athletic scholarships represented an opportunity not only to achieve equity in athletic departments but also to create financially reasonable programs.[30] Because of the dictates of Title IX, policy decisions of such magnitude had to be embraced by both factions of the athletic establishment. In the end, the AIAW was unable to persuade the existing male athletic community to consider an alternative to the athletic scholarship issue. As a result, by 1978 the AIAW had adopted athletic scholarship policies that were almost identical to those in effect for NCAA member institutions.

The pattern demonstrated in the case of the athletic scholarship issue was one that would be replicated on any number of issues pertaining to women's athletics throughout the decade of the 1970s. Time and time again the recommendations of women athletic leaders on fundamental philosophical issues would be overshadowed and overpowered by the existing men's inter-collegiate athletic structure. The organization that would cast the biggest shadow over the AIAW was the NCAA.

PARTNER OR PREDATOR? THE NCAA's TRANSFORMATION TO COED

Crucial to an understanding of contemporary intercollegiate athletics is the transformation of the NCAA from an all-male sport-governing body to a coeducational entity that eventually cornered the market on athletic govern-ance nationwide. Although representatives of the NCAA have claimed in the past that the association sustained an interest in women's athletics as early as the 1960s, the relationship between the NCAA and the women's athletic community was fraught with contradictions, mixed messages, and, some would argue, breaches of trust.

In 1964 Marguerite Clifton and Sara Staff Jernigan, as representatives of the DGWS, addressed the 1964 NCAA convention about developments in women's competition and the intention of the DGWS to serve as the governing body of women's athletics. Presumably in recognition of Clifton and Jernigan's visit the year before, the NCAA convention acted in 1965 to officially limit participation in NCAA championships to men only.[31]

As the DGWS readied itself to appoint their Commission on Intercolle-giate Athletics for Women (CIAW) in 1966, it once again sought an assurance from the NCAA that it had no interest in women's athletics. Richard Larkin, director of athletics at Ohio State University, contacted Charles Neinas, assistant to the director of the NCAA, on behalf of the DGWS, to inform him of its continuing plans. In a March 1966 letter to Larkin, Neinas reiterated that the NCAA had intended to limit its direction and authority only to male student athletes. As a consequence, "A national organization assuming responsibility for women's intercollegiate athletics would not be in conflict with this Association." Neinas added that "We wish the DGWS well in this important endeavor." Notably, Neinas blindcopied his boss, NCAA executive director Walter Byers, on that piece of correspondence.[32]

Although the matter of what roles the DGWS and the NCAA would perform in the respective governance of women's and men's athletics appeared to be made clear by Neinas's letter, portents of the future surfaced the following year when the NCAA appointed a "study committee" to explore the feasibility of the NCAA establishing machinery to provide for the development and supervision of women's intercollegiate athletics. When DGWS president Katherine Ley asked Walter Byers if this study committee represented a reversal of the NCAA's laissez-faire position on women's athletics, Byers responded by commenting, "I don't know precisely what you mean by our 'hands off' policy or who told you this was the official position of the Association."[33]

Given the fact that Byers had been blindcopied on the Neinas letter, his response to Ley seems somewhat disingenuous. Throughout the next fifteen years, the actions of the NCAA would repeat the pattern of the first few years. Often issuing equivocations about their interest in governing women's sport while simultaneously proclaiming support for the growth of women's athletics, the NCAA nevertheless consistently appointed various committees charged with studying women's athletics. The existence of these committees, which usually allowed for one or two representatives from the women's athletic community to participate, inextricably tied women's sport to the NCAA. Although denials abound that the NCAA intentionally set out to take over what would eventually become the AIAW, or women's athletics, there is ample evidence to support the assertion that the NCAA throughout the formative growth years, was positioning itself to play a major role in the way in which women's sport emerged on college and university campuses.

Following the passage of Title IX, the NCAA's once mild and occasional interest, which had been distilled into a wait-and-see attitude, took on the dimensions of a daily preoccupation. As women's college sport progressively assumed the form and character of its brother enterprise, assisted in its metamorphosis by Title IX, the NCAA no longer perceived women's athletics as a benign campus activity. Instead, women's athletics, with the AIAW as its symbol, became a competitor that was perceived to threaten the very economic foundation and security of men's college sport. In his memoir about the NCAA, Walter Byers captures the full weight of this realization when he wrote that "Almost instantaneously, the law [Title IX] brought the NCAA in conflict with the Association for Intercollegiate Athletics for Women (AIAW)."[34]

In response to fear and concern about Title IX and the AIAW, male athletic officials devised a two-part approach to intervening in the growth of women's athletics. First, by capitalizing on the legal assistance at its disposal and harnessing the ability of its members to gain access to political figures, the NCAA sought relief from legislators and lawmakers in limiting the power of Title IX in the intercollegiate athletic arena. In tandem with that lobbying effort, the NCAA also debated the organizational and legislative merits of controlling women's athletics by offering women's championships through the NCAA.

THE NCAA's OPPOSITION TO TITLE IX

Taking on the government in the halls of the U.S. Congress, the conference rooms of the Department of Health, Education, and Welfare (HEW, the agency charged with the enforcement of Title IX), and the federal courts, the NCAA established a substantial record of opposition to Title IX throughout the 1970s and into the 1980s. In the beginning, the NCAA attempted to undermine the application of Title IX to intercollegiate athletics by having it removed from the jurisdictional scope of the legislation itself.

Arguing that the federal government was overstepping its bounds by interceding in the business of higher-educational institutions, Senator John Tower was the first to carry the NCAA's preferred message to Congress. In 1974 Tower proposed an amendment that would have excluded all intercollegiate athletics from the jurisdiction of Title IX. Although the Tower Amendment was defeated by a joint Senate-House conference committee, a second amendment brought forward by Jacob Javits, which called for HEW to consider the nature of particular sports in its evaluation of athletic departments, did become part of the developing Title IX regulations.[35]

As the compliance year of 1978 loomed ever larger on the horizon, some NCAA schools remained unsatisfied with the developing Title IX regulations and implementation guidelines. Objecting on grounds that ranged from inappropriate governmental intervention in higher education to the suspicion that the interpretations were being written by radical feminists who were "entrenched in their thinking" to the need to limit Title IX reviews to nonrevenue-producing sports only, the NCAA tried and failed on several fronts to receive support for their position.

However, the dimensions of the resistance effort organized by the NCAA reveal a great deal about the inner workings of the intercollegiate athletics community. For example, the power of the NCAA to receive an attentive hearing from governmental officials extended all the way to the White House. In March 1975, NCAA president John Fuzak wrote to Gerald Ford, then-president of the United States, saying, "the HEW concepts of Title IX as expressed could seriously damage if not destroy the major men's intercollegiate athletic programs."[36] In turn, President Ford communicated a similar concern to Harrison A. Williams, chair of the Senate Committee on Labor and Public Welfare in July of that same year.[37]

In addition to direct access to power, the NCAA member institutions also had available sources of revenue to fund their lobbying initiatives that warrant some consideration. As a case in point, William (Bud) Davis, the president of New Mexico University, started a fund drive to hire a lobbyist in Washington, D.C., to work on the Title IX problem. What is of interest about this initiative is that he simply contacted athletics directors from various institutions and requested from each a $5,000 contribution. There was neither an apparent proposal made to the NCAA nor any apparent need for those athletics directors to seek approval from their chief executive officers to contribute. About the fund drive being undertaken, Don Canham, the director of athletics at the University of Michigan wrote, "I received a call from New Mexico University where they are attempting to raise $60,000 to hire a lobbyist and they wanted $5,000 from us which we gave in a hurry. . . . I know they have Notre Dame and several other large schools in on this."[38] What this would suggest is that lobbying efforts against Title IX were being initiated on university campuses whether college presidents wanted those initiatives to be undertaken or not.

Whereas the NCAA's overt attempts to defuse the impact of Title IX on intercollegiate athletics for the most part failed, they were enormously success-ful in setting the stage for the legislation to be derailed through a suit involving a single institutional complainant. In what appears to have been a contingency plan, the NCAA fought the battle regarding the jurisdiction and scope of Title IX on two fronts, not one. The direct approach included their own lawsuits in the courts and the lobbying efforts they made in Washington D.C.

While they were arguing in public forums, behind the scenes, however, they were also attempting to locate an institution that would advance their argument that Title IX should be applied at an institutional rather than a programmatic level. The "institutional vs. programmatic" argument per-tained to the focus of Title IX's applicability. In effect, it raised the question, Does the word "program" in the language of Title IX refer to the entire institution or only to the subunit actually receiving federal dollars? In other words, if an athletic program did not receive federal funds, would Title IX apply to athletic programs? In a related question, the NCAA sought clarifica-tion on the point of whether or not indirect funding, as constituted by federal financial aid loans, was sufficient to trigger Title IX jurisdiction.

In August 1977, NCAA officials were exploring the possibility of whether a small institution from South Carolina, Columbia Bible College, would achieve what the NCAA was hoping for if the college went to court. The profile presented by Columbia Bible College seemed ideal. With an enrollment of 664 students, the college was private, co-ed, and Fundamentalist in its religious orientation. The NCAA's interest in Columbia Bible College is evidenced in a memo to Walter Byers from Assistant Executive Director Tom Hansen, who wrote, "*Not* an NCAA member. Can we recruit?"[39]

Although the NCAA's interest in Columbia Bible College appears to have gone no further than the inquiry stage, the NCAA did identify the institution that would bring such a case forward when Grove City appeared on the scene in 1978. Beginning in that year, the NCAA through their legal counsel, the firm of Squire, Sanders, and Dempsey, provided assistance to Grove City as it contested HEW in court over the matter of Title IX's jurisdiction.[40] In the final ruling in *Grove City v. Bell,* issued in 1984, Grove City prevailed and for a four-year window of time (from 1984 through 1988), Title IX's application to athletic departments was basically rendered moot.[41]

THE PLANNED DEATH OF THE AIAW

The style of resistance adopted by the NCAA in its fight to limit the scope of Title IX and its subsequent behind-the-scenes involvement in the *Grove City* case, which employed both a very public agenda as well as a private plan of action, was honed to perfection when the NCAA sought a takeover of the Association for Intercollegiate Athletics for Women. Beginning in 1975, the NCAA began to discuss legislative initiatives that would result in the offering of championships for women. On the surface, the NCAA leadership justified the necessity for these deliberations by referring to the fact that approximately 46 percent of their membership did not belong to the AIAW and therefore did not provide access to women's championships for their female students.[42] Furthermore, the NCAA also maintained that as an exclusively male institution, it was obligated by Title IX to provide services to female athletes.

When the NCAA finally reached closure on this issue, voting to support Division I championships for women at its 1980 convention, concern for equal access was interwoven into the public statements made by several prime proponents of the NCAA decision to incorporate women into their structure. As Judith Holland, the former AIAW president who later shifted her support to the NCAA, remarked, "What we're asking for is simply a choice. We are trying to allow more options for women, the same types of opportunities men have."[43] Similarly, at the news conference following the vote to offer Division I women's championships, Walter Byers as the executive director of the NCAA observed that the vote represented "a historic commitment by the NCAA to enhance opportunities for women" that had the potential to give "fresh and renewed impetus to intercollegiate athletics for women at all levels" (175).

The rhetoric of equal opportunity, however attractive it might have been delivered in the midst of the Title IX debate, is shown to have been hollow when examined in light of a memorandum issued by Thomas Hansen to Walter Byers in September 1978. While strategizing over ways to control the growth of women's athletics, NCAA decision makers were keenly aware that the duplication of women's championships would have a dire effect on the ability of the AIAW to continue in their quest to serve as a representative of women's athletic interests on the national scene. In reporting on an executive council meeting held in Chicago, Hansen noted to Byers that "All present agreed [that to make rules applicable to women and to offer championships to women] will mean . . . the death of the AIAW. . . . It is significant that Margot Polivy [legal counsel for the AIAW] argued very hard that Title IX does not require common rules." Hansen further noted that President Hubbard "feels this is discrimination at its worst—putting women where they have no voice (within the NCAA)."[44]

It appears that the NCAA leadership knew full well that their actions constituted a takeover by fiat and that the impact of their decisions would not only remove a competing athletic governance body from the landscape but would, more importantly, eliminate the threat of an alternative model of athletics. In remarking upon the good fortune that the NCAA had realized when several dissatisfied AIAW leaders, Mary Alice Hill from San Diego State and Linda Estes of the University of New Mexico, had approached Walter Byers to explore the possibility of an alliance, Byers noted that "They rejected the all-comers philosophy of the AIAW—were committed to the NCAA philosophy—*to the winner belongs the spoils*" (emphasis added).[45] Having successfully removed the AIAW as a major obstacle to that philosophy, the NCAA was then relatively unencumbered in their efforts to restrain the future growth of women's athletics and to continue in their promotion of a commercialized and professionalized form of athletics on college campuses.

THE LONG-TERM IMPACT OF THE AIAW's DEMISE

Symbolically, the demise of the AIAW signaled the fact that despite the increasing numbers of female collegiate athletes, the male-dominated decision-making machinery within the intercollegiate athletic community and higher education had not been altered to any great degree and continues in the 1990s to remain relatively unchanged. As researchers Linda Carpenter and Vivian Acosta have pointed out, Title IX did little to ensure that women's voices would be accounted for within the central power structure of the NCAA and individual athletic departments.[46] In 1994, only 21 percent of women's athletic programs were headed by a female administrator. According to the findings of a study released in 1994 by the NCAA, those individuals designated as Senior Women Administrators (SWAs) by their institutions (an NCAA title that is intended to recognize the highest-ranking female administrator involved in the conduct of member institutions' intercollegiate athletic programs) have little access to direct decision making.[47] Whereas 66 percent of SWAs nationwide reported that they had had the opportunity to represent their institutions at the NCAA Convention, only 10 percent indicated that they had been permitted to vote on behalf of their institutions. (Notably, despite the definition, at least 1 percent of the SWAs listed were male.)[48]

Relative to progress made since Title IX, the connection between the male power structure and the NCAA's documentable resistance to equity appears to have translated into very real discrepancies on college campuses. In a survey completed by the Women's Sports Foundation in the spring of 1997 that reported on the state of gender equity in athletics during the 1995–1996 academic year, the findings revealed that while females comprised 55 percent of undergraduate enrollment, they constituted roughly 37 percent of the collegiate athletic population. Furthermore, male athletes had access to 63 percent of available scholarship funds; 73 percent of operating budgets were allocated to men's programs; and over 72.6 percent of recruitment dollars were dedicated to men's programs.[49]

Even in the wake of tremendous public debate on these discrepancies in the 1990s, the figures continue to register disparate treatment of female athletes. After a twenty-five year window within which change was presumably occurring, 90 percent of all intercollegiate athletic programs still are reported to be out of compliance with Title IX guidelines. At the Division I level, only 9 percent of institutions are said to satisfy the substantial proportionality test for Title IX compliance. Although when broken down further, Division IAAA (nonfootball-playing institutions) show a better compliance rate overall, with 15 percent reporting participation figures that match substantial proportionality standards, the fact that only 15 percent of those institutions in 1997 complied speaks to the powerful resistance effort that has been in force since Title IX was adopted in 1972.[50]

More profound than the numbers and percentages themselves are the parameters that now define women's athletics. Reliant on scholarships and the potential for television revenue generation, women's intercollegiate athletics has become subject to the same standards used to assess "successful" men's athletic programs. Through a process that Christine Grant, the director of women's athletics at the University of Iowa, has called the co-optation of women's programs, commercial interests and the professionalization of female athletes serve as the hallmarks that now distinguish "successful" women's programs.[51] And accompanying this conversion from an educational to a commercial enterprise, the problems that have long plagued men's athletics have started to make an appearance within women's athletics as well.

Researcher Murray Sperber (1990), for example, reported an increase in cheating among women's athletic programs. He noted that according to David Berst, head of NCAA Enforcement in 1985, "the pressure to win in Division

I was behind the multiplication of incidents and that more coaches [of women's teams] were willing to go the extra mile for the one player that might lift them up the plateau of wins."[52] Similarly, the academic integrity with which female student athletes are recruited has come into question following well-publicized stories such as the Tanya Harding softball incident at UCLA. In the spring of 1995, Harding, a world-renowned softball pitcher from Australia, was permitted to enroll at UCLA in March of that year, seemingly for the primary purpose of capitalizing on her pitching skills rather than ensuring that she would have a reasonable chance of being a successful student (UCLA won the Division I women's softball championship in 1995).[53]

In examining the historical struggle out of which women's athletics has emerged on college campuses, the commercial/professional framework wherein men's sport has evolved comes into focus more sharply. The seemingly irreconcilable differences that manifest themselves in discussions about equality between men's and women's athletic programs derive almost solely from the credence that higher-educational institutions have given to the commercial/professional model. If there is one lesson to be learned from the debate and controversy surrounding women's athletics on college campuses, it is the fact that alternatives to the prevailing male model have consistently failed to penetrate the halls of power. As a consequence, women's athletics, slowly and in a controlled way, has become ever more similar to men's athletics, for good and for bad.

Part III

Suggestions for Reform

8

Putting the
Amateur Myth to Rest

ROOTING FOR THE UNDERDOG

As the twentieth century comes to a close, it appears that athletic professionalism in the form of athletic scholarships and other financial subsidies has
become a permanent fixture in most spectator-oriented collegiate sport. And
as the previous chapter indicates, the corporate model seems destined to set
the tone for both men's and women's athletics well into the next century.
Proposals for truly amateur models, grounded in need-based financial aid, seem
quixotic in an era when Nike, Reebok, and television networks shape collegiate
athletic policy. Even the Patriot League, one of the last islands of amateur sport
in Division I, has recently set aside its opposition to athletic scholarships in
order to join the race for college basketball's "pot of gold."[1]

Although the future looks bleak for genuinely amateur collegiate sport, one
should not discount the sport cliché that "it is never over until it is over." In
fact, even at amateurism's darkest hour, the NCAA is supporting policies that
could conceivably have the unintended consequence of letting the underdogs
back into the game. The NCAA's 1997 decision to restructure so that each
division has greater autonomy is a case in point.[2] On the face of it, giving
Division I football conferences freedom to run their businesses as they please
seems to reaffirm the dominance of the professional model. However, by
distancing themselves from schools with smaller athletic budgets and with
histories of putting the academic needs of athletes first, the superpowers may
have actually increased their vulnerability to a number of legal challenges.[3]

For years the claim that Florida State, Michigan, and Notre Dame belong under the same amateur umbrella as Swarthmore College and Amherst has given the college sport industry a privileged legal status. By giving the impression that big-time college sport is merely a variant of the amateur contests staged by nonscholarship-granting institutions, college sport has generally avoided income taxes, antitrust scrutiny, and other laws that apply to businesses. But now that Division IA no longer has to listen to or accommodate the views of academically oriented amateur programs, it is an open question whether judges, legislators, and others will continue to accept the argument that major sports conferences are as concerned about education as they are about television revenue and corporate sponsors.

No one can say how the courts, legislative bodies, and government agencies will respond to the NCAA's restructuring initiative, but according to sports attorney Gary Roberts, the NCAA's action may in years to come put Division IA schools in serious antitrust risk, subject athletic revenue to unrelated business income taxes, and lead to players being viewed as employees, with a right to unionize and to be covered by workers' compensation laws.[4] If any of these outcomes were to occur, the costs of running a big-time college sports program would become so prohibitive that some form of amateurism based on need-based aid might become a practical alternative.

A much more urgent reason for giving true amateurism a serious look is the pressing need, both ethically and educationally, to comply with Title IX. Recent court rulings and actions by the federal government make it clear that Title IX is going to be aggressively enforced. In a speech commemorating the twenty-fifth anniversary of Title IX, President Bill Clinton instructed government agencies to increase their vigilance in enforcing the legislation. Said Clinton: "Every school and every educational program that receives federal assistance in the entire country must understand that complying with Title IX is not optional. It is the law and must be enforced."[5]

In many schools, enforcement will require innovative approaches to athletic financing that would not have been considered previously. This is especially likely where men's revenue-producing sports consume substantial university resources but seldom, if ever, show a profit.[6] Not only will Title IX inspire introspection regarding finances, but its premise that sport is a vital aspect of the total educational experience of both male and female athletes is likely to stimulate debate about sport's academic role. In this new Title IX environment, it would not be surprising to see universities giving serious consideration to some form of amateurism based on need-based aid.

The remainder of this chapter will examine a two-tiered proposal for collegiate sport reform that calls for a substantial increase in the number of colleges and universities engaged in truly amateur sport while at the same time creating a "super division" of sports teams that can openly operate much like the professional sports franchises they have already become. A brief history of various need-based proposals that have come before the NCAA in recent decades will first be presented, followed by an assessment of the costs and benefits of implementing an amateur model. Finally, an outline of a nonexploitative approach to professional college sport will be presented that synthesizes the views of others who have proposed similar reforms.

PROPOSALS FOR NEED-BASED AID IN RECENT DECADES

Logic and sound ideas are seldom enough in and of themselves to bring about social change. Also essential is an atmosphere conducive to change. In the 1970s, a set of economic, political, and social conditions came together that led the NCAA to take a serious look at the concept of need-based aid. The decade began with a large number of athletic departments operating at a deficit, and as the decade advanced, a national energy crisis and runaway inflation made the financial crisis in college sport even worse.[7] Title IX, which had been passed in 1972, was also forcing many institutions to begin thinking about how they were going to finance the kind of program expansion required to guarantee gender equity. Among the options considered was cutting athletic scholarships.

One of the first proposals for need-based aid appeared in a 1971 report prepared by a special committee on financial aid established by the NCAA.[8] This committee, chaired by William Flynn of Boston College, proposed that financial aid at all schools, including those with big-time football programs, be based on financial need and that there be a limitation on the number of financial aid awards. Among the benefits of such a system, the committee cited: savings in costs, the broader dispersion of athletic talent, fewer invited athletes "riding the bench," placing athletes in the same financial aid stream as nonathletes, increasing financial support for low- or non-revenue sports, and "helping to identify the non-professional character and purpose of intercollegiate athletics."[9]

The Special NCAA Committee Report was sent out to chief executive officers of member institutions for reactions. The letters received at NCAA headquarters revealed a philosophical split within the organization relating to need-based aid that has lasted into the present. Not surprisingly, most major football schools opposed the proposal. For instance, Reverend Edmund P. Joyce, executive vice president of Notre Dame, responded that the proposal would be difficult to administer and impossible to enforce. He was especially concerned that a need-based system of financial aid "might encourage a tendency to 'skirt' the rules, especially on the part of well-meaning alumni."[10]

Gordon H. Chalmers, athletic director at Indiana State University, shared Joyce's concern about cheating. Referring to the Big Ten's experiment with need-based financial aid in the 1950s and 1960s, Chalmers warned that "we will again be burdened with the back door policy of the school giving the need scholarship and the Alumni picking up the difference. . . ."[11] Chalmers was also concerned that the National Association of Intercollegiate Athletes would get a "shot in the arm" and build their football and basketball programs overnight. Athletes who could not qualify for need-based aid, he reasoned, would migrate to NAIA programs, where they could still receive athletic grants.

Another theme in the letters from CEOs of big-time football schools was that need-based aid violated the basic American value of rewarding merit. Exceptional athletes, like exceptional scholars, should be rewarded regardless of the economic circumstances of their parents. A related argument was that need-based aid might drive the middle and upper classes away from athletics. C. G. Taylor, chancellor of Louisiana State University, warned against a "welfare system syndrome" where there would be "a tendency toward the withdrawal from the athletic program by students from middle and upper socio-economic income levels with the result that their value system would be lost to the program."[12] Taylor saw this as leading to reduced attendance and economic loss.

The philosophical chasm separating the big-time programs from the truly amateur ones was strikingly revealed in the letters of presidents of liberal arts colleges. In his letter in support of need-based financial aid, President John William Ward of Amherst College argued that athletic scholarships are at the very core of all that is wrong with collegiate sport. "Contracted grants-in-aid at many schools," wrote Ward, "force athletes to remain on a team in order to continue their education. Athletic programs which depend on huge media-oriented audiences compel college athletes to perform like professionals without anything near commensurate compensation. In the marketplace such practices run counter to standard labor ethics; in an educational context they affront common sense."[13]

President Robert F. Oxnam of Drew University supported the need-based proposal because it would help to pare athletic costs. He also argued that need-based aid would offer an opportunity to make athletics an integral part of the academic program "rather than a reflection of the Roman coliseum. . . ."[14] In general, the liberal arts colleges were suspicious of athletic scholarships because they contractually obligated an athlete to engage in an activity that diverted significant energy away from academic pursuits. According to President Ward of Amherst, "There is *no* defensible reason for a young man or woman to be required to practice for and compete in a sport in order to complete a college education (emphasis in original)."[15]

The 1971 report of the Committee on Financial Aid was a precursor of the aid-based-on-need proposal that came before the NCAA in 1973. Unlike the 1971 report, however, the 1973 legislation contained a compromise measure whereby tuition and fees would be rewarded regardless of need while additional aid would be permitted only if need could be documented. Allowing merit awards for tuition controlled for wide differences in tuition between public and private schools, thus allaying some concerns about maintaining a competitive balance. However, the combined merit-need system cut substantially the savings that could have been realized from a totally need-based approach.

Even with this concession to the proponents of athletic scholarships, the 1973 legislation was defeated by a show of hands. In 1976 a very similar need proposal was introduced at the NCAA convention, and again it was voted down. This time, however, the outcome was so close that it resulted in the first roll-call vote in NCAA history. The desire to cut program costs was clearly keeping the need proposal on the front burner. In 1977 the need proposal was reintroduced with an amendment that would have exempted football and basketball. Both the amendment and the proposal were defeated. Essentially the same legislation was introduced in 1978 and 1979, and again it was defeated, the major objection being that the measures would create two classes of athletes.[16]

After a decade-long string of defeats, one would expect the proponents of need-based aid to have fled the field. However, in 1981, spurred on by institutional financial stresses and concerns about Title IX, an ad hoc committee was appointed by the NCAA council to again recommend financial aid legislation that could cut program costs. After reviewing earlier legislation and considering the interests and sensibilities of the membership, the committee recommended a carefully crafted proposal that would allow an institution to award tuition and fees and course-related books on a merit basis, with any remaining aid being based on need. The legislation also featured a need-analysis methodology that is used by universities nationally and conforms to U.S. Department of Education standards.[17]

The floor debates at the 1981 NCAA convention indicated that in the minds of many delegates, need-based aid was a reasonable strategy for absorbing some of the costs of granting women equal access to college sports. Rising in support of the proposal, Charles D. Lein of the University of South Dakota warned that "Title IX, and the financial commitments that go along with it, are for real."[18] He then added that without cost-cutting legislation like the financial aid proposal on the floor, "we are going to witness the disappearance of the non-revenue sports from all sizes and types of institutions of higher learning" (112).

When Reverend Edmund P. Joyce of Notre Dame rose to oppose the need proposal, he spoke for the majority of college administrators and coaches at universities with big-time football programs. For Father Joyce, it was "the height of folly" to not recognize that athletes in revenue-producing sports deserve different treatment than other students when it comes to financial aid. The football player, said Joyce, is rigorously recruited for his special abilities, and once enrolled "he is absorbed into a Spartan regime that places demands upon him both academically and athletically that very few other students experience. By exercising his talents, he also helps to bring in millions of dollars of revenue that generally redounds to the benefit of his fellow students in the non-revenue sports. He, thus, makes a major contribution toward balanced budgets in athletic departments" (116).

Father Joyce's position came very close to an open admission that big-time college sport operates primarily as an unrelated business, whose contribution to the university is more in the area of producing revenue than in providing athletes with the same quality educational experience available to other students. In a statement that must have shocked delegates from elite liberal arts colleges, Joyce asserted that "football players cannot and should not be treated the same as the generality of students" (116). In subsequent floor debate, Penn State football coach Joe Paterno and University of Arkansas football coach Frank Broyles stood solidly behind Father Joyce in opposing need-based aid and emphasized the unique status of revenue-producing college sport (120–123).

When the vote was finally taken, the proposal for need-based aid was defeated among Division I schools by 148 to 101. In addition to reaffirming the NCAA's commitment to a form of athletic professionalism, the 1981 vote revealed a growing consensus about how college sport would be governed and financed in the future. With regard to the governance issue, it was becoming clear that schools with major football and basketball programs wanted to break free from everyone else. One of the things that people like Father Joyce and Frank Broyles found most frustrating about the proposal for need-based aid was the possibility that it might be forced on them by schools whose philosophies of collegiate sport differed quite radically from their own. In his speech opposing need-based aid, Joyce argued for reorganization within the NCAA that would give the football powers greater autonomy (118). In 1997 that reorganization was finally achieved.

The need-based aid proposal of 1981 had again been viewed by many as a way of cutting costs and offsetting some of the expenses that were likely to accompany the implementation of Title IX. The failure of that proposal suggested that universities were committed to an alternate strategy for solving their financial difficulties, one that emphasized increasing revenues in big-time programs more than cutting costs across the board. In the 1980s and 1990s, the NCAA placed its financial future in the hands of a relatively small number of Division IA superpowers whose profits are expected to pay for nonrevenue-producing sports at big-time schools and to trickle down in various ways to the entire membership. In other words, the way to pay the bills, including the cost of Title IX, is to further obscure any demarcation that may have existed between intercollegiate athletics and professional sport.

That spectator-oriented college sport performs functions enumerated by Father Joyce at the 1981 NCAA convention seems beyond dispute. What is open to question, however, is whether or not the benefits associated with this industry require a system that denies athletes basic rights and protections, undermines education, and justifies its actions on the fraudulent grounds that big-time college sport is an amateur enterprise. It is the major contention of this book that such a system is not necessary. On the contrary, an alternative model is possible that not only makes room for both professional and amateur college sport but also lays the amateur myth to rest.

EXTENDING THE REALM OF BONA FIDE AMATEUR SPORT

A truly amateur model of collegiate sport has, of course, been adopted with considerable success in Division III schools and in the Ivy League.[19] It was also the preferred model of the early AIAW. However, an amateur model based on need-based aid and strictly enforced across all schools and conferences has never been tried in the history of American college sport. Before 1949 the NCAA lacked the power to enforce such a system. In the 1950s the NCAA increased its enforcement powers but lost the battle to preserve amateurism in big-time collegiate sport when it caved into pressure to award athletic scholarships. Although it has never been tried, it is possible to assess some of the likely consequences of extending amateurism to schools whose revenue-producing sports cannot support themselves.

THE EDUCATIONAL IMPACT OF AMATEURISM

One major consequence of extending the amateur model to all but the most financially successful athletic programs would be to bring collegiate sport more into line with a university's tax-exempt function of educating young men and women. A number of critics of collegiate sport have argued that amateurism is a nineteenth-century anachronism, which has no place in the world of modern sport.[20] This position is only partially correct. When the term "amateur" is used to deny high-performance athletes fair financial compensation for what they do for a living, it is not only anachronistic but highly exploitative. However, when the term is applied to collegiate athletes, competing during their free or unobligated time, it captures the true spirit of what collegiate sport ought to be.

Amateurs can and often do compete as fiercely as high-level professionals. It is not the desire to win that separates amateurs from professionals but the amount of time and specialized training that the latter must devote to sport. In a university setting, the time demands of pursuing an education full time are inconsistent with pursuing sport as a profession. Thus, universities are among the few places remaining in the modern world where amateur sport ought to flourish and where athletic professionalism is out of place. Any effort to extend the domain of true amateur college sport can only enhance the educational opportunities of student athletes and bring sport into line with a university's mission.

One contribution of extending the amateur model beyond Division III would be to substantially reduce the need for Proposition 48 and the wasteful bureaucratic apparatus necessary for its enforcement.[21] Under current rules the NCAA can prevent a college freshman from playing sports for a year if he or she fails to meet certain academic standards. In the amateur model proposed here, just as in the model embraced by the early AIAW, all students admitted would be immediately eligible to play sports. Student athletes who have difficulty reconciling the demands of sport and schoolwork could simply decide (ideally, with input from an academic adviser) to give up sports for a while with no financial loss. No single reform would do more for athletes from disadvantaged educational backgrounds.

A truly amateur model of collegiate sport would also place the college athlete in the same financial aid stream as other students, thereby avoiding the often-held impression that athletes are a privileged elite and have little in common with the rest of the student body. In an amateur model, athletic excellence becomes one factor among others that should be considered in admissions decisions. Once in school, however, a star athlete could end up working alongside a regular student in the campus cafeteria to offset expenses.

It is likely that the amateur model would weigh most heavily on athletes whose families do not qualify for financial aid. The point that must be understood, however, is that amateur sport is an extracurricular recreational activity, not a form of employment. Therefore, amateur college athletes are no different from the thousands of other students whose parents mortgage their houses and take out loans to pay for a college education. Athletic directors at the amateur level must realize that athletes are often juggling the demands of school, sports, and a part-time job. And coaches must be ready to make adjustments in practice time and other sport-related activities to best meet students' needs.

THE FINANCIAL IMPACT OF AMATEURISM

In order to determine the feasibility and impact of adopting an amateur model of college sport that rests on the framework of need-based financial aid, consideration must be given to the quality of financial information available on college sport and the financial management practices used to gather these data. Ideally, this kind of feasibility study would occur under circumstances where there existed accurate and uniform methods of accounting and reporting athletic department revenues and expenses. However, college and university athletic departments, over the years, have been remarkably lacking in such standard forms of budgeting practices.

In a 1993 report produced by the National Association of College and University Business Officers (NACUBO), it was noted that expenses itemized by individual sport are rarely available and when provided are often listed under a category entitled "Expenses Not Related to Specific Sports."[22] The report addressed the seriousness of this lack of specificity by pointing out that whether or not an institution was interested in fiscal accountability, scaling back its program, or responding to the needs of gender equity, "accurate information by sport is particularly important."[23] Although some schools have proclaimed for over two decades that their revenue-generating programs make a profit and pay for women's programs and nonrevenue men's programs, there is little substantive and reliable data to support that assertion.

Economist Kenneth Sheehan from the University of Notre Dame elaborates on the pitfalls of interpreting the data that are available for review about athletic budgets. He cautions:

Every college has its own set of accounting conventions some of which make no economic sense and serve to give a misleading picture of athletic finances. For example, Notre Dame's athletic budget excludes most of its television revenue from its football contract with NBC; Michigan's athletic revenue (like most schools) excludes licensing income; and Oregon with the highest reported football costs ($8.6 million) includes items generally excluded from football budgets.[24]

Despite the limitations of the available information, some discernible trends can be identified. According to the NCAA, the average Division IA program in 1995 operated at a $237,000 deficit when institutional support, such as state funds and student fees, was removed.[25] The NCAA report also found that over 60 percent of Division I men's basketball programs and Division IA football programs lost money.[26] It is undeniable that revenue from television, gate receipts, and corporate sponsorships has been increasing over the years, but so have the costs. A few universities make a handsome profit from college sports. But for the vast number of colleges and universities in all NCAA divisions, football and men's basketball barely pay for themselves, let alone for the entire athletic program.

Sheehan has taken a look at the specific question of whether or not football and men's basketball programs make a profit. In line with the NCAA data, Sheehan found that the percentage of those programs reporting profits is low as well. According to Sheehan's analysis, very few athletic departments record consistent and comfortable profits from football and men's basketball. Based on figures from 106 Division IA institutions, Sheehan found that only 41 made money from football and men's basketball and 31 earned more than $1 million a year.[27] Among the more profitable Division IA programs were those like Michigan's that had large stadiums, successful basketball programs, and lucrative licensing radio and television agreements.

Given these realities, it is highly unlikely that most schools are going to solve their financial problems by investing more money in revenue-producing sports. At a school such as Michigan, where football and men's basketball generate close to $18 million annually in net revenues, funding gender equity from major sports revenues may not be a problem. At most schools, however, achieving gender equity will require innovative cost-cutting measures in addition to aggressive fundraising and marketing.[28] One very viable cost-cutting alternative is to adopt a system of financial aid based on need.

Although a need-based proposal has not come before the NCAA for a vote since 1981, various NCAA committees have continued looking into the issue, and a report by the Committee on Financial Aid and Amateurism was presented to the NCAA as recently as 1995. The 1995 report contained the results of a rigorous study to determine exactly how much money could be saved by awarding financial aid beyond tuition and fees on the basis of need. According to the study, an average Division I institution that has 200 student athletes on athletics aid could expect to save around $200,000.[29] The predicted savings varied depending on such factors as whether the school was public or private, large or small.

The results of this NCAA study support the contention that even a need-based proposal that includes a merit award for tuition and fees could lead to substantial savings. It is difficult to estimate how much more money could be saved by adopting an amateur model that is totally need-based, but it seems reasonable to conclude that in some schools it could be several hundred thousand dollars. Over the past ten years, college presidents have reduced costs by making a modest 10 percent across-the-board cut in the number of athletic scholarships.[30] There is no doubt that scholarships constitute a major expense in the college sport industry and that major cuts in this area could help many athletics departments save men's nonrevenue sports and make progress toward gender equity.

An amateur model would definitely cut costs. But what is not clear is the effect that such a system would have on the revenue side, that is, the marketability of college sport as commercial entertainment. It can certainly be argued that the elimination of athletic scholarships would reduce the incentive for many blue-chip athletes to attend college. It could also limit the control that coaches have over the players they do get. If these changes in the quality and control of the athletic labor force were to make games less appealing to networks, corporate sponsors, and paying spectators, it could have a very negative impact on those schools that attempt to fund their entire athletics programs from commercial sport. These are legitimate concerns.

It is debatable whether the elimination of athletic scholarships would limit college sport's capacity to generate profit. To quote Mike Hamrick, athletics director at East Carolina University, "Technically, I-A football could be played without any scholarships as long as everyone has to abide by the same numbers rules, not just on scholarships but also on squad limits."[31] This may be true, but it would be politically naive to think that schools like Notre Dame and Michigan could be convinced to jeopardize their incredibly lucrative athletic programs by experimenting with need-based financial aid. At these schools, as well as the several dozen others where revenue-producing sports are self-supporting, the best strategy is probably to drop the amateur label altogether and let them operate much like the professional sports franchises they have already become.

At the vast majority of Division I and II schools, however, revenue-producing sports actually run deficits and therefore can only gain financially from turning amateur. Even without athletic scholarships, amateur programs could still attract paying spectators, corporate sponsors, media exposure, and revenue from the sale of licensed merchandise. As Walter Byers has argued, talented athletes would not stop playing collegiate sport merely because they could no longer receive scholarships.[32] And a need-based system might distribute these athletes across a broader range of schools than is the case today, thus revitalizing amateur sport at many of the nation's smaller colleges and universities.

IMPLEMENTATION AND ENFORCEMENT

Since 1956 a number of changes in American higher education have eliminated obstacles to the implementation of a truly amateur model. Forty years ago, as few as 2 percent of students at some schools received need-based financial aid.[33] Today, many millions of dollars in financial aid are available from universities, the states, and from the federal government. The argument that an amateur model based on need-based aid would limit college sport to a privileged economic elite simply does not fit the realities of late-twentieth-century America. The cost of education is admittedly escalating, and some schools are being forced to cut back on financial aid, but the tremendous increase in the availability of financial aid over the past forty years has opened opportunities for all classes to engage in truly amateur collegiate sport.

In addition to being labeled elitist, amateur college sport that is reliant on need-based financial aid has also been attacked for being impossible to administer. Changes in the administration of financial aid over the years have also made this argument less than convincing. Today, most colleges and universities have sophisticated management information systems and rely on a standardized method of determining financial need that was developed by the federal government. It is the rare family that does not go through the ritual of filling out the Financial Aid Form (FAF) when a child is applying to college, and most people are used to providing sensitive financial information to universities. Although the process still has its glitches, the system is generally efficiently managed.

A totally need-based model may tempt alumni and boosters to pick up the cost of education not covered by financial aid. However, cheating of this sort seems to be quite common, even at scholarship-granting institutions. Probably of greater concern than payments from alumni and boosters is the amount of discretion that individual financial aid officers would have in adjusting the needs analysis to accommodate a student athlete's individual circumstances. Because financial officers can use their professional judgment in making these decisions, a highly-sought-after student athlete could end up receiving more need-based aid at one institution than another. This has definitely been a problem in Division III schools and in the Ivy League.

One control over such irregularities in a financial aid program would be a federal audit. The passage of the Equity in Athletics Disclosure Act of 1994 (EADA) represents movement in the direction of a federal audit system of intercollegiate athletic finances. The level of disclosure called for by the legislation requires schools to report participation rates for female and male athletes, expenses for coaches' salaries, student financial aid, and operations. Individual conferences could also initiate audits to ensure fairness in the awarding of financial aid. This was recently done in the Ivy League.[34]

In addition to penalties for violating NCAA regulations, a school that awarded more aid than allowable by federal guidelines could find itself facing possible restrictions on the availability of federal funds. Another possible solution to the problem of unethical practices within financial aid offices themselves would be to create a central entity to standardize the processing of student athletes' needs analyses. Any costs involved in creating such a processing center could be offset by the savings from cutting the NCAA's academic clearinghouse, which currently monitors compliance with Proposition 48. Whatever the mechanism for awarding financial aid, the amateur model can operate only if coaches and athletic programs are kept out of financial aid decisions.

With the end of athletic scholarships, the NCAA's amateur divisional structure would be based on levels of commercialism rather than professionalism. Division I schools would continue to have a heavy spectator orientation, with criteria such as stadium size and average attendance determining membership. Division III would remain as it is now, a division for schools that place a greater emphasis on the impact of athletics on the participants than on the general entertainment needs of the public. Division II would fall somewhere in between. These differences in emphasis would provide a range of choices for athletes with different levels of ability. Athletes with hopes of becoming professionals would gravitate toward a new NCAA Division that would be set aside for schools that produce significant sports revenue and want to continue subsidizing athletes.

One final policy that would have to be implemented in schools that turned amateur is immediate and total compliance with Title IX, a law that 90 percent of colleges are violating right now. From the highest levels of competition to the lowest, amateur college sport adds a dimension to the total education of young athletes that complements, and in some ways goes beyond, what can be learned in the classroom. It is simply not sound educational policy to provide women with fewer opportunities to experience the social, physical, and educational benefits of college sport than men. And under an amateur model constructed on need-based aid, the economic and philosophical arguments for denying women equal access to sport are no longer tenable.

GETTING OUT FROM UNDER THE TABLE

It is the major thesis of this book that meaningful collegiate sports reform is impossible without first unmasking the NCAA's amateur myth. Once this myth has been dispelled, there are a number of options available to universities. One is for the majority of schools to give up athletic scholarships, return college sport to regular students, and get on with the task of educating America's youth. The other is to openly admit that scholarship athletes are paid professionals and to provide a nonexploitative context in which they can further develop their athletic skills. This second alternative would allow universities to operate a number of college sports teams primarily as profit centers and as training grounds for high performance athletes.

One fairly straightforward and workable approach to creating a nonexploitative model of professional college sport is to follow the contours of what exists now. The NCAA's Division IA would be set aside for schools that currently run one or more sports as unrelated businesses. What would be different is that sports in this category would have to be totally self-supporting. Money for administrative expenses, stadium upkeep, and other items that are often taken from the university's general fund would now come from sports revenues. Of course, line items such as coaches' salaries, player compensation, and travel and recruiting expenses would also be the total responsibility of each college sport franchise.

The sources of revenues would be much the same as they are today, including gate receipts, the sale of broadcast rights, corporate sponsorships, the sale of licensed merchandise, and money from alumni and boosters. Because these teams would continue to act as minor leagues for other professional sport organizations, such leagues as the NFL and the NBA would be expected to provide financial support. In Olympic sports such as gymnastics and swimming, the National Olympic Committee could be expected to expand the kinds of financial support they already provide. Although many nonrevenue-producing sports might be better served by the expanded and revitalized amateur college sport system, those that attract sufficient external funding could conceivably join the self-supporting professional teams in Division IA.

Rick Telander, in his book, *The Hundred Yard Lie*, made a similar proposal for the creation of a college football league he called the Age Group Professional Football League (AGPFL).[35] Just as in Telander's model, athletes in the system proposed here would not have to be registered college students. However, they could pursue degrees on a part-time or full-time basis depending on the demands of their sport. The basic compensation package would include, among other things, room and board, plus one year of college tuition for each of the four years of professional college sport completed. Athletes would have up to ten years to take advantage of these tuition credits.

Beyond these benefits, athletes could openly bargain for whatever the market will bear. As in Telander's league, there could be some kind of pay scale. Other options would include money from product endorsements, speaking engagements, television appearances, and the wide variety of entrepreneurial activities currently pursued by college coaches. Athletes could also accept salary advances from sports agents, a practice that is already quite common in college sports but (as is the case with many other forms of payment to college athletes) is kept "under the table." Compensation systems such as these are already receiving some attention from the NCAA as methods of preventing the loss of talented players to such professional leagues as the NBA.[36]

In a 1996 speech to a conference of collegiate athletic directors, Cedric Dempsey, the current executive director of the NCAA, suggested a number of financial incentives to encourage athletes to complete four years of athletic eligibility. Among these incentives, Dempsey mentioned loans based on anticipated earnings as well as opportunities to make product and corporate endorsements. One source of the loans, according to Dempsey, might be professional sports teams and leagues.[37] In his 1997 "State of the Association" speech, Dempsey stated that allowing amateurs to earn money based on athletic achievement was a "gray area" ethically, but he added that the NCAA should investigate legitimate ways to allow athletes to earn "athletically-related income."[38]

With the end of what Telander aptly labeled the "hundred yard lie" the unethical ambiguity of amateurism would be eliminated and professional college athletes would receive compensation that is commensurate with their market value. Issues such as how much money athletes should be allowed to earn during the academic year (in addition to their athletic grants) and whether they should be allowed to accept prize money for international tennis competition would no longer deserve serious consideration. Professional college athletes would be as free as their coaches to market their athletic skills and would have all of the rights of other university employees, including medical benefits and the right to workers' compensation when seriously injured.

SOME FINAL THOUGHTS

Aside from its relative freedom from fraud and duplicity, the professional model of college sport proposed here is remarkably similar to what exists now. Many big-time college athletes devote most of their time to sports and end up giving only one or two classes a semester their full attention. There is no better evidence of this than the rather large numbers of athletes who must take "incompletes" in classes or who end up taking courses during the intersession and summer, when professors tend to be less demanding.[39] For all intents and purposes, many big-time college athletes are already part-time students. And in some cases, athletes would prefer not to be bothered with school at all.

With regard to financial compensation, athletic scholarships have constituted payment for services rendered since 1956. In addition, a rather extensive under-the-table payment system has long been in place to supplement the incomes of college athletes whose services are highly in demand. In other words, under the present system, hundreds, and even thousands, of dollars are often funneled to blue-chip athletes that when combined with scholarship money roughly approximate what some athletes would be getting in an open market. By openly acknowledging that college athletes are in fact professionals, little would change except that athletes would get a bigger share of sports revenues and no longer be treated as criminals for accepting compensation they deserve.

A more openly professional model is likely to find support, even among some big-time college coaches. However, it does pose a number of problems for those who run the college sport industry. First, as has been mentioned repeatedly throughout this book, the IRS would likely renew its efforts to impose unrelated-business income taxes on sports revenue, as well as on players' benefits. Second, there is no guarantee that athletes in their newly recognized status as university employees would not decide to form unions to bargain collectively for a larger share of revenues. These developments would not be well received by college presidents and their boards.

Contrary to proclamations by coaches and others in the collegiate sport industry, most big-time college sport programs do not make much money. Because the number of teams that do is quite small, the new Division IA proposed here is likely to include only several dozen major athletic powers in a limited number of sports. Because these professional college teams would operate as separate corporations, thus deriving no financial support from the universities with which they are affiliated, they would be exempted from the jurisdiction of Title IX. This is precisely what the NCAA and the College Football Association (CFA) have been lobbying for over the years. This new arrangement would finally give the sports superpowers the freedom they have always wanted. Schools that could not afford professional college sport would simply return to the amateur level.

V. Lane Rawlins, president of the University of Memphis, has expressed his concern that universities whose revenue-producing sports do not generate much profit may find it difficult to comply with Title IX, at least as he interprets the law.[40] In the system proposed here, such Title IX concepts as proportionality, which makes perfectly good sense when sport is an integral part of the total educational experience of young college men and women, would be totally inappropriate in the Division IA pro leagues. It would be like saying that the Green Bay Packers must also support a women's field hockey team for educational reasons. Of course, the downside of running college sport like a real business is that teams would no longer be subsidized from the general university fund. Only the fittest would survive in this competitive environment. The rest would have to turn amateur.

The proposal for extending amateurism to schools such as those in Divisions I and II is in some ways more radical than openly paying athletes. Many college presidents and prominent members of their boards see the profits and the attention that college sport brings to schools like Michigan and Notre Dame and are willing to risk millions of dollars to emulate them. Temple University, for instance, spent $3.6 million on its football program in 1995–1996, but it attracted only an average of 6,500 spectators to its home games.[41] Many other colleges and universities at the Division I and II levels are equally deluded as to the kinds of returns they can expect for their investment in professional college sport.

Given this obsession with the glamor of the "big-time," it may not be easy to persuade schools to consider giving up athletic scholarships and the other trappings of professionalism. On the other hand, the additional responsibilities associated with Title IX might well be the catalyst needed to convince schools to think about alternate models for financing their athletics programs. In addition, there may also be college presidents who are less enamored with the professional model than one might think and who might view amateurism as a refreshing alternative. For all those who believe that college sport works best when it is an extracurricular activity, rather than a full-time occupation, amateurism is the best choice for the twenty-first century.

Notes

PREFACE

1. The 1966 season is best remembered for Notre Dame's 10–10 tie with Michigan State. See Mike Celizic, *The Biggest Game of Them All: Notre Dame, Michigan State, and the Fall of '66* (New York: Simon and Schuster, 1992), for a thoughtful analysis of that season and its impact on the development of commercialized college sport.

2. The biennial contract with a major television network for the right to broadcast college football jumped from $15.5 million for the 1966 and 1967 seasons to $24 million for the 1971 and 1972 seasons. See Paul R. Lawrence, *Unsportsmanlike Conduct: The National Collegiate Athletic Association and the Business of College Football* (New York: Praeger, 1987), 96.

3. Walter Byers, with Charles Hammer, *Unsportsmanlike Conduct: Exploiting College Athletes* (Ann Arbor: University of Michigan Press, 1995), 342.

INTRODUCTION

1. James F. Wright, "Fantastic Numbers," *NCAA News*, 4 January 1995, pp. 1, 14.

2. Michelle Lee Thompson, "Nike, Athletic Department Sign $7 Million Contract," *The Michigan Daily*, 21 October 1994.

3. Arthur Padilla and Janice L. Boucher, "On the Economics of Intercollegiate Athletics Programs," *Journal of Sport and Social Issues*, nos. 1 and 2 (1987): 61–73.

4. See "Sports Revenues and Expenditures of NCAA Institutions," *The Chronicle of Higher Education*, 7 September 1994, p. A58.

5. "Athletic Notes," *The Chronicle of Higher Education*, 20 July 1994, p. A31.

6. See, for instance, the transcript of the Kent Waldrep hearing before the Workers' Compensation Commission, Austin, Texas, at 24, A. Kent Waldrep, Jr., Bd. No. 75–12394 DN (12 March 1993).

7. Joseph B. Hoffman and Alexander Van der Bellen, "IRS, Taxes, and Corporate Sponsorship," *NCAA News*, 16 August 1995, pp. 4–5.

8. Walter Byers, *Unsportsmanlike Conduct* (Ann Arbor: University of Michigan Press, 1995), 342.

9. For a review of contrasting definitions of work and leisure, see John Neulinger, *The Psychology of Leisure* (Springfield, IL: Charles C. Thomas, 1974), and Stanley Parker, *Work and Leisure* (London: George Allen and Unwin, 1983).

10. Charles Brightbill, *The Challenge of Leisure* (Englewood Cliffs, NJ: Prentice Hall, 1963), 4.

11. Bennett M. Berger, "The Sociology of Leisure: Some Suggestions," in *Work and Leisure*, ed. Erwin O. Smigel (New Haven, CT: College and University Press, 1963), 21–40.

12. Ibid., 29.

13. The concepts of instrumental and normative constraints are based on the work of Amitai Etzioni, *A Comparative Analysis of Complex Organizations* (New York: The Free Press, 1975), and closely parallel Berger's distinction between activities constrained by moral norms and those primarily constrained by expediency.

14. According to the NCAA, sport participation for student athletes is an avocation that is primarily motivated by the educational, physical, mental, and social benefits derived. See *NCAA Manual*, 1995-96, p. 4.

15. Ibid., 374.

16. Ibid., 367.

17. See Jim Naughton, "Athletes on Top-Ranked Teams Lack Grades and Test Scores of Other Students," *The Chronicle of Higher Education*, 25 July 1997, pp. A43–44.

18. See Ron Smith, *Sports and Freedom: The Rise of Big-Time College Athletics* (New York: Oxford University Press, 1988), for an excellent discussion of the intrusion of professionalism into collegiate sport before the founding of the NCAA.

CHAPTER 1

1. Barrington Moore, Jr., *Social Origins of Dictatorship and Democracy* (Boston: Beacon Press, 1966), 488.

2. Ibid.

3. Bliss Perry, *The Amateur Spirit* (New York: Houghton, Mifflin and Company, 1904), 25.

4. Thorstein Veblen, *The Theory of the Leisure Class* (New York: Mentor Books, 1953), 42.

5. George C. Brodrick, "A Nation of Amateurs," *The Nineteenth Century* 284 (October 1900), 523.

6. Sir Lewis Namier, *England in the Age of the American Revolution* (New York: St. Martin's Press, 1961), 14–15.

7. John Keegan quoted in Dominic Lieven, ed., *The Aristocracy in Europe, 1815–1914* (Hampshire, England: MacMillan, 1992), 192–93.

8. Brodrick, "A Nation of Amateurs," 524.

9. Ibid.

10. David Cannadine, *The Decline and Fall of the British Aristocracy* (New Haven, CT: Yale University Press, 1990), 239.

11. Ronald A. Smith, *Sports and Freedom: The Rise of Big-Time College Athletics* (New York: Oxford University Press, 1988), 6.

12. Harold A. Harris, *Sport in Britain: Its Origins and Development* (London: Stanley Paul, 1975), 49.

13. Howard Savage, *Games and Sports in British Schools and Universities* (New York: The Carnegie Foundation for the Advancement of Teaching, 1927), 78.

14. Eugene A. Glader, *Amateurism and Athletics* (West Point: Leisure Press, 1978), 19.

15. Ibid., 111.

16. Christopher Dodd, "Rowing," in *Sport in Britain: A Social History*, ed. Tony Mason (Cambridge: Cambridge University Press, 1989), 286.

17. Glader, *Amateurism and Athletics*, 172.

18. The practice of awarding "broken time" payments to athletes for time away from the job caused controversy in British rugby in the nineteenth century and in the Olympics throughout the twentieth. See John H. Smith, "Northern Union Football," *The Encyclopedia of Sports and Games*, vol. 2 (London: William Heineman, 1911), 256–57.

19. For a discussion of the problems of amateurism in the Olympics, see William O. Johnson, *All That Glitters Is Not Gold: The Olympic Games* (New York: G. P. Putnam's Sons, 1972), and Geoffrey Miller, *Behind the Olympic Rings* (Lynn, MA: H. O. Zimman, Inc., 1979). See especially Chapter 4, "Who May Compete?"

20. David C. Young, *The Olympic Myth of Greek Amateur Athletics* (Chicago: Ares, 1985). See Chapter XII for an interpretation of amateurism in American colleges.

21. Richard D. Mandell, *Sport: A Cultural History* (New York: Columbia University Press, 1984), 178–79.

22. Samuel Eliot Morison, Henry Steele Commager, and William E. Leuchtenburg, *The Growth of the American Republic*, vol. 1 (New York: Oxford University Press, 1980), 57.

23. Mandell, *Sport: A Cultural History*, 178.

24. Benjamin G. Rader, *American Sports: From the Age of Folk Games to the Age of Televised Sports* (Englewood Cliffs, NJ: Prentice Hall, 1990), 13.

25. Smith, *Sports and Freedom*, 10.

26. James M. Whiton, "The First Harvard–Yale Regatta," *Outlook* LXVIII (June 1901), 288.

27. Ibid.

28. Charles W. Eliot, letter to Ellen Peabody, in Henry James, *Charles Eliot, President of Harvard College*, vol. 1 (New York: Houghton, Mifflin Company, 1930), 80.

29. Howard J. Savage et al., *American College Athletics*, Bulletin Number Twenty-three (New York: Carnegie Foundation for the Advancement of Teaching, 1929), 21.

30. Melvin L. Adelman, *A Sporting Time: New York City and the Rise of Modern Athletics, 1820–70* (Urbana: University of Illinois Press, 1986), 191.

31. D. Stanley Eitzen and George H. Sage, *Sociology of North American Sport* (Dubuque, IA: Brown and Benchmark, 1991), 43.

32. Rader, *American Sports*, 70.

33. Donald Chu, "The American Conception of Higher Education and the Formal Incorporation of Intercollegiate Sport," in *Sport Sociology: Contemporary Themes*, eds. Andrew Yiannakis et al. (Dubuque, Iowa: Kendall/Hunt, 1976), 151.

34. Lawrence R. Veysey, *The Emergence of the American University* (Chicago: University of Chicago Press, 1965), 326.

35. Ibid.

36. Richard Hofstadter, *Anti-Intellectualism in American Life* (New York: Vintage Books, 1963), 25.

37. Hal A. Lawson and Alan G. Ingham, "Conflicting Ideologies concerning the University and Intercollegiate Athletics: Harper and Hutchins at Chicago, 1892–1940," *Journal of Sport History* 7, no. 3 (Winter 1980): 42.

38. Ibid., 41.

39. Merle Curti and Vernon Carstensen, *The University of Wisconsin: A History*, vol. 1 (Madison: University of Wisconsin Press, 1949), 709–10.

40. Edward S. Jordan, "Buying Football Victories," *Colliers*, 18 November 1905, pp. 19–20.

41. Samuel Eliot Morison, *Three Centuries of Harvard* (Cambridge, MA: Harvard University Press, 1936), 409.

42. Alexander Meiklejohn, "The Evils of College Athletics," *Harpers Weekly*, 2 December 1905, p. 1751.

43. Henry P. Wright, letter to Walter Camp, 28 November 1902, Walter Camp Papers, Box 44, Folder 2, Manuscripts and Archives, Yale University.

44. Smith, *Sports and Freedom*, 186.

45. Frederick Rudolph, *The American College and University* (New York: Vintage Books, 1962), 199.

46. Frank Presbrey and Paul Moffatt, *Athletics at Princeton* (New York: Frank Presbrey, 1901), 135.

47. "No Football Reform; Delay by New Body," *New York Times*, 30 December 1905, p. 7.

48. Henry Beach Needham, "The College Athlete," *McClure's Magazine*, June–July 1905, pp. 115–28.

49. Meiklejohn, "The Evils of College Athletics," p. 1751.

50. Veysey, *The Emergence of the American University*, 69.
51. Charles W. Eliot, "Inaugural Address," at Harvard, 19 October 1869, p. 22, HUA.
52. Charles W. Eliot, *Report of the President and Treasurer of Harvard College*, 1882–83, 22–23.
53. Charles W. Eliot, "Eliot on Athletics," *Yale Alumni Weekly*, 6 February 1895.
54. See Smith, *Sports and Freedom*, 127–31, for a discussion of the athletic committee concept at Harvard.
55. Ibid., 127.
56. Savage, *American College Athletics*, 34.
57. David Starr Jordan, "The Thought of the Nation," *Colliers*, 10 December 1904, p. 22.
58. Rader, *American Sports*, 178.
59. Presbrey and Moffatt, *Athletics at Princeton*, 135.
60. Carl D. Voltmer, *A Brief History of the Intercollegiate Conference of Faculty Representatives* (New York: Western Intercollegiate Conference, 1935), 6–7.
61. *Report on Intercollegiate Sports*, by a subcommittee appointed at the Conference on Intercollegiate Athletics, 1898, Brown University Archives.

CHAPTER 2

1. Notre Dame was a relatively unknown Midwestern college when a 1913 upset football victory over Army in New York City put "the Fighting Irish" in the national limelight. Notre Dame became the center of pride for millions of ethnic Americans for whom a Notre Dame victory over Yale or Harvard was a symbolic victory of working people over their bosses.
2. Benjamin G. Rader, *American Sports: From the Age of Folk Games to the Age of Televised Sports* (Englewood Cliffs, NJ: Prentice Hall, 1990), 182.
3. David L. Goldberg, "What Price Victory? What Price Honor? Pennsylvania and the Formation of the Ivy League, 1950–1952," *The Pennsylvania Magazine of History and Biography* (April 1988), p. 246.
4. James Hammond Moore, "Football's Ugly Decades, 1893–1913," *Smithsonian Journal of History* 2 (1967): 59.
5. Some of the major magazines that attacked the evils of college sport include *Colliers, Harper's Weekly, McClures*, and *Outlook*.
6. This discussion of the Roosevelt meeting and the creation of the NCAA comes primarily from Jack Falla, *NCAA: The Voice of College Sports* (Mission, KS: National Collegiate Athletic Association, 1981), 9–17.
7. Ibid.
8. Intercollegiate Athletic Association of the United States, NCAA, *Proceedings of the First Annual Convention*, 29 December 1906, p. 33.
9. Intercollegiate Athletic Association of the United States, NCAA, *Proceedings of the Second Annual Convention*, 28 December 1907.

10. Howard Roberts, *The Big Nine* (New York: G. P. Putnam's Sons, 1948), 14.

11. Rader, *American Sports, 176.*

12. Intercollegiate Conference, [*Big Ten*] *Minutes of the Meeting of Faculty Representatives*, January 1927.

13. National Collegiate Athletic Association, *Proceedings of the Eleventh Annual Convention*, 28 December 1916, p. 118.

14. National Collegiate Athletic Association, *Proceedings of the Seventeenth Annual Convention*, 29 December 1922.

15. *Family Encyclopedia of American History* (Pleasantville, NY: The Reader's Digest Association, Inc., 1975), 903.

16. Howard J. Savage et al., *American College Athletics*, Bulletin Number Twenty-six (New York: Carnegie Foundation for the Advancement of Teaching, 1929).

17. Ibid., 201.

18. John R. Thelin, *Games Colleges Play: Scandal and Reform in Intercollegiate Athletics* (Baltimore, MD: Johns Hopkins University Press, 1994), 28–31.

19. Savage, *American College Athletes*, 242.

20. Ibid., 259.

21. President Wilbur Papers, Box 77, Folder "Board of Athletic Control," "Alumni Association Tuition Scholarship Fund," Stanford University Archives (ca. Spring 1932).

22. Savage, *American College Athletics*, 256.

23. *New York Herald*, 21 January 1922 clipping found in President Wilbur Papers, Box 51, Folder 14, Stanford University Archives.

24. Ibid.

25. Joseph K. Hart, "The Faculty Loses the Ball," *The Survey* 49 (1 December 1922): 304.

26. "Story of a Graduate Manager," 1925 Transcript found in President Lowell Papers, 1922–25, Folder 6B, Harvard University Archives.

27. Ibid.

28. Adryn L. Sponberg, "The Evolution of Athletic Subsidization in the Intercollegiate Conference of Faculty Representatives [Big Ten]" (Ph.D. diss., University of Michigan, 1968), 41.

29. "What Football Players Are Earning This Fall," *Literary Digest*, 15 November 1930, p. 28.

30. Ibid.

31. Falla, *The Voice of College Sports*, 130.

32. "Sheep Skin or Pig Skin?" *Washington Post*, 18 December 1935 clipping found in President Newcomb Papers, II, Box 4, Folder "Athletics," University of Virginia Archives.

33. "South Relaxes Rules on Help to Athletes," *New York Times*, 19 December 1938, p. 28.

34. "Recommendations of the Presidents of Six Member Institutions of the Southern Conference," Document found in President Frank P. Graham Files, dated 10 January 1936, Box 3, Folder 1/1/4, University of North Carolina Archives.

35. Ibid.

36. Charles L. Van Noppen, letter to Graham, 12 December 1933, President Frank T. Graham Files, "Football: Coach Collins Controversy, 1933–34," Box 20, Folder 2/2/3, University of North Carolina Archives.

37. J. F. Patterson, M.D., letter to Graham, 17 December 1935, President Frank P. Graham Files, Box 3, Folder 1/1/4, University of North Carolina Archives.

38. Montgomery County Alumni Association of the University of North Carolina Resolution, 28 January 1936, President Frank P. Graham Files, Box 3, Folder 1/1/4, University of North Carolina Archives.

39. Frank Graham, letter to Howard Savage, 21 December 1935, President Frank P. Graham Files, Box 3, Folder 1/1/4, University of North Carolina Archives.

40. Ibid.

41. Frank Graham, letter to Jonathan Daniels, *Raleigh News and Observer*, 30 December 1935, President Frank P. Graham Files, Box 3, Folder 1/1/4, University of North Carolina Archives.

42. National Collegiate Athletic Association, *Proceedings of the Thirty-Sixth Annual Convention*, 29–31 December 1941, 144.

43. "Ivy Group Agreement," released to the press 20 November 1945, President A. W. Griswald Presidential Records, Box 38, Folder 340, Yale University Manuscripts and Archives.

44. Sponberg, *The Evolution of Athletic Subsidization*, 53.

45. For a discussion of circumstances leading up to the Sanity Code, see National Collegiate Athletic Association, *1946–47 Yearbook*, pp. 78–79.

46. Ibid., 77–79.

47. National Collegiate Athletic Association, *1947–48 Yearbook*, pp. 212–13.

48. Ibid., 213.

49. National Collegiate Athletic Association, *1946–47 Yearbook*, p. 77.

50. See *1947–48 Yearbook*, p. 191, for a discussion of the politics of changing the language regarding recruiting.

51. Ibid., 222.

52. *New York Times*, 24 May 1949, p. 38.

53. Tim Cohane, "Let's Take the Hypocrisy out of College Football," *Look Magazine*, December 1950, pp. 60–63.

54. *New York Times*, 10 August 1948, p. 28.

55. President Blake R. Van Leer of Georgia Tech, letter to the presidents of the Southern, Southeastern, and Southwestern Conferences, 25 January 1949, Records of the Office of the President, 1949–66, Box 16, Folder "NCAA Regional Conference," 28 May 1949, Georgia Tech Archives.

56. "A Joint Meeting of the Southern, Southeastern, and Southwestern Conferences, 28 May 1949," Memo, Records of the Office of the President, 1946–1966,

Box 16, Folder "NCAA Regional Conference, May 28, 1949," Georgia Tech Archives.

57. *New York Times*, 15 January 1950, p. 42.

58. *New York Times*, 12 January 1950, p. 37.

59. National Collegiate Athletic Association, *1949–50 Yearbook*, p. 197.

60. Ibid., 199.

61. *New York Times*, 20 January 1950, p. 34.

62. *New York Times*, 15 January 1950, p. 42.

63. National Collegiate Athletic Association, *1951–52 Yearbook*, p. 254.

64. National Collegiate Athletic Association, *1956–57 Yearbook*, p. 4.

65. Ibid.

66. Walter Byers, *Unsportsmanlike Conduct: Exploiting College Athletes* (Ann Arbor: University of Michigan Press, 1995), 73.

67. Southern Conference Minutes, 9 December 1955, Records of the Office of the President, 1949–1966, Box 19, Folder "Southeastern Conference, 1954–59," Georgia Tech Archives.

68. Ibid.

69. Joseph M. Sheehan, "Notes on College Sports," *New York Times*, 16 January 1957, p. 35.

70. Richard N. Current et al., *American History: A Survey*, vol. 2 (New York: Alfred A. Knopf, 1983), 864.

71. Falla, *The Voice of College Sports*, 110.

72. "Ivy Group Agreement," released to the press on 11 February 1954, President A. W. Griswald Presidential Records, Box 38, Folder 343, "Athletics: Ivy League Presidents," 1954, Yale University Manuscripts and Archives.

CHAPTER 3

1. Linda K. Kerber and Jane Sherron De Hart, eds., *Women's America: Refocusing the Past* (New York: Oxford University Press, 1995), 5.

2. Elizabeth S. Eschbach, *The Higher Education of Women in England and America, 1865-1920* (New York: Garland Publishing, Inc., 1993), 83.

3. Mary Ashton Rice Livermore, *What Shall We Do with Our Daughters?* (Boston, MA: Lee and Shephard Publishers, 1883), 22.

4. Barbara Miller Solomon, *In the Company of Educated Women: A History of Women and Higher Education in America* (New Haven, CT: Yale University Press, 1985), 27.

5. Eschbach, *The Higher Education of Women*, 34.

6. Solomon, *In the Company of Educated Women*, 27.

7. Edward H. Clarke, *Sex in Education, or A Fair Chance for the Girls* (Boston, MA: James R. Osgood and Company, 1873), 62.

8. Charles W. Eliot, "Woman's Work and Woman's Wages," *North American Review* CCCVIII (July 1882), 161.

9. Roberta Frankfort, *Collegiate Women: Domesticity and Career in Turn-of-the-Century America* (New York: New York University Press, 1977), 41.

10. Solomon, *In the Company of Educated Women*, 58; Charlotte Williams Conable, *Women at Cornell: The Myth of Equal Education* (Ithaca, NY: Cornell University Press, 1977), 65–66.

11. Solomon, *In the Company of Educated Women*, 55-56.

12. Ibid.

13. G. Stanley Hall, *Adolescence: Its Psychology and Its Relation to Physiology, Anthropology, Sociology, Sex, Crime, Religion, and Education* (New York, 1908), Chapter 2; Solomon, *In the Company of Educated Women*, 61.

14. Livermore, *What Shall We Do with Our Daughters*, 22; Elizabeth Blackwell, *The Laws of Life with Special Reference to Physical Education of Girls* (1852) found in the library archives at Hobart and William Smith Colleges, Geneva, New York.

15. Harriett Isabel Ballintine, *The History of Physical Training at Vassar College 1865-1915* (Poughkeepsie, NY: Lansing & Brothers, n.d.), 5.

16. L. Clarke Seelye, Inaugural Address (Smith College Collection, 1875), 27–28.

17. Frederick Rudolph, *The American College and University* (Athens: University of Georgia Press, 1990), 325–26.

18. Reet Howell, *Her Story in Sport: A Historical Anthology of Women in Sports* (West Point, NY: Leisure Press, 1982). For a full discussion on the emergence of the array of curricular areas associated with physiology, hygiene, and women's health, see J. A. Mangan and Roberta J. Park, eds., *From Fair Sex to Feminism: Sport and the Socialization of Women in the Industrial and Pre-Industrial Eras* (Totowa, NJ: Frank Cass and Company Limited, 1987); and, Patricia Vertinsky, *The Eternally Wounded Woman: Women, Doctors, and Exercise in the Late Nineteenth Century* (Manchester, England: Manchester University Press, 1990). Another very good overview of women's health at the turn of the century is provided in Helen Lenskyj, *Out of Bounds: Women, Sport, and Sexuality* (Toronto, Ontario, Canada: The Women's Press, 1986).

19. Susan K. Cahn, *Coming on Strong: Gender and Sexuality in Twentieth-Century Women's Sport* (New York: The Free Press, 1994), 26.

20. Roberta J. Park, "Sport, Gender and Society in a Transatlantic Victorian Perspective," In J. A. Mangan and Roberta J. Park, eds., *From Fair Sex to Feminism: Sport and the Socialization of Women in the Industrial and Pre-Industrial Eras* (Totowa, NJ: Frank Cass and Company Limited, 1987); Ellen W. Gerber, Jan Felshin, Pearl Berlin, and Waneen Wyrick, eds., *The American Woman in Sport* (Reading, MA: Addison-Wesley Publishing Company, 1974).

21. Harriett Isabel Ballintine, *The History of Physical Training at Vassar College, 1865-1915* (Poughkeepsie, NY: Lansing & Brothers, n.d.), 9.

22. A pamphlet outlining the customs, fashions, and sentiments involving women's lives is published by the Women's Rights National Historical Park, Seneca Falls, New York (National Park Service, U.S. Department of the Interior). The publication, dated July 10, 1994, is entitled "Women's Rights." The specific section

is called "Fashion vs. Health." Also see Wendy Lebing, "The Way It Was when Women Were under Wraps," *Sports Illustrated* (February 9, 1987): n.p.

23. Women's Rights National Historical Park, Pamphlet, Section called "Fashion vs. Health." Also see Thorstein Veblen, *The Theory of the Leisure Class* (Fairfield, NJ: Augustus M. Kelley, Publishers, 1991), 180.

24. Lenskyj, *Out of Bounds*, 60.

25. At the time that James Naismith had invented the game, basket ball was spelled as two words. Berenson wrote about the game of basket ball in an article entitled "Basket Ball for Women," *Physical Education* 3 (September 1894): 107. Joan S. Hult, "Introduction to Part I," in Joan S. Hult and Marianna Trekell, eds., *A Century of Women's Basketball: From Frailty to the Final Four* (Reston, VA: AAHPERD Publications, 1991), 3–8; Betty Spears, "Senda Berenson Abbott—hisNew Woman: New Sport," in Joan S. Hult et al., *A Century of Women's Basketball*, 30.

26. Joan Paul, "Clara Gregory Baer: Catalyst for Women's Basketball," in Joan S. Hult et al., *A Century of Women's Basketball*, 39.

27. Paul, "Clara Gregory Baer," 42–44.

28. Spears, "Senda Berenson Abbott," 27; Howell, *Her Story in Sport*.

29. Gerber et al., *The American Woman in Sport*, 62.

30. Spears, "Senda Berenson Abbott," 27; italics in original.

31. Joan S. Hult, "The Governance of Athletics for Girls and Women: Leadership by Women Physical Educators, 1899–1949," in Hult et al., *A Century of Women's Basketball*, 55.

32. For a complete discussion of the various forms of interclass, intramural, extramural, and intercollegiate competition in which female college students participated, see Gerber et al., *The American Woman in Sport*, 56–68.

33. For a full discussion of the topics of sport, masculinity, education, and changing America, see Part I of Michael A. Messner and Donald F. Sabo, eds., *Sport, Men, and the Gender Order: Critical Feminist Perspectives* (Champaign, IL: Human Kinetics Publishers, 1990); Donald J. Mrozek, *Sport and American Mentality, 1880–1920* (Knoxville, TN: The University of Tennessee Press, 1983); and Mangan et al., *From Fair Sex to Feminism*.

34. Richard Hofstadter, *Anti-Intellectualism in American Life* (New York: Vintage Books, 1963), 18.

35. Todd Crosset, "Masculinity, Sexuality, and the Development of Early Modern Sport," in Messner et al., *Sport, Men, and the Gender Order*.

36. Ibid., 52. The quotes contained in this paragraph refer to the work of G. J. Barker-Benfield, *The Horrors of the Half-Known Life* (New York: Harper & Row) as quoted in Crosset.

37. Ibid., 53.

38. Murray Sperber, *Shake Down the Thunder: The Creation of Notre Dame Football* (New York: Henry Holt and Company, 1993), 76.

39. Crosset, "Masculinity, Sexuality. . . ," 45-54; Mrozek, *Sport and American Mentality*; David Whitson, "Sport in the Social Construction of Masculinity," in Messner et al., *Sport, Men, and the Gender Order*.

CHAPTER 4

1. Joan Paul, "Heroines Paving the Way," in Greta L. Cohen, ed. *Women in Sport: Issues and Controversies* (Newbury Park, CA: Sage Publications, 1993), 30–31.

2. Janet Woolum, *Outstanding Women Athletes: Who Are They and How They Influenced Sports in America* (Phoenix, AZ: Oryx Press, 1992), 174.

3. Gerber et al., *The American Woman in Sport*, 63.

4. Joan S. Hult et al., "The Governance of Athletics for Girls and Women," 65.

5. For a full history of the evolutionary changes that the National Women's Basketball Committee underwent between 1899 and 1949, see Hult, "The Governance of Athletics for Girls and Women." Women's intercollegiate athletic governance derives its roots from the National Women's Basketball Committee. From 1899 until 1982, the National Women's Basketball Committee would be transfigured and reinvented several times, eventually emerging as the Division for Girls and Women in Sport in the 1950s. Under the rubric of the DGWS, the Commission on Intercollegiate Athletics for Women (CIAW) was formed in 1967 to respond to the rapid changes occurring in women's sport at the college level. The CIAW would eventually become the Association for Intercollegiate Athletics for Women (AIAW). The AIAW served as the female counterpart to the NCAA from 1971 through 1982. For an overview of that history, see Joan S. Hult, "The Story of Women's Athletics: Manipulating A Dream 1890–1985," in D. Margaret Costa and Sharon R. Guthrie, eds., *Women and Sport: Interdisciplinary Perspectives* (Champaign, IL: Human Kinetics Publishers, 1994), Chapter 6.

6. Hult, "The Governance of Athletics for Girls and Women," 66.

7. Larry Engelmann, *The Goddess and the American Girl: The Story of Suzanne Lenglen and Helen Wills* (New York: Oxford University Press, 1988), 291; Cahn, *Coming on Strong: Gender and Sexuality in Twentieth-Century Women's Sport*, 47. Covers of magazines such as *Physical Culture* also depicted female athletes as mythical, graceful figures. See the cover of *Physical Culture*, December 1927, for an example.

8. Paula Dee Welch, "The Emergence of American Women in the Summer Olympic Games, 1900–1972," (D.Ed. diss., University of North Carolina, Greensboro, 1975), 24–51.

9. Ibid.

10. Cahn, *Coming on Strong: Gender and Sexuality in Twentieth-Century Women's Sport*, 59.

11. Ibid.

12. Ellen Gerber, "The Controlled Development of Collegiate Sport for Women," *Journal of Sports History* (Spring 1975): 6.

13. Hult, "The Governance of Athletics for Girls and Women," 68; Gerber, "Chronicle of Participation," in Gerber et al., eds., *The American Woman in Sport*, 71; Gerber, "The Controlled Development of Collegiate Sport for Women," 8.

14. Paula Welch, "Governance: The First Half Century," in Greta L. Cohen, ed., *Women in Sport: Issues and Controversies* (Newbury Park, CA: Sage Publications, 1993), 71–73.

15. Ibid.

16. Reprint of the "Women's Division—National Amateur Athletic Federation Platform," in *Women and Athletics* (New York: A. S. Barnes and Company, 1930), 3–4. Original platform adopted at the first annual meeting of WD–NAAF in Chicago, Illinois, April 22, 1924.

17. Carole A. Oglesby, *Back to the Future: Reexamining Women's Sport*. Paper presented at the AAHPERD National Convention, Las Vegas, Nevada, 1988; also Carole A. Oglesby, "Epilogue," in Michael Messner and Donald F. Sabo, eds., *Sport, Men, and the Gender Order: Critical Feminist Perspectives* (Champaign, IL: Human Kinetics Publishers, 1990), 242.

18. Gerber, "The Controlled Development of College Sport for Women," 21. See Hult, "The Governance of Athletics for Girls and Women," for a crucial distinction between competition that could be engaged in within the context of sport-for-all versus varsity and elite types of competition; Gerber et al., eds., *The American Woman in Sport*, 73; Agnes R. Wayman, "Competition," *American Physical Education Review*, vol. 34 (October 1929): 469.

19. Murray Sperber, *Shake down the Thunder: The Creation of Notre Dame Football* (New York: Henry Holt and Company, 1993), 73. It should be noted that Rockne's remarks were directed toward a small but growing number of women with physical education majors emerging during the 1920s, one of which was housed at the University of Notre Dame. Although female physical educators were most successful for a time in implementing an alternative form of athletics on college campuses, male physical educators (as distinct from male coaches) often subscribed to a democratic, inclusive ideal of sport competition as well.

20. Walter Byers and Charles Hammer, *Unsportsmanlike Conduct* (Ann Arbor, MI: University of Michigan Press, 1995), 243.

21. Guttman, *Women's Sport: A History*, 135. Also, Welch, "Governance: The First Half Century," in Cohen, ed., *Women and Sport: Issues and Controversies*. See section titled "Anti-Competitive Era," 71. In Mary A. Boutilier and Lucinda SanGiovanni, eds., *The Sporting Woman* (Champaign, IL: Human Kinetics Publishers, 1983), the notion that women themselves were anti-competitive is also discussed.

22. See the Women's Division Platform.

23. A statement entitled "Competition" was circulated by the Women's Division—National Amateur Athletic Federation in the publication *Women and Athletics* (New York: A. S. Barnes and Company, 1930), 39.

24. Gerber, "The Controlled Development of Collegiate Sport for Women," 12–14.

25. John Dewey, *Democracy and Education* (New York: The Free Press, 1968). See chapter entitled "The Democratic Conception in Education," particularly p. 83.

26. Florence C. Burnell, "Intercollegiate Athletics for Women in Coeducation Institutions," *American Physical Education Review*, vol. 22 (1917): 17.

27. Agnes Wayman, "Women's Athletics—All Uses—No Abuses," *American Physical Education Review*, vol. 29 (November 1924): 519.

28. Ibid., 517.

29. Ibid., 517.

30. Mabel Lee, "The Case for and against Intercollegiate Athletics for Women and the Situation as It Stands Today," *American Physical Education Review*, vol. 29 (January 1924): 15.

31. John M. Cooper, "A Magna Carta for the Girl and Woman of Athletics," *The Catholic Charities Review* (January 1925). Reprinted in the Women's Division—National Amateur Athletic Federation, *Women and Athletics*, 21.

32. John R. Tunis, "Women and the Sport Business," *Harper's Weekly*, Volume 159 (July 1929): 218. Reprinted in the Women's Division—National Amateur Athletic Federation, *Women and Athletics*, 26.

33. Harry E. Stewart, "A Survey of Track Athletics for Women," *American Physical Education Review*, vol. 21 (January 1916): 13. The phrases "physical training" and "physical straining" were used by Mabel Lee in "The Case for and against Intercollegiate Athletics for Women," 13.

34. E. H. Arnold, "Athletics for Women," *American Physical Education Review*, vol. 29 (October 1926): 452–457.

35. Trilling, "Safeguarding Girls' Athletics," 12.

36. See aims numbered 9, 10, 12, and 13 of the Women's Division Platform.

37. Barbara Solomon, *In the Company of Educated Women* (New Haven, CT: Yale University Press, 1985), 103–104.

38. See aims numbered 7 and 8 in the Women's Division Platform.

39. Gerber, "The Controlled Development of Intercollegiate Athletics for Women," 10. The five associations included the Committee on Women's Athletics of the American Physical Education Association, the Association of Directors of Physical Education for Women in Colleges and Universities, the Athletic Conference of American College Women, the American Association of University Women, and the National Association of Deans of Women.

40. Ronald Smith, paper presented at AAHPERD National Convention, April 1996. In this presentation, Smith outlines the negative response that the women's physical education leadership had to Palmer's ideas about intercollegiate athletics for women. Additional information on Gladys Palmer's views on intercollegiate competition can be found in Gladys Palmer, "Policies in Women's Athletics," *Journal of Health and Physical Education*, vol. 9 (November 1938): 565–567, and Hult, "Governance of Athletics for Girls and Women," 72–73.

41. Lee, *Memories beyond Bloomers*, 225–226. Correspondence addressed to Miss Applebee from Lillian Schroeder, executive secretary of the Women's Division, dated

March 3, 16, and 20, 1925, reveals a testy exchange on the thorny question of what Schroeder referred to as "inter-competition." Applebee sought clarification with regard to whether or not the Women's Division would support intercollegiate and international competition for women. Although Schroeder indicates that the Women's Division does not have the power to shut down programs that might engage in those forms of competition, she was clear in the March 20 letter that "The N.A.A.F. *does not* approve of international competition for women" (emphasis hers). Further evidence of the tension that Applebee had created among physical educators can be found in a letter submitted to the March 1 edition of *The Sportswoman* (a publication owned and managed by Applebee) that questioned the desire "to encourage competition in field hockey through the United States Field Hockey Association," pointing out that it was "premature in the case of undergraduate women." See letter from Mary Wheeler, *The Sportswoman*, vol. 1, no. 12 (March 1, 1925): 2.

42. Lee, *Memories beyond Bloomers*, 226.

43. "Intercollegiate Sports for Women," editorial, *American Physical Education Review*, vol. 29 (April 1924): 198–199.

44. Ethel Perrin, "More Competitive Athletics for Women—But of the Right Kinds," *American Physical Education Review*, vol. 34 (October 1929): 473.

45. Helen Lefkowitz Horowitz, "A Man's and A Woman's World," *Academe* (July–August, 1995): 10–14. Some sense of the social significance of women obtaining the right to vote is conveyed in the words of M. Carey Thomas, president of Bryn Mawr College and leader in the National American Woman Suffrage Association, who said in 1908, "Giving women the ballot is the visible sign and symbol of stupendous social revolution, and before it we are afraid."

46. Martha S. West, "Women Faculty: Frozen in Time," *Academe* (July–August 1995): 26.

47. Helen Smith, "Evil of Sports for Women," *Journal of Health and Physical Education*, vol. 2 (January 1932): 50–51.

48. Mabel B. Gummings, "Adaptations of the Physical Education Program for Girls to the Strengths and Abilities of the Individual," *American Physical Education Review*, vol. 30 (1925): 325–329.

49. Lee, "The Case for and against Intercollegiate Athletics for Women," 13–16.

50. Helen N. Smith and Helen L. Coops, *Play Days—Their Organization and Correlation with a Program of Physical Education and Health* (New York: A. S. Barnes & Company, 1928).

51. Norma M. Leavitt and Margaret M. Duncan, "The Status of Intramural Programs for Women," *Research Quarterly*, vol. 8 (March 1937): 68–69. Note that in this report as well as in other previous reports, interpretation of the data needs to be viewed with caution. Although in the Leavitt and Duncan study, for example, they report that 70 percent of colleges had engaged in play days in 1936, the total number of responding schools was seventy-one. Thus, the figure represents 70 percent of the responding schools, not necessarily 70 percent of all women's programs in the country. The importance of this is seen very clearly in the article published by Mabel

Lee entitled "The Case for and against Intercollegiate Athletics for Women and the Situation since 1923"), printed in *Research Quarterly*, vol. 2 (March 1931): 93–127. Although she reports that "Intercollegiate athletic competition for women does not exist in colleges of the United States except in a very limited number and percentage," it is notable that at least seven institutions with varsity athletic programs for women failed to respond (or were not invited to respond) to the survey.

52. David Sherman, *Ursinus College Field Hockey 75th Anniversary 1919–1994* (Collegeville, PA: Ursinus College Sports Information, Fall 1994), 24.

53. "Girls Athletics at Ursinsus," *The Ruby*, 1923.

54. Carolyn Kane, "Foremothers: Constance M. K. Applebee—Field Hockey's Feisty First Lady" (n.d., n.p.). Found in Constance Applebee Papers, Box 3, Correspondence and Miscellaneous, Bryn Mawr College, Bryn Mawr, Pennsylvania.

55. Ibid.

56. Personal communication with Dave Sherman, sports information director at Ursinus College, June 27, 1996. Sherman pointed out that the "All Time Field Hockey" records reported in the *Ursinus College Field Hockey 75th Anniversary 1919–1994* publication did not reflect the fact that Ursinus had four teams that had competed well into the 1970s.

57. Lee, *Memories beyond Bloomers*, 225-226.

58. Editorial, *The Sportswoman*, vol. 1, No. 13 (March 1, 1925): 1. Although no author is specifically named, it appears that Constance Applebee, as the editor of the publication, was the author.

CHAPTER 5

1. Nell Irvin Painter, *Standing at Armageddon: The United States, 1877–1919* (New York: W. W. Norton and Company, 1987), 231.

2. According to Walter Byers, "in 1956, the colleges, acting through the NCAA in the name of 'amateurism,' installed their own pay system called the athletics 'scholarship.' " See Walter Byers, *Unsportsmanlike Conduct: Exploiting College Athletes* (Ann Arbor: The University of Michigan Press, 1995), 2–3.

3. This discussion is taken from *Van Horn v. Industrial Accident Commission*, 33 Cal. Rptr. 169 (1963).

4. Ibid., p. 170.

5. Marcus L. Plant, letter to Walter Byers, 8 July 1964, Walter Byers Papers, Workman Compensation Folder, NCAA Headquarters, Overland Park, Kansas.

6. Robert F. Ray, president of the NCAA, and Everett D. Barnes, secretary-treasurer of the NCAA, memorandum to Faculty Representatives and Athletic Directors of Member Institutions; Officers of Allied Conferences, 21 December 1964, Walter Byers Papers, Workman Compensation Folder, NCAA Headquarters, Overland Park, Kansas. Earlier drafts of this memo, written by Marcus Plant, are also included in the Workman Compensation Folder.

7. Byers, *Unsportsmanlike Conduct*, 75.

8. Ray and Barnes, memorandum to Faculty Representatives and Athletic Directors, 2–3.

9. Everett D. Barnes, letter to Walter Byers, 6 July 1964, Walter Byers Papers, Workman Compensation Folder, NCAA Headquarters, Overland Park, Kansas.

10. Clyde B. Smith, letter to Walter Byers, 6 December 1966, Walter Byers Papers, Long Range Planning Folder, NCAA Headquarters, Overland Park, Kansas.

11. National Collegiate Athletic Association, *Proceedings of the 61st Annual Convention*, 9–11 January 1967, 122.

12. M. R. Clausen, the person who proposed this amendment, argued that it would allow an athlete who had voluntarily quit sport to be referred for disciplinary action. See NCAA, *Proceedings of the 61st Annual Convention*, 122.

13. *NCAA Manual*, 1968–69, p. 15.

14. Byers, *Unsportsmanlike Conduct*, 163.

15. David Swank, quoted in NCAA, *Proceedings of the 61st Annual Convention*, 123.

16. See Gary Shaw, *Meat on the Hoof* (New York: St. Martin's Press, 1972), for a discussion of the running off of athletes (coaches making sports activities grueling so athletes voluntarily give up their scholarships) in the Southwest Conference in the 1960s.

17. The 90-second estimated time comes from Walter Byers, *Unsportsmanlike Conduct*, 164.

18. J. E. Sullivan, letter to George H. Gangwere, 25 June 1979, Walter Byers Papers, Vol. CXIX, Folder "Legal, 1979," NCAA Headquarters, Overland Park, Kansas.

19. *Rensing v. Indiana State University*, 444 N.E. 2d. 1173 (1983).

20. Walter Byers, *Unsportsmanlike Conduct*, 9.

21. Mark Alan Atkinson, "Worker's Compensation and College Athletics: Should Universities Be Responsible for Athletes Who Incur Serious Injury?" *Journal of College and University Law*, no. 2 (Fall 1983–84): 203.

22. *Askew v. Macomber*, 398 Mich. 212, 247 N.W. 2d. 288 (1976).

23. *Coleman v. Western Michigan University*, 336 N.W. 2d. 225–226 (1983).

24. Carolyn E. Thomas, "The Golden Girl Syndrome: Thoughts on a Training Ethic," NAPEHE, *Annual Conference Proceedings*, Vol. 2 (1980), p. 139.

25. In *NCAA Manual*, 1983–84, p. 263, a hypothetical case was described where a scholarship athlete made token appearances at practice or did not show up at all. The question was whether or not aid could be terminated immediately. The NCAA response was "yes, such an action on the part of the grantee would be a fraudulent misrepresentation of information on the grantee's application, letter of intent, or tender."

26. *Morgan v. Win Schuler's Restaurant*, 64 Mich. App. 37, 234 N.W. 2d. 885 (1975).

27. *Coleman v. Western Michigan University*, 336 N.W. 2d. 226 (1983).

28. *Board of Regents of the University of Oklahoma v. National Collegiate Athletic Association*, 52 LW 4937.

29. This account of the *McEwen* case was taken from "Athletic Aid Is Ending for Phillip's Victim," *New York Times*, 19 April 1996, p. B16.

30. Jim Naughton, "Women in Division I Sports Programs: 'The Glass is Half Empty and Half Full,'" *The Chronicle of Higher Education*, 11 April 1997, pp. A39–40.

31. Douglas Lederman, "Athletic Merit vs. Academic Merit," *The Chronicle of Higher Education*, 30 March 1994, p. A37.

32. In 1994 the average NCAA athletic program in every division ran a deficit when institutional support had been excluded. See *The Chronicle of Higher Education*, 7 September 1994, p. A58.

33. Goldie Blumenstyk, "Money-Making Champs," *The Chronicle of Higher Education*, 19 April 1996, pp. A49–A50.

34. Ibid., A49.

35. Bob Baum, "In Sports World, Apparel Is Champ," *New Haven Register*, 14 April 1996, pp. A1, A6–A7.

36. Goldie Blumenstyk, "Georgia Tech and McDonalds Sign $5.5-Million Deal," *Chronicle of Higher Education*, 3 February 1995, p. A44.

37. Rick Pitino, the coach of the 1996 national champion Kentucky Wildcats, made $3 million in salary and other benefits, including contracts with sneaker companies. See Selena Roberts, "Pitino Turns down the Nets to Stay in the Bluegrass," *New York Times*, 31 May 1996, p. B9.

38. See, for instance, Vincent J. Dooley, "Student Athletes Well Compensated," *NCAA News*, 1 March 1995, pp. 4–5.

39. This description of Nike trips for coaches is taken from J. B. Strasser and Laurie Becklund, *Swoosh: The Unauthorized Story of Nike and the Men Who Played There* (New York: Harcourt, Brace and Jovanovich, 1991), 438–439.

CHAPTER 6

1. These data were derived from *Barron's Profiles of American Colleges*, 1997 edition, and the *1996 NCAA Division I Graduation-Rates Report*.

2. Jim Naughton, "Athletes on Top-Ranked Teams Lack Grades and Test Scores of Other Students," *The Chronicle of Higher Education*, 25 July 1997, A43.

3. An overview of the 1.6 rule was taken from Jack Falla, *NCAA: The Voice of College Sports* (Mission, Kansas: National Collegiate Athletic Association, 1981), 145-146.

4. Wilford S. Bailey, "NCAA Eligibility Requirements for Athletes," unpublished speech to the National Association for Equal Opportunity in Higher Education, Walter Byers Papers, Proposition 48 Folder 1986, Box "Professional Relations 1983–84," NCAA Headquarters, Overland Park, Kansas, pp. 1–2.

5. Walter Byers, letter to Wilford S. Bailey, 21 April 1986, Walter Byers Papers, Proposition 48 Folder 1986, Box "Professional Relations 1983–84," NCAA Headquarters, Overland Park, Kansas.

6. Robert F. Goheen, memorandum to Everett D. Barnes and the Council of the NCAA, 13 April 1966, Walter Byers Papers, Helms Athletic Foundation Folder, Box "Golf 1966," NCAA Headquarters, Overland Park, Kansas.

7. Ibid.

8. NCAA, *Proceedings of the 67th Annual Convention*, 11–13 January 1973.

9. Falla, *The NCAA*, 117.

10. An excellent review of research on college sport during this period appeared in *The Journal of Sport and Social Issues* 11, nos. 1 and 2 (1987). The papers in this volume were commissioned by the Amateur Athletic Foundation of Los Angeles to help inform the work of the Presidents Commission of the NCAA.

11. This discussion of the early version of Proposition 48 was taken from a NCAA News Release, 1 November 1985, Walter Byers Papers, Proposition 48 Folder 1985, Box "Professional Relations 1985," NCAA Headquarters, Overland Park, Kansas.

12. Walter Byers, *Unsportsmanlike Conduct: Exploiting College Athletes* (Ann Arbor: The University of Michigan Press, 1995), 297.

13. A detailed table describing NCAA Division I eligibility standards in 1996–1997 and thereafter appears in the *NCAA News*, 16 August 1995, p. 8. It should also be noted that the College Board has recentered SAT scores so that a 700 is now 820. The table in the *NCAA News* adjusts for this change by converting to the old scoring system.

14. Henry S. Pritchett, quoted in Savage et al., *American College Athletics*, xxi.

15. The most comprehensive review of this literature appears in *The Journal of Sport and Social Issues* 11, nos. 1 and 2 (1987).

16. The Center for Athletes Rights' and Education was funded by the Department of Education's Fund for the Improvement of Post-Secondary Education and was cosponsored by the National Football League Players Association and the National Conference of Black Lawyers.

17. See Allen L. Sack, "College Sport and the Student Athlete," *The Journal of Sport and Social Issues* 11, nos. 1 and 2 (1987): 33–34.

18. Patricia A. Adler and Peter Adler, *Backboards and Blackboards* (New York: Columbia University Press, 1991).

19. *Report No. 1: Summary Results from the 1987–88 National Study of Intercollegiate Athletics* (Palo Alto, CA: American Institutes for Research, 1988).

20. *Report No. 4: Women in Intercollegiate Athletics at NCAA Division I Institutions* (Palo Alto, CA: American Institutes for Research, 1989).

21. See, for instance, Arthur Ashe, "Send Your Children to Libraries," *New York Times*, 6 February 1977, p. 2S.

22. An athletic director at Lamar University firmly believed that BEOG money should be used this way. In his opinion, "To do otherwise might force institutions to actually waste 'hard to come by' athletic money when it could be available from other sources." James B. Higgins, Athletic Director, Lamar University, letter to J. Neils

Thompson, Secretary-Treasurer, NCAA, 29 October 1976, Walter Byers Papers, Television Committee Folder, 1978, Box "TV Communications, 1978," NCAA Headquarters, Overland Park, Kansas.

23. According to Walter Byers, the NCAA's executive director during this period, "The diversion of poverty funds to athletic programs never became the public issue it should have." Byers, *Unsportsmanlike Conduct*, 236.

24. NCAA, *1996 NCAA Division I Graduation-Rates Report* (Overland Park, Kansas: NCAA, 1996), 387.

25. See Murray Sperber, "Affirmative Action for Athletes."

26. Arthur Ashe, "Send Your Children to the Libraries."

27. Naughton, "Athletes on Top-Ranked Teams Lack Grades," p. A44.

28. Marc Ethier, "Male Basketball Players Continue to Lag in Graduation Rates," *The Chronicle of Higher Education*, 3 July 1997, p. A39.

29. See Sally Huggins, "NCAA's D.C. office served Association well in its first year," *NCAA News*, 17 June 1996, pp. 1, 24.

30. C. C. Johnson Spink, "Tax Threat to Colleges," *The Sporting News*, 4 June 1977, clipping found in Walter Byers Papers, Legal Folder 1977, Box "Legal 1977–79," NCAA Headquarters, Overland Park, Kansas.

31. J. M. Moudy, letter to The Honorable Jim Wright, 12 May 1977, Walter Byers Papers, Legal Folder 1977.

32. Jim Wright, letters to Michael Blumenthal and Jerome Kurtz, 17 May 1977, Walter Byers Papers, Legal Folder 1977.

33. Ibid.

34. J. M. Moudy and James Zumberge, mailgram to J. Neils Thompson, 18 May 1977, Walter Byers Papers, Legal Folder 1977.

35. Charles W. Neinas, letter to Senator Robert Dole, 2 June 1977, Walter Byers Papers, Legal Folder 1977.

36. R. L. Phinney, letter to J. Neils Thompson, 18 May 1977, Walter Byers Papers, Legal Folder. According to this letter, Sheldon Cohen recommended against an aggressive congressional lobbying effort. In a 1996 interview for this book, Cohen said that he felt that the case could have been won on its merits and would have been won even without aggressive lobbying efforts.

37. The letters from Robert F. Drinan, Thomas P. O'Neill, Jr., and Edward M. Kennedy that were sent to William J. Flynn between June 15 and 21 are in the Walter Byers Papers, Legal Folder 1977.

38. The NCAA attorneys at the time were well aware that the need of an organization for income for its exempt functions was not a compelling factor in deciding the unrelated-business issue. See George H. Gangwere, letter to Walter Byers, 8 April 1977, Walter Byers Papers, Legal Folder 1977.

39. Richie T. Thomas, letter to Thomas C. Hansen, 23 June 1977, Walter Byers Papers, Legal Folder 1977.

40. Ibid.

41. Spink, "Tax Threat to Colleges."

42. Sections 511–513 of the Internal Revenue code were enacted in the 1950s to prevent a so-called not-for-profit organization from avoiding tax liability on income derived from activities that are unrelated to the organization's tax-exempt function.

CHAPTER 7

1. Bruce Horowitz, "A Basketball League of Their Own: Women Athletes Leap through Hoops to Live Their Dreams," *USA Today*, 18 October 1996, p. 1C; David Kindred, *Colorado Silver Bullets: For the Love of the Game* (Fairfield, NJ: Horowitz/Rae Publishers); Valerie Lister, "Fans Turn Out; Marketing's a Huge Success," *USA Today*, 29 July 1997, p. 2C.

2. Donald F. Sabo, Project Director, "The Women's Sports Foundation Gender Equity Report Card: A Survey of Athletic Opportunity in American Higher Education," 23 June 1997. This report can be obtained by contacting the Women's Sports Foundation at Eisenhower Park, East Meadow, New York 11554.

3. Linda Carpenter, "Letters Home: My Life with Title IX," in Greta L. Cohen, ed., *Women in Sport: Issues and Controversies* (Newbury Park, CA: Sage Publications, 1993), 79–94; Sue Durrant, "Title IX—Its Power and Its Limitations," *Journal of Health, Physical Education, Recreation, and Dance*, 60–64.

4. Katherine Ley, "Increasing Opportunities for Girls' Sports." Paper presented at the National Federation of High School Athletic Directors, Williamsburg, Virginia, June 28, 1965, p. 1.

5. Joan S. Hult, "The Story of Women's Athletics: Manipulating a Dream 1980–1985," in D. Margaret Costa and Sharon R. Guthrie, eds., *Women and Sport: Interdisciplinary Perspectives* (Champaign, IL: Human Kinetics Publishers, 1994), 83–101.

6. Joan S. Hult, "The Story of Women's Athletics," and Joan S. Hult, "College Governance, Championships, and Memories," In Joan S. Hult & Marianne Trekell, *A Century of Women's Basketball* (Reston, VA: AAHPERD, 1991), 281–307; Leotus L. Morrison, "The AIAW: Governance by Women for Women," in Greta L. Cohen, ed., *Women in Sport: Issues and Controversies* (Newbury Park, CA: Sage Publications, 1993), 60–68.

7. Jack Falla, *NCAA: The Voice of College Sports: A Diamond Anniversary History (1906–1981)* (Mission, KS: National Collegiate Athletic Association, 1981); Ronald A. Smith, *Sports & Freedom: The Rise of Big-Time College Athletics* (New York: Oxford University Press, 1988), 191–208.

8. Morrison, "The AIAW: Governance by Women for Women," 62.

9. Hult, "The Legacy of the AIAW," 281.

10. Bonnie Slatton, "AIAW: The Greening of American Athletics," in James Frey, ed., *The Governance of Intercollegiate Athletics* (West Point, NY: Leisure Press, 1982), 144–154.

11. Ibid.

12. Ibid., 148.

13. Hult, "The Legacy of the AIAW"; Hult, "College Governance, Championships, and Memories"; Morrison, "The AIAW: Governance by Women for Women"; Slatton, "AIAW: The Greening of American Athletics."

14. Ibid.

15. DGWS, *Procedures for Intercollegiate Athletic Events* (Washington, DC: AAHPER, 1969), AAHPERD Archives, AAHPERD Headquarters, Reston, Virginia.

16. "AIAW White Paper on Women's Sports," 19 March 1973. AIAW Archives, AIAW Financial Aid Resolution Folder, Box 37, University of Maryland Library Archives, College Park, Maryland.

17. Throughout the 1970s, the gap between AIAW and NCAA policies on matters of eligibility, financial aid, recruiting, and other athletic matters became less pronounced than at the start of the decade. See Ruth Hammock Alexander, "An Explanation of the Variances in AIAW–NCAA Rules Eligibility and Standards," in *Athletic Administration* (Winter 1980), 19–21, for a sense of how far things had advanced just prior to the NCAA takeover of women's intercollegiate athletics.

18. Morrison, "The AIAW: Governance by Women for Women," 62–64; Hult, "The Story of Women's Athletics," 96–100.

19. Ibid.

20. Slatton, "AIAW: The Greening of American Athletics," 145.

21. Hult, "The Story of Women's Athletics," 97.

22. Ibid., 99.

23. Ibid., 95.

24. Ibid., 97.

25. Two articles appeared in the *Washington Post* during January 1973 that provide an overview of the issues as viewed from the student complainants on the "no athletic scholarship" position taken by the AIAW. See "Coeds Protest Sports Bar" from January 16, 1973, and "Miss Carr Relinquishes Scholarship" from January 13, 1973, for more details.

26. "Philosophical Background to Athletic Scholarship Statement," AIAW Archives, AIAW Financial Aid Resolution Folder, Box 37, University of Maryland Library, College Park, Maryland.

27. Linda Estes, letter to Carole Oglesby, 12 March 1973, AIAW Archives, Special Meeting—AIAW Historical—March 25–27, 1973, Box 67, University of Maryland Library, College Park, Maryland.

28. Quotes from Roberta Howells and Doris Soladay contained in a summary of comments accompanying votes on the athletic scholarship question put forward to AIAW voting members, compiled by Elizabeth Hoyt in a memorandum to Members of Special Committee to Reword DGWS Scholarship Statement and Revise AIAW Rules and Regulations, 22 March 1973, AIAW Archives, Special Meeting—AIAW Historical—March 25–27, 1973 Folder, Box 67, University of Maryland Library, College Park, Maryland.

29. Donna Mae Miller and Mary Pavich Roby, letter to Betty Hartman, Carole Oglesby, and Mary Reksted, 12 March 1973, AIAW Archives, Special Meeting—

AIAW Historical—March 25–27, 1973 Folder, Box 67, University of Maryland Library, College Park, Maryland.

30. Christine Grant, "AIAW Financial Aid Resolution," 15 January 1976, AIAW Archives, AIAW Financial Aid Resolution Folder, Box 37, University of Maryland Library, College Park, Maryland.

31. Donna Lopiano, memorandum to AIAW Executive Board, Committee on Men's Athletics, AIAW Past Presidents, Katherine Ley, Joanne Thorpe, Rachel Bryant, and Mary Roby, 8 December 1980, AIAW Archives, CIAW-AIAW-NCAA Chronology Folder, Box 37, University of Maryland Library, College Park, Maryland.

32. Charles Neinas, letter of Richard Larkin, Walter Byers Papers, Women's Athletics 1960 Folder, Box "Women's Athletics 1960," NCAA Headquarters, Overland Park, Kansas.

33. Lopiano, memorandum to AIAW Executive Board, 8 December 1980, 3.

34. Walter Byers and Charles Hammer, *Unsportsmanlike Conduct: Exploiting College Athletes* (Ann Arbor, MI: University of Michigan Press, 1995), 240.

35. Linda Carpenter, "Letters Home: My Life with Title IX," 79–94; Durrant, "Title IX—Its Power and Its Limitations," 60–64.

36. John Fuzak, letter to Gerald Ford, 20 March 1975, Walter Byers Papers, 1/75–6/75 Folder, Box "HEW-Title IX," NCAA Headquarters, Overland Park, Kansas.

37. Gerald Ford, letter to Harrison A. Williams, 21 July 1975, Walter Byers Papers, 7/75–12/75 Folder, Box "HEW-Title IX," NCAA Headquarters, Overland Park, Kansas.

38. Don Canham, letter to Walter Byers, 26 September 1978, Walter Byers Papers, 7/78–12/78 Folder, Box "HEW-Title IX," NCAA Headquarters, Overland Park, Kansas.

39. Tom Hansen, memorandum to Walter Byers, 15 August 1977, Walter Byers Papers, 7/77–12/77 Folder, Box "HEW-Title IX," NCAA Headquarters, Overland Park, Kansas; Skipper Zipperlen, memorandum to Walter Byers, 16 August 1977, Walter Byers Papers, 7/77–12/77 Folder, Box "HEW-Title IX," NCAA Headquarters, Overland Park, Kansas.

40. Ritchie T. Thomas, letter to Thomas Hansen, 30 October 1978; William D. Kramer, letter to David M. Lascell, 20 November 1978; and William D. Kramer, letter to Thomas Hansen, 19 December 1978, Walter Byers Papers, 7/78–12/78 Folder, Box "HEW-Title IX," NCAA Headquarters, Overland Park, Kansas.

41. Carpenter, "Letters Home"; Durrant, "Title IX—Its Powers and Its Limitations."

42. Byers, *Unsportsmanlike Conduct*, 244. For additional data, see Falla, *NCAA: The Voice of College Sports*, 157–175.

43. Falla, *NCAA: The Voice of College Sports*, 174.

44. Thomas Hansen, memorandum to Walter Byers, 5 September 1978, Walter Byers Papers, 7/78–12/78 Folder, Box "HEW-Title IX," NCAA Headquarters, Overland Park, Kansas.

45. Byers, *Unsportsmanlike Conduct*, 245.

46. R. Vivian Acosta and Linda Jean Carpenter, "Women in Intercollegiate Sport: A Longitudinal Study—Seventeen-Year Update 1977–1994," unpublished manuscript, Brooklyn College, Brooklyn, New York, 1994.

47. Laura Bollig, ed., *The 1995–1996 NCAA Manual* (Overland Park, KS: NCAA Publishing, 1995): 21.

48. *Summary of the Survey to Review the Roles of Senior Woman Administrators at NCAA Member Institutions* (Overland Park, KS: NCAA Publishing, 1994).

49. Sabo, "The Women's Sports Foundation Gender Equity Report Card."

50. Erik Brady, "Title IX Improves Women's Participation," *USA Today*, 3 March 1997, 4C.

51. Christine Grant and Charles Darley, "Equity: What Price Equality?," in Greta L. Cohen, ed., *Women and Sport: Issues and Controversies* (Newbury Park, CA: Sage Publications, 1993), 251–263.

52. Sperber, *College Sport Inc.*, 328.

53. D. Stanley Eitzen and George H. Sage, "*Sociology of North American Sport*" (Dubuque, IA: Brunon and Benchmark Publishers, 1997), 294.

CHAPTER 8

1. Jim Naughton, "Why a League with an Academic Focus Started Allowing Basketball Scholarships," *The Chronicle of Higher Education*, 17 January 1997, p. A45.

2. For an excellent review of the restructuring that took place at the 1997 NCAA convention, see Jim Naughton, "NCAA Completes Action on Its New Structure and Approves Academic-Year Jobs for Athletes," *The Chronicle of Higher Education*, 24 January 1997, p. A33.

3. This argument is eloquently presented in Gary Roberts, "Consider Everything Else before Restructuring," *NCAA News*, 19 September 1994, pp. 4–5.

4. Ibid.

5. Bill Clinton, quoted in Sally Huggins, "Clinton Urges Vigorous Enforcement of Title IX Law," *NCAA News*, 30 June 1997, p. 5.

6. See V. Lane Rawlins, "Don't Make Title IX a Zero-Sum Game," *NCAA News*, 7 July 1997, p. 5, for an elaboration on this theme.

7. *Preliminary Report by Special NCAA Committee on Financial Aid*, p. 1, Committee Draft No. 3, Walter Byers Papers, Financial Aid, Special Committee Folder, 1970, NCAA Headquarters, Overland Park, Kansas.

8. *Final Report of the Committee on Financial Aid of the National Collegiate Athletic Association*, Walter Byers Papers, Financial Aid, Special Committee Folder, 1971, NCAA Headquarters, Overland Park, Kansas.

9. Harry M. Cross, "Principal Remarks to Council of Presidents of Association of State Universities and Land Grant Colleges, 10 November 1970, pp. 3–4, in Walter Camp Papers, Financial Aid, Special Committee Folder, 1970, NCAA Headquarters, Overland Park, Kansas.

10. Reverend Edmund P. Joyce, C.S.C., letter to Earl M. Ramer, 20 September 1971, Walter Byers Papers, Financial Aid, Special Committee Folder, 1971, NCAA Headquarters, Overland Park, Kansas.

11. Gordon H. Chalmers, letter to Walter Byers, 5 November 1970, Walter Byers Papers, Financial Aid, Special Committee Folder, 1970, NCAA Headquarters, Overland Park, Kansas.

12. C. G. Taylor, letter to Earl M. Ramer, 30 September 1971, Walter Byers Papers, Financial Aid, Special Committee Folder, 1971, NCAA Headquarters, Overland Park, Kansas.

13. John William Ward, letter to Walter Byers, 26 July 1972, Walter Byers Papers, Financial Aid, Special Committee Folder, 1971, NCAA Headquarters, Overland Park, Kansas.

14. Robert F. Oxnam, letter to Walter Byers, 24 June 1972, Walter Byers Papers, Financial Aid, Special Committee Folder, 1972, NCAA Headquarters, Overland Park, Kansas.

15. Ward, letter to Byers.

16. For a summary of these legislative initiatives, see David P. Seifert, memo to Walter Byers, 25 September 1980, Walter Byers Papers, Box Financial Aid, Special Committee to Review Financial Aid Legislation Folder, 1980, NCAA Headquarters, Overland Park, Kansas.

17. National Collegiate Athletic Association, *Proceedings of the 75th Annual Convention*, 12–14 January 1981, 110.

18. Ibid., 112.

19. It should be noted that Division III and the Ivy League do have problems when it comes to keeping athletic and financial aid decisions separate. See, for instance, David Goldin, "Ivy League Plans an Audit to Enforce Its Policy against Athletic Scholarships," *New York Times*, 5 April 1996, p. A16, and Chris Murphy, "Illicit Financial Aid Casts Shadow on Division III," *NCAA News*, 25 November 1996, p. 4.

20. Ronald A. Smith, in *Sports and Freedom: The Rise of Big-Time College Athletics* (New York: Oxford University Press, 1988) takes the position that amateurism is "an untenable concept in a free and open society."

21. Difficulties in administering the NCAA's academic clearinghouse, which determines whether students have met Proposition 48 standards, are discussed in Jim Naughton, "Hundreds of Students Lose Scholarships in Widespread Confusion Over NCAA Rules," *The Chronicle of Higher Education*, 27 September 1996, pp. A49–50.

22. "Athletics and Their Costs: Exerpts from a Revealing New Report," *Academe* 79, no. 6 (November/December 1993): 26–36.

23. Ibid.

24. Kenneth G. Sheehan, *Keeping Score: The Economics of Big-Time Sports* (South Bend, IN: Diamond Communications, 1996), 263.

25. "Study: Typical I-A Program is $1.2 Million in the Black," *NCAA News*, 18 November 1996, pp. 1, 10.

26. Christine H. B. Grant, quoted in Jim Naughton and Rachanee Srisavasdi, "Data on Funds for Men's and Women's Sports Become Available as New Law Takes Effect," *The Chronicle of Higher Education*, 25 October 1996, pp. A45–46.

27. Sheehan, *Keeping Score*, 277.

28. Since 1982 more than a third of the schools that once sponsored wrestling have dropped their programs. The drop in men's gymnastics has been even greater. Rather than cutting costs in other ways, some schools seem to be cutting men's nonrevenue-producing sports. See Jim Naughton, "More Colleges Cut Men's Teams to Shift Money to Women's Athletics," *The Chronicle of Higher Education*, 21 February 1997, pp. A39–A40.

29. NCAA Committee on Financial Aid and Amateurism, "Need-Based Financial Aid Report to the 1995 NCAA Convention," 22 November 1994.

30. Sheehan, *Keeping Score*, 290.

31. Mike Hamrick, quoted in "Opinions," *NCAA News*, 19 July 1997, p. 4.

32. Walter Byers, interview for this book, 7 November 1996, Overland Park, Kansas.

33. According to Stephen Horn, financial aid in 1981 had changed significantly from the days when the Sanity Code was considered in 1949. The amount of available money had increased, and financial administrators had become more competent to handle such a system. See National Collegiate Athletic Association, *Proceedings of the 75th Annual Convention*, 12–14 January 1981.

34. Goldin Davidson, "Ivy League Plans an Audit to Enforce Its Policy against Athletic Scholarships," *New York Times*, 5 April 1996.

35. Rick Telander, *The Hundred Yard Lie: The Corruption of College Football and What We Can Do to Stop It* (New York: Simon and Schuster, 1989).

36. The kinds of accommodations being considered are discussed in some detail in William E. Kirwan, "Protecting College Athletes from Unscrupulous Agents," *The Chronicle of Higher Education*, 21 January 1996, p. A31.

37. Goldie Blumenstyk, "Playing Sports and Making Money," *The Chronicle of Higher Education*, 21 January 1996, p. A31.

38. Jim Naughton and Andrew Mytelka, "Gripes about Bowls, a Fight with 'USA Today,' and Proposals on Loans for Athletes," *The Chronicle of Higher Education*, 24 January 1997, p. A34.

39. See the work of Richard M. Brede and Henry J. Camp discussed in Allen L. Sack, "College Sport and the Student-Athlete," *The Journal of Sport and Social Issues* 11, nos. 1 and 2 (1987): 39.

40. Rawlins, "Don't Make Title IX a Zero-Sum Game," 5.

41. Mike Waller, "A Shakey Football Conference: Fears, Defections, and Collapse," *The Chronicle of Higher Education*, 6 June 1997, p. A37.

Further Reading

Boutilier, Mary A., and Lucinda SanGiovanni. *The Sporting Woman*. Champaign, IL: Human Kinetics Publishers, 1983.

Byers, Walter, with Charles Hammer. *Unsportsmanlike Conduct: Exploiting College Athletes*. Ann Arbor: University of Michigan Press, 1995.

Cahn, Susan. *Coming on Strong: Gender and Sexuality in Twentieth Century Women's Sport*. New York: Free Press, 1994.

Cannadine, David. *The Decline and Fall of the British Aristocracy*. New Haven, CT: Yale University Press, 1990.

Celizic, Mike. *The Biggest Game of Them All: Notre Dame, Michigan State, and the Fall of '66*. New York: Simon and Schuster, 1992.

Cohen, Greta L. *Women in Sport: Issues and Controversies*. Newbury Park, CA: Sage Publications, 1993.

Costa, Margaret, and Sharon Guthrie. *Women and Sport: Interdisciplinary Perspectives*. Champaign, IL: Human Kinetics Publishers, 1994.

Falla, Jack. *NCAA: The Voice of College Sports: A Diamond Anniversary History, 1906–1981*. Mission, KS: National Collegiate Athletic Association, 1981.

Fleisher, Rather A., III, Brian L. Goff, and Robert D. Tollison. *The National Collegiate Athletic Association: A Study in Cartel Behavior*. Chicago, IL: University of Chicago Press, 1992.

Gerber, Ellen, Jan Felshin, Pearl Berlin, and Waneen Wyrick. *The American Woman in Sport*. Reading, MA: Addison-Wesley Publishing Company, 1974.

Hart-Nibbrig, Nand, and Clement Cottingham. *The Political Economy of College Sports*. Lexington, MA: Lexington Books, 1986.

Hofstadter, Richard. *Anti-Intellectualism in American Life*. New York: Vintage Books, 1963.

Howell, Reet. *Her Story in Sport: A Historical Anthology of Women in Sports*. West Point, NY: Leisure Press, 1982.

Hult, Joan S., and Marianne Trekell. *A Century of Women's Basketball: From Frailty to Final Hour*. Reston, VA: American Alliance for Health, Physical Education, Recreation, and Dance, 1991.

Lawrence, Paul R. *Unsportsmanlike Conduct: The National Collegiate Athletic Association and the Business of College Football*. New York: Praeger, 1987.

Lenskyj, H. *Out of Bounds: Women, Sport, and Sexuality*. Toronto, Ontario, Canada: The Women's Press, 1986.

Mangan, J. A., and Roberta J. Park. *From Fair Sex to Feminism: Sport and the Socialization of Women in the Industrial and Pre-Industrial Eras*. Totowa, NJ: Frank Cass and Company Limited, 1987.

McMillen, Tom, with Paul Coggins. *Out of Bounds: How the American Sports Establishment Is Being Driven by Greed and Hypocrisy—and What Needs to be Done about It*. New York: Simon and Schuster, 1992.

Messner, Michael, and Don Sabo. *Sport, Men, and the Gender Order: Critical Feminist Perspectives*. Champaign, IL: Human Kinetics Publishers, 1990.

Rader, Benjamin G. *American Sports: From the Age of Folk Games to the Age of Televised Sports*. Englewood Cliffs, NJ: Prentice-Hall, 1990.

Rudolph, Frederick. *The American College and University*. New York: Vintage Books, 1962.

Savage, Howard J. *Games and Sports in British Schools and Universities*. New York: The Carnegie Foundation for the Advancement of Teaching, 1927.

Savage, Howard J., with Howard W. Bentley, John T. McGovern, and Dean F. Smiley. *American College Athletes* (Bulletin Number Twenty-Three). New York: Carnegie Foundation for the Advancement of Education, 1929.

Smith, Ron. *Sports and Freedom: The Rise of Big-Time College Athletics*. New York: Oxford University Press, 1988.

Sperber, Murray. *College Sports Inc.: The Athletic Department vs. the University*. New York: Henry Holt, 1990.

————. *Shake Down the Thunder: The Creation of Notre Dame Football*. New York: Henry Holt and Company, 1993.

Sponberg, Adryn, "The Evolution of Athletic Subsidization in the Intercollegiate Conference of Faculty Representatives (Big Ten)" Ph.D. diss., University of Michigan, 1968.

Telander, Rick. *The Hundred Yard Lie: The Corruption of College Football and What We Can Do to Stop It*. New York: Simon and Schuster, 1989.

Thelin, John R. *Games Colleges Play: Scandal and Reform in Intercollegiate Athletics*. Baltimore, MD: Johns Hopkins University Press, 1994.

Veysey, Lawrence R. *The Emergence of the American University*. Chicago: University of Chicago Press, 1965.

Woolum, Janet. *Outstanding Women Athletes: Who They Are and How They Influenced Sports in America*. Phoenix, AZ: Oryx Press, 1992.

Index

About the Authors

ALLEN L. SACK is Professor of Sociology and Management at the University of New Haven. He played defensive end on Ara Parseghian's 1966 National Championship football team and was drafted by the Los Angeles Rams. In 1981–82 he was the Director of the Center for Athletes Rights and Education, and he is currently the Coordinator of the Management of Sports Industries Program at the University of New Haven.

ELLEN J. STAUROWSKY is Associate Professor of Sport Sciences at Ithaca College. As a former college athlete, coach, and athletic director, she brings a unique blend of academic credentials and practical insight to the problems facing intercollegiate athletics.

HICKSVILLE PUBLIC LIBRARY

3 1911 00348 4582

796.043   Sack, Allen L.
S
          College athletes for
          hire.

8/98

DATE			

HICKSVILLE PUBLIC LIBRARY
HICKSVILLE, N.Y.

BAKER & TAYLOR